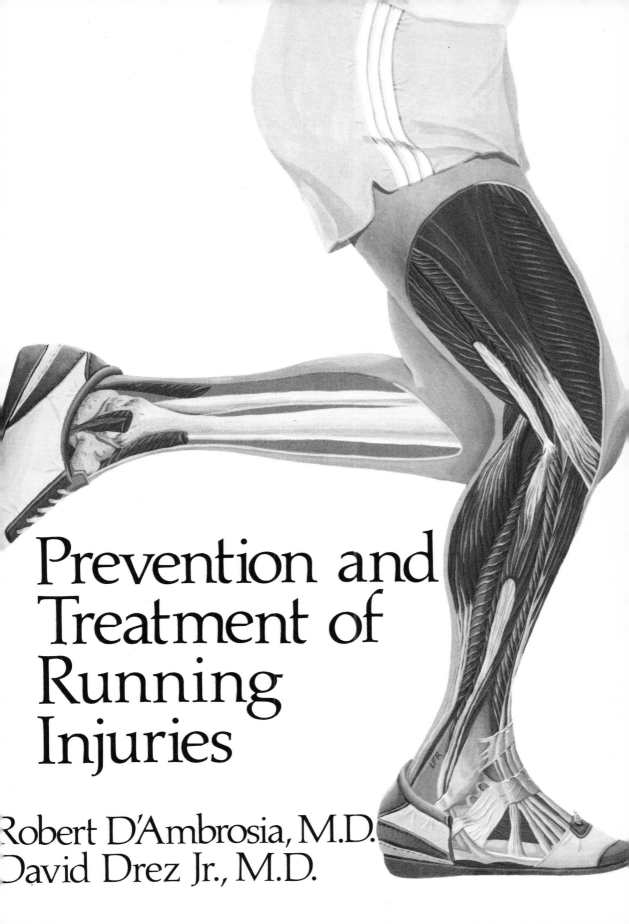

Prevention and Treatment of Running Injuries

Robert D'Ambrosia, M.D.
David Drez Jr., M.D.

To

BARBARA   JUDY
Lisa   Susan
Chris   Catherine
Matt   David
Peter

Acknowledgments

Editing a multiauthored text can be a time-consuming project not only for the editors, but also for the many authors on whom the editor depends for contributions. The authors who wrote this text did outstanding jobs with their individual chapters, and their efforts combined to make this book what it is.

This task was simplified for the editors, and the final product was largely made possible through the efforts of one person, Rose Pintado. Rose works in the LSU Department of Orthopaedic Surgery as a research associate and as such guided and directed the development of this book from beginning to end. Her dedication and perseverance is deeply appreciated by the editors who humbly acknowledge that this book would not have been possible without her special effort.

Our deepest gratitude also goes to Virginia Howard and the LSU Editorial Office who aided us in the copy editing. Their pleasant dedication to excellence is sincerely appreciated.

We also acknowledge the help of the Secretarial Staff of the LSU Department of Orthopedic Surgery under the guidance of Myrna Gemelli.

Preface

No sport has captured the imagination of such a large segment of our population as running. The enthusiasm generated for this activity has approached overwhelming proportions—it has become not only a sport, but a philosophy of life. This over-zealousness has pushed runners to try to make their bodies reach new physical limits. Understandably, many running injuries have resulted.

As physicians who have enjoyed the avocation of running since high school track, we recognize the fact that runners naturally seek physicians who have some empathy for their running problem. Four years ago, because of the increase in running injuries presented to us, we decided to establish a running clinic to accomodate the needs of our running population. We found that the team approach was essential for the best care for our runners. Our team consists of orthopedists, a physical therapist, and an orthotist. This approach has proved to be exceedingly beneficial in helping runners with musculoskeletal problems; we have also gained much knowledge about running problems, and especially about how best to prevent such injuries from occurring.

Similar clinics have been set up in diverse areas of the United States, and the sharing of our various experiences has been valuable. This book evolved from our contact with other running-oriented physicians, physical therapists, orthotists, and nutritional experts throughout the United States and Canada. The editors took great care to seek out authorities for the different subject areas of the text in an attempt to amass the most current knowledge presently available on ways to prevent and treat running injuries.

Table of Contents

Editor

Robert D. D'Ambrosia, M.D
Professor and Head
Department of Orthopedics
Louisiana State University
School of Medicine
New Orleans, LA

Associate Editor

David Drez, Jr., M.D.
Clinical Associate Professor
Department of Orthopedics
Louisiana State University
School of Medicine
New Orleans, LA

Contributors

William G. Clancy, Jr., M.D.
Associate Professor
Health Sciences, Medicine, and Surgery
University of Wisconsin Medical School
Madison, WI

Virginia B. Davis, L.P.T., M.A.
Director of Physical Therapy
Hotel Dieu Hospital
New Orleans, LA

Roy Douglas
Certified Prosthetist
Assistant Professor
Louisiana State University Medical Center
New Orleans, LA

Peter G. Hanson, M.S., M.D.
Associate Professor of Medicine
Center for Health Sciences
University of Wisconsin
Madison, WI

Diane M. Huse, R.D., M.S.
Instructor, Mayo Medical School
Nutritionist, Mayo Clinic
Rochester, MN

Douglas W. Jackson, M.D.
Director of Sports Medicine Clinic and Knee
  Fellowship
Memorial Hospital Medical Center
Long Branch, CA
Assistant Clinical Professor of Surgery
University of California
Irvine, CA

Robert E. Leach, M.D.
Professor and Chairman
Department of Orthopedic Surgery
Boston University School of Medicine
Boston, MA

Roger A. Mann, M.D.
Associate Clinical Professor of Orthopedic
  Surgery
University of California Medical School
Clinical Director
Gait Analysis Laboratory
Shriner's Hospital for
  Crippled Children
San Francisco, CA

Angus McBryde, Jr., M.D.
Clinical Professor of Orthopedic Surgery
Duke University Medical Center
Durham, NC

Lyle J. Micheli, M.D.
Director Division of Sports Medicine
Children's Hospital Medical Center
Boston, MA

Scott Mubarak, M.D.
Assistant Professor
Division of Orthopedics and Rehabilitation
University of California
San Diego, CA

William Stanish, M.D.
Director of Nova Scotia Sport Medicine Clinic
Assistant Professor of Surgery
Dalhousie University
Nova Scotia, Canada

1

Biomechanics of Running

Roger A. Mann, M.D.

The biomechanics of running are somewhat difficult to discuss because of the great variability of the activity; ie, from the slow recreational jogger to the world class sprinter. In the biomechanical studies of "normal" human walking, subject variability is minimal and the speed of gait is constant, as is the range of motion of the joints of the lower extremity, phasic muscle activity, and forces. In running, there is a broad spectrum of speed, resulting in extreme variability in the range of motion of the joints, phasic muscle activity, and ground reactions. To fully appreciate the biomechanical aspects of running, I believe we should compare it with an established standard. Because walking has been carefully studied, it will be used as the standard to which various speeds of running will be compared. All the data will be for steady-state walking and running. The acceleration or deceleration of gait will not be discussed.

All unreferenced data presented have been obtained from work carried out at the Gait Analysis Laboratory at Shriner's Hospital for Crippled Children in San Francisco, California.

Gait Cycle

The gait cycle is a useful framework by which the various events that occur during human locomotion can be expressed. The gait cycle begins and ends with heel strike of the same foot. That sequence also constitutes a stride, which consists of two steps. In the case of a person running on his toes, the gait cycle will obviously be from the time of initial ground contact until the same extremity once again comes into contact with the ground. The cycle is further divided into a stance phase and a swing phase. During walking

WALK CYCLE PHASES

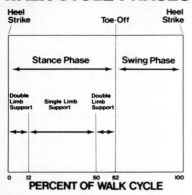

Fig. 1.1: Phases of the walking cycle.

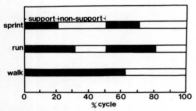

Fig. 1.2: The support or stance phase is in black and the non-support or swing phase is in white. Note: As the speed of gait increases, the period of support decreases and the period of non-support increases.

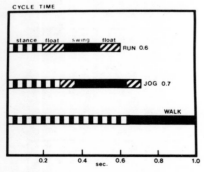

Fig. 1.3: As the speed of gait increases, there is a period of time in which both feet are off the ground. This period is known as the float phase. As the speed of gait increases, the length of the stance phase decreases and the period of float phase increases.

the stance phase occupies about 60% of the gait cycle and the swing phase 40%. Two periods of double-limb support occur during the first 12% and the last 12% of the stance phase, and a period of single-limb support occupies about 35% of the walking cycle. During walking there is no period in which both feet are off the ground (Fig. 1.1).

As the speed of gait increases, the period of stance phase decreases and swing phase increases (Fig. 1.2). As the speed of gait continues to increase, there is a period, termed the non-support or float phase, in which both feet are off the ground. So as the speed of running increases, the stance phase decreases, swing phase increases, and float phase increases (Fig. 1.3).

Angular Rotation of the Lower Extremity

During normal locomotion, motion occurs in the lower extremities in the transverse, sagittal, and frontal planes. In walking, this motion has been well documented and has been measured by many laboratories.[1,2] The results of the measurements basically agree with one another. When a person starts to run, however, the measurement of the rotation in the transverse plane becomes much more difficult and as a result, no reliable quantitative measurement of the transverse plane rotation have been made yet (Fig. 1.4). The sagittal plane motion, however, has been well documented;[3] the sagittal plane rotation of the hip, knee, and ankle, during walking, jogging, and running is presented (Fig. 1.5). Frontal plane motion of the hip joint, namely hip abduction and adduction, is also presented (Fig. 1.6).

Forceplate Analysis of Gait

During locomotion, forces are exerted against the ground. These forces are measured by use of a forceplate. The forces that are measured consist of the vertical, fore and aft shear, medial and lateral shear, and torque. The force data for walking are presented here (Fig. 1.7). The forceplate analysis for running and jogging demonstrates much more variability from step to step, as compared with walking. The vertical, fore and aft shear, and medial and lateral shear for jogging and running are also presented here (Fig. 1.8).

A comparison of the force data for walking and running readily demonstrates the marked increase in the ground reaction of running. The magnitude

2

Roger A. Mann, M.D.

of the vertical force in walking at a cadance of 120 steps per minute (60 strides) rarely exceeds 115 to 120% of body weight. The inclination and magnitude of the initial spike on a vertical force curve are much greater for running than for walking. In walking the initial spike is about 70% of body weight, whereas running barefooted increases the spike to slightly less than 200% of body weight. Also interestingly, the two peaks that are normally seen in the vertical force curve for walking are no longer present during running, probably because only one extremity is on the ground at a time during the stance phase of running, whereas the stance phase of walking includes two periods of double-limb support.

The fore and aft shear pattern demonstrates the same basic configuration for walking, jogging, and running; however, the magnitude is increased about 50% for running. The medial and lateral shear curves for walking, jogging, and running also demonstrate the same general pattern, although again magnitude is increased in running.

The torque measurement during walking demonstrates an initial internal torque followed by an external torque against the ground. This sequence correlates well with the transverse rotation curve of the lower extremity, in that internal rotation occurs in the lower extremity at the same time that an internal torque occurs against the ground, and conversely, external rotation occurs in the lower extremity, associated with an external torque against the ground. Because torque has been adequately measured only for walking, no data are presented for jogging and running.

Electromyography of the Lower Extremities

The phasic activity of the muscles of the lower extremities during walking is shown (Fig. 1.9). The phasic activity has been presented by muscle groups such as the hip flexors and extensors, knee flexors and extensors, and ankle dorsiflexors and plantar flexors, because these muscles are essentially functioning as a unit, rather than as individual muscles. The muscles of the lower extremities do not have a fine neurologic and cerebral representation, as do the muscles of the upper extremities. The overall muscle function is much more gross in the lower extremity than in the upper extremity, and as the speed of gait increases, it has been found that the phasic activity

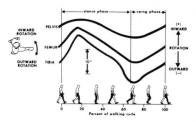

Fig. 1.4: Transverse plane rotation of the pelvis, femur, and tibia. Note that maximum internal rotation is achieved by approximately 15% of the walking cycle and maximum external rotation at the time of toe-off.

Fig. 1.5: Sagittal plane motion of the lower extremity during walking, jogging, and running.

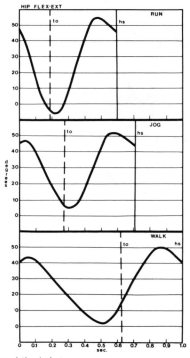

a. Hip joint

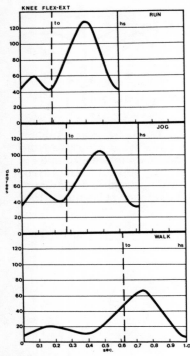

b. Knee joint

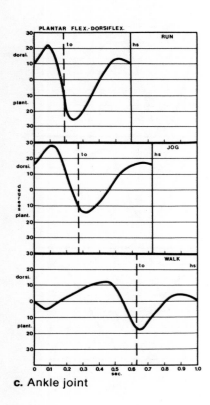

c. Ankle joint

of the various muscles function even more as a group than during walking. Electromyographic activity of the muscles of the lower extremity for jogging and running is presented (Fig. 1.10).

Biomechanical Principles

Several basic principles should be kept firmly in mind when evaluating the changes in the biomechanics of the lower extremities as the speed of gait increases. The transverse rotation that occurs in the lower extremity during the walking gait has been documented both qualitatively and quantitatively, but quantitative data of running has been difficult to obtain. Qualitative data obtained from high-speed movies show that the same basic type of rotation occurs during running and the rotation seems to be of somewhat greater magnitude than that observed during walking. The transverse rotation, which occurs in the lower extremity at the time of initial ground contact, is transmitted across the ankle joint to the subtalar joint. The subtalar joint is an oblique hinge that is aligned at about 45° to the horizontal plane and deviates 16° from medial to lateral in relation to the foot (Fig. 1.11). The subtalar joint, acting as an oblique hinge, translates the transverse rotation of the lower extremity into inversion and eversion of the calcaneus.[4,5,6]

Internal rotation of the lower extremity everts the calcaneus, and conversely, external rotation of the lower extremity inverts the calcaneus (Fig. 1.12). The motion in the subtalar joint essentially controls the subsequent stability of the forefoot through its control of the transverse tarsal joint and therefore, controls the stability of the longitudinal arch of the foot. The function of the transverse tarsal joint, which is composed of the talonavicular and calcaneocuboid joints, is such that its stability is increased by inversion of the calcaneus and conversely, is decreased by eversion of the subtalar joint (Fig. 1.13).[7]

Rotation in the mid-tarsal area of the foot is minimal, and the next joint that plays a significant role in the biomechanics of the foot is the metatarsophalangeal joint. Two mechanisms that function at the level of the metatarsophalangeal joint help to stabilize the foot. The first (Fig. 1.14), is the metatarsal break.[8,9] This obliquely placed axis acts to cam the foot in such a manner as to help produce inversion of the calcaneus and external rotation of the lower extremity. The second mechanism that is functioning is that of

Roger A. Mann, M.D.

the plantar aponeurosis,[10] which arises from the tubercle of the calcaneus, passes forward, and inserts into the base of the proximal phalanges. As the toes are forced into dorsiflexion during the latter part of stance phase, the plantar aponeurosis is wrapped around the metatarsal heads in such a way that it not only stabilizes the metatarso-phalangeal joints but helps to elevate the longitudinal arch (Fig. 1.15). At the same time that the plantar aponeurosis is functioning, the intrinsic muscles of the foot are active, and these also help to stabilize the longitudinal arch as well.

Functional Biomechanics

Thus far, some of the biomechanical principles of the lower extremity have been presented. Needless to say, the function of the lower extremities is a dynamic one, and as the speed of gait increases, not only is the speed by which each of these mechanisms occurs increased but the magnitude of the force involved increases greatly.

At the time of initial ground contact, internal rotation occurs in the lower extremity, and as the foot is loaded, concomitant eversion occurs in the calcaneus. The eversion of the calcaneus starts a series of movements that results in pronation of the longitudinal arch. The eversion of the calcaneus results in a flexible transverse tarsal joint, which permits a certain degree of collapse of the longitudinal arch as the foot is applied to the ground. This mechanism of eversion of the calcaneus along with flexibility of the longitudinal arch is purely passive and is not under any muscle control *per se*. The factors limiting the degree of collapse of the longitudinal arch after initial ground contact appears to be only those provided by the axis of motions of the joints of the foot, shape of the bones of the foot, and their connecting ligaments. Pronation is a normal occurrence in the foot at the time of initial ground contact (Fig. 1.16).

Once the foot is firmly on the ground, progressive external rotation occurs in the lower extremity. This external rotation passes across the ankle joint to the subtalar joint. In response to this external rotation, the subtalar joint brings about inversion of the calcaneus, which in turn stabilizes the transverse tarsal joint, and helps to create a rigid longitudinal arch. As the weight bearing progresses along the foot to the metatarsal head area, bringing about dorsiflexion of the metatarso-phalangeal joints, the oblique metatarsal break

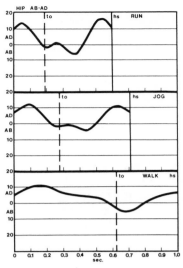

Fig. 1.6: Frontal plane motion of the hip joint, namely, hip abduction and adduction during walking, jogging, and running.

Fig. 1.7: Forceplate analysis of walking.

VERTICAL FORCE

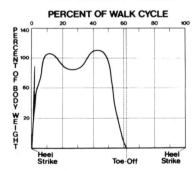

a. Vertical force

FORWARD-AFT SHEAR

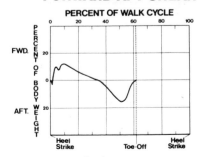

b. Fore and aft shear

MEDIAL-LATERAL SHEAR

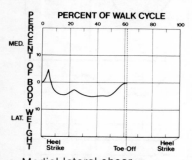

c. Medial lateral shear

TORQUE

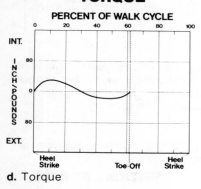

d. Torque

Fig. 1.8: Comparison of the force-plate analysis for walking, running, and jogging.

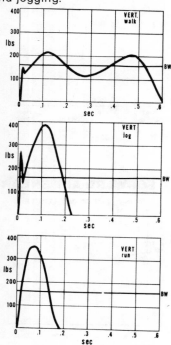

a.

further helps to bring about inversion by increasing external rotation of the tibia. Stability of the foot is further enhanced by the action of the plantar aponeurosis and intrinsic muscles of the foot. The actions that have just been described are active mechanisms, as opposed to the passive mechanism of pronation. The external rotation of the stance limb is initiated by the forward motion of the swing leg, which helps to bring the swing leg side of the pelvis forward. As this occurs, the stance leg femur, which is fixed to the pelvis by the electrically active adductor muscles of the thigh, is externally rotated. The external rotation of the femur passes across the knee joint, which is stabilized by its ligaments, as well as by the popiteus muscle. This external rotation force passes through the tibia and across the ankle joint to the subtalar joint, which through its control of the calcaneus and transverse tarsal joint then stabilizes the longitudinal arch, creating a rigid level of the foot.

The motion occurring in the sagittal plane at the hip, the knee, and the ankle demonstrates some interesting changes as the speed of gait increases. Generally speaking, the total range of motion increases in each of these joints during jogging and running (Fig. 1.5). At the time of *initial ground contact* there is an increased amount of flexion at the hip joint, rapid flexion at the knee joint, and dorsiflexion at the ankle joint. This increased joint motion functions mainly to help the body absorb the sharply increased impact of initial ground contact. The most significant change is at the ankle joint, where at the time of initial ground contact, plantar flexion occurs during walking, but during running rapid dorsiflexion occurs. Our laboratory has obtained high-speed movies of many long-distance runners, and with few exceptions, initial ground contact is either heel first or foot flat. Even a sprinter's foot, which lands in plantar flexion, undergoes a certain degree of dorsiflexion after initial ground contact, although the degree of dorisiflexion is not sufficient to permit the sprinter's heel to strike the ground. During the *mid-stance phase,* progressive extension occurs at the hip joint and continues until after toe-off. The knee joint, after undergoing rapid flexion during the first half of stance, rapidly extends during the remainder of the stance until toe-off. The ankle joint, after rapid dorsiflexion which peaks at mid-stance, undergoes rapid plantar flexion. This continues until after toe-off.

6

Roger A. Mann, M.D.

In contrast to the runner, the few sprinters we have studied had gradual extension of the hip joint after initial ground contact and progressive flexion of the knee joint, but the same type of rapid dorsiflexion of the ankle joint until mid-stance, when rapid plantar flexion began.

The frontal plane motion of the hip joint demonstrates adduction at the time of initial ground contact, which increases in magnitude with increased speed of gait (Fig. 1.6). This adduction at the hip joint accounts for the initial medial force spike noted in the forceplate data (Fig. 1.8). We then see progressive abduction of the hip, which reaches its peak after toe-off, and this is what accounts for the lateral force curve noted throughout the remainder of stance phase.

Electromyography

The electromyographic data of the phasic activities of the muscle in the lower extremities also change as the speed of gait increases. Generally speaking, by percentage the muscles have a longer period of stance phase activity than that normally seen in walking. As an example, it is rare to see a muscle group active for more than 50% of the stance phase during walking, but in jogging and running, there is activity during 70 to 80% of the stance phase. The muscle function about the hip joint demonstrates that during walking, the gluteus maximus is active from the end of the swing phase until the foot is flat on the ground. It is probably functioning to help decelerate the swinging thigh and to provide stability at the hip joint at the time of initial ground contact. During jogging and running, the gluteus maximus likewise has terminal swing phase activity but remains active during the first 40% of the stance phase. During that period, rapid hip extension occurs and the gluteus maximus appears to help bring this about. The hip abductors function during terminal swing and throughout the first 50% of the stance phase during walking, jogging, and running. The abductors function to stabilize the stance leg side of the pelvis at the time of initial ground contact, which helps prevent excessive sagging of the swing leg side of the pelvis.[11] The period of activity in the hip adductors definitely changes as the speed of gait increases. During walking, the hip adductors are active during the last third of the stance phase, whereas during jogging and running they appear to demonstrate activity throughout the entire stance and swing

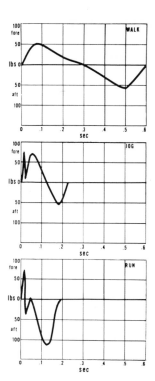

b.

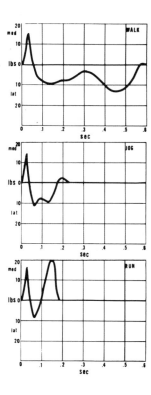

c.

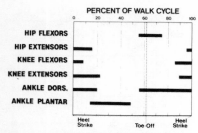

Fig. 1.9: Electromyographic activity of the muscle groups of the lower extremity during walking.

Fig. 1.10: Electromyographic activity of the muscle of the lower extremity during walking, jogging, and running in relationship to the range of motion of the joint.

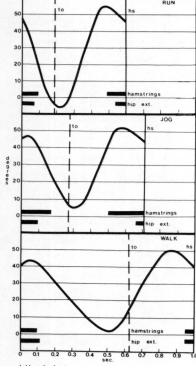

a. Hip joint

phase. Data about the activity of the hip adductor muscles have always been difficult to collect and are highly variable. A larger series of runners should be studied to further our knowledge regarding phasic activity.

The quadriceps group of muscles about the knee joint appears to perform the same functions during both walking and running. At the end of swing phase they bring about terminal knee extension and stabilize the knee after initial ground contact, through the period of initial knee flexion. These muscles, however, remain active during about 50 to 60% of the stance phase in running, as compared with only 25% during walking. The period of swing phase activity during running and sprinting increases considerably, probably to help bring about the rapid knee extension that is required as the speed of gait increases. During walking, knee extension is a fairly passive mechanism. The hamstring muscles are active during the end of swing and into mid-stance phase until the foot is flat on the ground, which is about 10% of the walking cycle. As the speed of gait increases, the hamstrings become active during the last third of swing phase, at which time the hip and knee joints become extended. Because this is a two-joint muscle, it probably helps to initiate extension of the hip joint, which occurs simultaneously. Once stance begins, the hamstrings remain active for about 60% of the stance phase, during which time rapid extension continues, whereas the knee rapidly flexes.

A significant change occurs about the ankle joint in the phasic activity and the function of the anterior and posterior calf muscles. During walking, the anterior compartment is active from late stance through the first 50% of stance phase. The anterior compartment still initially undergoes a concentric contraction at the time of toe-off, and the concentric contraction continues after initial ground contact until maximum dorsiflexion is reached at about 50% of stance phase. During walking, the anterior compartment functions to restrain plantar flexion of the foot after initial ground contact, but during running, the anterior compartment appears to be accelerating the tibia over the fixed foot. This may be one of the mechanisms by which the body maintains and possibly increases its velocity of gait. Further study of the function of the anterior compartment is needed to elucidate this possibility.

Roger A. Mann, M.D.

During walking, the posterior calf muscles restrain the forward movement of the tibia over the fixed foot. The posterior calf muscles are active from about 25% of the stance phase until 50% of the stance phase and for the most part undergo an eccentric type of contraction. It is only during the last 25% of their activity that this muscle group starts to undergo a concentric contraction that initiates active plantar flexion. This muscle group, by functioning to restrain the forward movement of the tibia, permits the body to lean forward and to take a longer stride.[12,13] Active plantar flexion, causing push-off or forward propulsion of the body during walking, does not seem to occur. During jogging and running, the posterior calf becomes functional at the end of swing phase and undergoes a rapid eccentric contraction at the time of initial ground contact as rapid dorsiflexion of the ankle joint occurs. The posterior calf then continues its activity for about 60% of the stance phase. Activity ceases, however, after about half of the plantar flexion of the ankle joint has occurred. The posterior calf probably functions initially to help stabilize the ankle joint at the time of initial ground contact by controlling the forward movement of the tibia. In the latter part of the stance phase, the posterior calf probably provides some degree of propulsion, but how much it provides remains to be determined.

The posterior calf does perform push-off during the acceleration phase of running as well as during sports that require rapid starting, such as squash, racquetball, or tennis, but in steady-state running, push-off appears to be minimal.

Pronation

As pointed out previously, pronation is a normal function of the foot at the time of initial ground contact. Pronation itself is a passive event brought about by the weight of the body against the lower extremity and the subsequent loading of the subtalar joint, which will normally collapse into an everted position at ground contact, due to the configuration of the joint. The constraints of pronation are the shape of the joints of the subtalar joint complex along with their ligamentous support, and to a lesser degree the muscle support. As pronation occurs, the tibia rotates internally, which again is secondary to the eversion movement of the subtalar joint. Hypothetically, if one were to place the calcaneus in a device that would not permit eversion and then

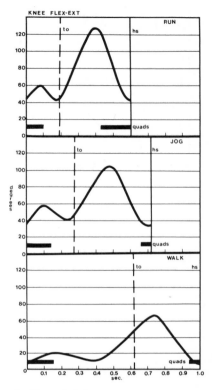

b. Knee joint

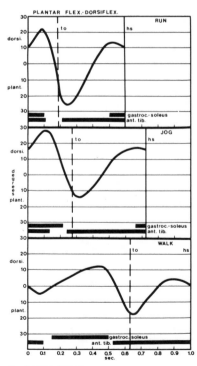

c. Ankle joint

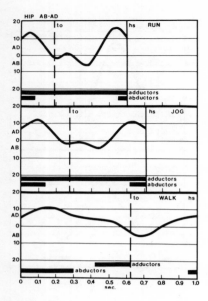

d. Hip joint

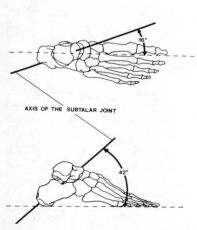

Fig. 1.11: Axis of the subtalar joint.

load the extremity, there would be little or no internal rotation of the tibia; conversely, if the calcaneus were to be held into extreme eversion, there would be extreme flattening of the longitudinal arch along with an increased internal rotation of the lower extremity.

This sequence of events is observed clinically in people who have a flat foot or a cavus foot. In a person with a flat foot, at the time of initial ground contact eversion of the subtlar joint increases, which results in an increase in the degree of internal rotation of the lower extremity, as well as increased flattening of the longitudinal arch. In the cavus foot, the opposite occurs; ie, the motion of the subtalar joint decreases and as a result, internal rotation of the subtalar joint and flattenting of the longitudinal arch are both minimal. The flat foot represents an increase in the absorption of the impact, in which we observe increased motion in the lower extremity; with repetitive stress, this situation may cause various clinical problems in some persons. In the cavus foot, the absorption of the impact actually decreases, which results in increased stresses being placed on the lower extremity. Just because someone has this type of foot configuration, however, does not necessarily mean the foot will be symptomatic.

Runners develop problems mainly because of the repetitive stress imparted to the lower extremity. An average 150-lb man who is walking with a step length of 2½ feet and taking about 2,110 steps to walk a mile, will absorb at initial ground contact, considering an impact of 80% of the body weight, a total of 253,440 pounds (127 tons) or 63½ tons per foot. If the same person were running a mile, taking a step of 3½ feet and taking about 1,175 steps, he would absorb at initial ground contact, considering an impact of 250% of body weight, a total of 440,625 pounds (220 tons) or 110 tons per foot.

The other factor that must be taken into account when considering pronation is the time interval in which the pronation occurs. In walking, pronation is completed by about 15% of the walking cycle or 25% of the stance phase. The internal rotation of the lower extremity usually reaches its peak at the same time, according to the torque measurements of the forceplate. In real time, for a person walking at a normal pace of 120 steps per minute, full pronation occurs within about 150 milliseconds (total stance time of about 600 milliseconds), whereas for a person who is running at a six-

Roger A. Mann, M.D.

minute-mile pace, maximum pronation occurs within 30 milliseconds (total stance time about 200 milliseconds). Therefore, the pronation that occurs during running takes place in about one fifth of the time as that observed during walking. In a study by Cavanagh *et al*,[14] an estimate was made of the angular velocity of pronation, and they noted that although the maximum degree of pronation occurs by 30 milliseconds, the actual angular velocity of the subtalar joint reaches its maximum at 15 milliseconds. High-speed movies in our laboratory have shown that, as the foot strikes the ground, the heel is in a slightly inverted position so that on initial ground contact, the calcaneus is rapidly brought out of this slightly inverted position, and as it is loaded with about 2½ times the body weight, it rapidly passes into eversion. The remainder of the weight acceptance and associated pronation is carried out at a slightly slower rate, possibly because of the impact absorption mechanism of the limb, namely the rapid dorsiflexion of the ankle joint and flexion of the knee joint. An interesting correlation in data of Cavanagh *et al*, was that the medial shear reached its peak after about 10 milliseconds and is probably accounted for in part by the inverted position of the subtalar joint at initial ground contact, after which the direction of the force changes to that of a lateral shear, which reaches its peak by 30 milliseconds, probably because maximum pronation has occurred.

Effect of Orthotic Devices on Hindfoot Motion

In a small percentage of runners an overuse syndrome can occur as a result of the repetitive stress of running. Such persons generally tend to have a more pronated foot than the average population but a few may also have a cavus type of foot. Other malalignment problems, such as genu varum and valgum, and toeing in and toeing out, can also lead to clinical problems secondary to the stress of running. Various types of orthotic devices have been used by runners and the question that always arises is what, if anything, does an orthosis do from a biomechanical point of view. One of the problems in making such a determination is the actual measurement of tibial and subtalar joint rotation during running. Unfortunately, no reliable method is available at this time, but a fairly good estimate of subtalar joint motion can be

Fig. 1.12: Model of the function of the subtalar joint as it translates motion from the tibia above into the calcaneus below.

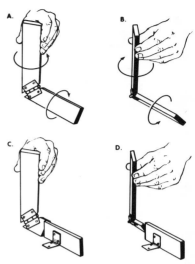

a. Action of a mitered hinge demonstrating translation of rotation across a 45° hinge. This is analogous to the subtalar joint. Inward rotation of the upper stick causes outward rotation of the lower stick and this is analogous to the inward rotation of the tibia, producing eversion of the calcaneus.

b. Conversely, it is demonstrated that outward rotation of the tibia will produce inward rotation of the calcaneus.

c. & d. The addition of a pivot between two segments of the mechanism presents the analogy as above but with the addition of the transverse tarsal joint. This is depicted by the pivot point beyond the 45° hinge working against the distal segment which is fixed on the ground. This distal segment represents the forefoot that is firmly planted on the ground. The inward rotation of the tibia, which produces eversion of the calcaneus, will obviously have an effect on the transverse tarsal joint. (See text for further explanation.)

Fig. 1.13: Axes of the transverse tarsal joint (TN = talonavicular and CC = calcaneocuboid joint).

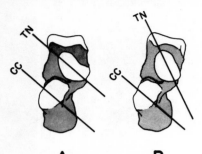

A   **B**

a. When the calcaneus is in eversion, the conjoint axes between the talonavicular and calcaneocuboid joints are parallel to one another so that there is increased motion in the transverse tarsal joint.

b. When the calcaneus is in eversion the conjoint axes between the talonavicular and calcaneocuboid joints are parallel to one another so that there is increased motion in the transverse tarsal joint.

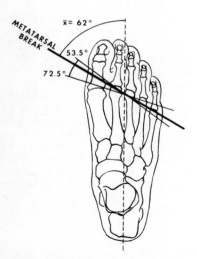

Fig. 1.14: Variation in the angulation of the metatarsal break.

obtained by placing a series of dots along the posterior aspect of the calf, the heel, and the shoe. By a photometric method of analysis, a general quantitation of the motion of the subtalar joint has been obtained. In a review of several of the studies, in most cases the overall configuration of the curve of pronation of the hindfoot seemed to follow along the same general pattern as obtained for walking. The use of some type of a support along the medial side of the foot will bring about a decrease in the amount of eversion of the calcaneus and subsequent pronation of the longitudinal arch. The thicker the material, the greater the decrease in eversion of the calcaneus. The study by Cavanagh *et al*, in which increasing thicknesses of felt were selectively placed along the medial border of the foot (eventually equivalent to 9.5 millimeters), showed a decrease in the degree of pronation and a sharp decrease in the angular velocity of the pronation. They further studied the subject, using a forceplate, and the only significant change was in the medial and lateral shear, in which the medial shear was decreased considerably in the subject using the medial support.

By careful laboratory study of high-speed motion pictures of runners, we have been able to demonstrate a qualitative decrease in pronation as well as medial deviation of the inner border of the foot and ankle, with increased support along the medial side of the foot.

An orthosis providing a medial arch support therefore appears to play a role in the control of the foot by decreasing the total number of degrees, as well as the rate, of pronation of the foot. This type of device would be of clinical benefit in a certain select group of symptomatic runners.

References

1. Levens AS, Inman VT, Blosser JA: Transverse rotation of the segments of the lower extremity in locomotion. J Bone Joint Surg 30A:859-1948.
2. University of California (Berkeley), Prosthetic Devices Research Project, Subcontractor's Final Report to the Committee on Artificial Limbs National Research Council; Fundamental studies of human locomotion and other information relating to design of artificial limbs, 1947. Two volumes.
3. Sutherland DH, Hagy JL: Measurement of gait movements from motion picture films. J Bone Joint Surg 54A:787-797, 1972.
4. Wright DG, Desai ME, Henderson BS: Action of the subtalar and ankle-joint complex during the stance phase of walking. J Bone Joint Surg 46A:361, 1964.
5. Close JR, Inman VT: The action of the subtalar joint.

Roger A. Mann, M.D.

Univ Calif Prosthet Devices Res Rep Ser 11, Issue 24, May 1953.

6. Manter JT: Movements of the subtalar and transverse tarsal joints. Anat Rec 80:397, 1941.
7. Elftman H: The transverse tarsal joint and its control. Clin Orthop 16:41, 1960.
8. Inman VT: The Joints of the Ankle. Baltimore, Waverly Press, 1976.
9. Isman RE, Inman VT: Anthropometric studies of the human foot and ankle. Bull Prosthet Res 10-11:97, 1976.
10. Hicks JH: The mechanics of the foot, II. The plantar aponeurosis and the arch. J Anat 88:25, 1954.
11. Inman VT: Functional aspects of the abdutor muscles of the hip. J Bone Joint Surg 29:607, 1947.
12. Simon SR, Mann RA, Hagy JL, Larsen LJ: Role of the posterior calf muscles in the normal gait. J Bone Joint Surg 29:607, 1947.
13. Sutherland DH: An electromyographic study of the plantar flexor of the ankle in normal walking on the level. J Bone Joint Surg 48A:66-71, 1966.
14. Cavanagh PR, Clarke T, Williams K, Kalenak A: An evaluation of the effect of orthotics on force distribution and rearfoot movement during running. Presented at the Am Orthop Soc Sports Med Meeting, Lake Placid, NY June, 1978.

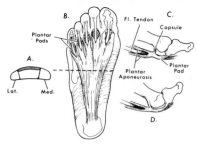

Fig. 1.15: The plantar aponeurosis.

a. Cross section.

b. The plantar aponeurosis divides as it proceeds distally to allow the flexor tendons to pass through the aponeurosis.

c. The plantar aponeurosis combines with the joint capsule to form the plantar pad of the metatarsophalangeal joint.

d. Dorsiflexion of the toes forces the metatarsal head into plantar flexion and brings the plantar pad over the head of the metatarsal.

Fig. 1.16: A model of the linkage between the tibia, hindfoot, and forefoot demonstrating the effect on the longitudinal arch.

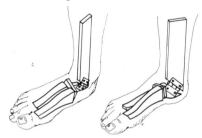

a. Internal rotation of the tibia produces eversion of the calcaneus, which in turn produces a flexible transverse tarsal joint and flattens the longitudinal arch, bringing about pronation of the foot. This occurs at the time of initial ground contact.

b. External rotation of the tibia brings about inversion of the heel, stability of the transverse tarsal joint with elevation of the longitudinal arch, giving rise to a supinated firm forefoot.

2

Examination of the Lower Extremity in Runners

David Drez, Jr., M.D.

As should be evident from the previous chapter on biomechanics, doing a detailed examination of the lower extremity in the runner is a necessity. Such an examination permits one to recognize anatomic abnormalities that could cause the runner problems. Even subtle anatomic deviations can produce injury because of the large forces that the lower extremity is subjected to during running and jogging.

This chapter discusses possible sites of injury in the lower extremity.

General Principles

The lower extremity should be examined while the runner is sitting, reclining, and standing, while walking, and in some cases while running. Dynamic evaluation is important because some abnormalities that are accentuated under certain conditions might otherwise be overlooked. In addition, the runner should be scrutinized from the front, the back, the side, close, and at a distance. The examining room surface should preferably be hard rather than soft or carpeted, in case certain alterations in the foot are obscured. In addition to the lower extremity, the entire torso should be examined.

Examination of the Erect Patinet
Standing

Spinal alignment is observed while the patient is erect and with forward flexion. The spine must also be viewed laterally. *Spinal mobility* and *hamstring tightness* can be ascertained by forward flexion with the arms extended to touch the toes.

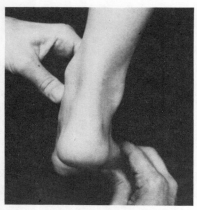

Fig. 2.1: With patient prone, the foot is held at the fourth and fifth metatarsal heads with the thumb and index fingers of one hand while the other index finger and thumb palpate the talar head.

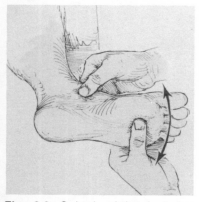

Fig. 2.2: Subtalar joint is being everted and inverted.

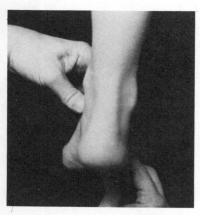

Fig. 2.3: Eversion of the foot.

Leg length discrepancies can be detected by palpating and marking the iliac crests or anterior superior spines and noting any difference in height of the marking in one side compared with the other.

Extremity alignment is observed next. The area of the knee is of prime importance. Any *genu varum* or *genu valgum* is measured with goniometer. Some degree of genu valgum in women is not uncommon, but in my opinion should not exceed 5°. Genu varum in men is likewise not uncommon. Five degrees again probably represents the upper limits of normal. Flexion contractures or recurvatum at the knee are noted as well. *Patellar position* is observed and the Q angle is measured.

Walking

While the patient walks back and forth, the examiner looks for *asymmetrical arm motion, excessive pelvic tilt,* and any other *deviations in the gait pattern. Femoral rotation, patellar position, patellar tracking,* and *knee alignment* are noted. The entire foot is again evaluated. *Dynamic gastroc-soleus tightness,* not seen at rest, may become more pronounced during walking; the heel may never touch the floor. *Heel and toe walking* should be done.

Running

Observing the patient running or jogging is helpful in some cases, although it demands a degree of dedication that time constraints make difficult in the usual practice situation. In cases that are difficult to diagnose, however, this examination is recommended.

Examination of the Sitting Patient

Leg lengths are checked again by having the runner sit with the back against the wall and knees extended. *Hamstring tightness* and *sciatic nerve irritation* can be evaluated by the examiner's passively extending each of the seated patient's legs. Full extension should be possible without undue lumbar extension or discomfort. The *deep tendon reflexes* should be checked also.

Patellar position and *patellar tracking* are observed on flexion and extension. The anterior aspect of the knee is palpated as it is flexed and extended. Extension of the knee against resistance may provide information regarding *patellofemoral pathology.*

David Drez, Jr., M.D.

Areas about the knee—in particular, the *patella*, the *patellar tendon*, the *tibial tubercle*, the *lateral femoral epicondyle*, and *pes anserinus tendon* area—should be palpated. The degree of *tibial torsion* is also observed.

Examination of the Reclining Patient
Supine

Leg lengths are again determined by measuring from the anterior superior iliac crest to the medial malleolar area. *Strength of the abdominal muscles* is evaluated by having the patient do sit-ups with the knees flexed.

Range of motion of the hips and knees is checked. A thorough examination of the knee is mandatory.

The amount of *hip flexion with the knee extended* allows assessment of *hamstring flexibility*. In my opinion, at least 60° of hip flexion should be possible in the runner.

Hamstring stretchability should be measured as outlined in Chapter 11, Figs. 11.8 and 11.8a).

With the patient in the supine position, have him flex the hip to 90° with the knee also flexed. The patient should maintain 90° of hip flexion throughout the test by placing both hands around his thigh. Extend the flexed knee as far as possible and measure the angle at the knee to determine hamstring flexibility/tightness (Fig. 11.8a). The long axes of the fibula and the femur should have an angle of 0°. Hamstring tightness is present if the angle is greater than 0°.

Ankle dorsiflexion with the leg extended is measured; I believe at least 10° should be possible in the runner.

Peripheral pulses are palpated and *muscle strength* in the lower extremity is grossly evaluated. Palpation of major muscle masses, such as the quadriceps, to ascertain any differences in *muscle tone* is important. A *sensory examination* can be rapidly and easily done.

Prone

With the patient prone, the knees are flexed and the amount of *hip rotation* is measured. External rotation and internal rotation of the hip in most cases are equal; a difference of 30° in one side compared with the other is significant.[2]

The amount of *ankle dorsiflexion* is again checked with the foot in slight eversion. It should be at least 10°.

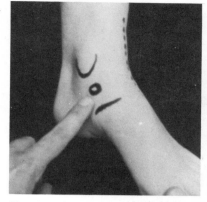

Fig. 2.4: Area where talar head is palpated when foot is everted.

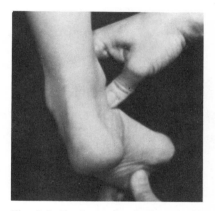

Fig. 2.5: Foot maximally inverted.

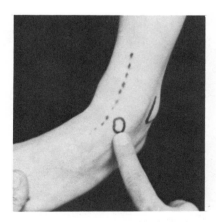

Fig. 2.6: Area where talar head is palpated when foot is inverted.

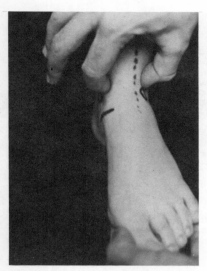

Fig. 2.7: Neutral position of subtalar joint—no bulge of talus medialy or laterally.

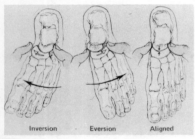

Inversion   Eversion   Aligned

Fig. 2.8: Neutral position of subtalar joint.

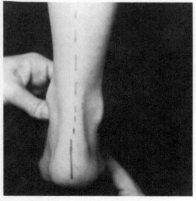

Fig. 2:9 Heel-leg alignment.

The amount of *inversion and eversion of the subtalar joint* is measured. Normally, inversion is around 30°, and eversion, 10°.[3,4]

The neutral position of the subtalar joint should be determined by the following technique.[5,6,7] With the patient prone, the foot is grasped over the fourth and fifth metatarsal heads with the index finger and thumb. The other index finger and thumb are used to palpate the talar head (Fig. 2.1). The foot is maximally everted and the subtalar joint is palpated medially just anterior to and below the medial malleolous (Figs. 2.2—4).

The foot is now maximally inverted and the talar head is felt to bulge just lateral to the midline, and just anterior to the lateral malleolus (Figs. 2.5 and 2.6). The subtalar joint is then placed in a position in which no bulge is felt medially or laterally (Fig. 2.7). The subtalar joint is now said to be in a neutral position and congruently aligned with the tarsal navicular (Fig. 2.8).

After the neutral position has been achieved, observations are made for abnormalities of alignment. The first measurement is that of the *leg-heel alignment.* A line drawn to bisect the lower third of the leg just before the gastrocnemius muscle belly should fall directly over or parallel to a line that bisects the bony outline of the calcaneus (Fig. 2.9). Some 2-3° of varus of the heel is normal. Next, *heel-forefoot alignment* is determined. A line bisecting the bony outline of the os calcus should be perpendicular to the plane of the first through the fifth metatarsal heads (Fig. 2.10).

Abnormalities or deviations of the leg-heel alignment are present if the heel is in a varus or valgus position to the line bisecting the lower one third of the leg (Fig. 2.11). These deviations are measured with a goniometer and are recorded as degrees of heel valgus or heel varus.

Deviations of heel-forefoot alignment exist when the forefoot is either in a valgus or varus relationship to the normal perpendicular arrangement between the heel and forefoot (Fig. 2.12). These deviations are measured with a goniometer and recorded as degrees of forefoot valgus or forefoot varus.

Mobility of the mid tarsal joints and *first ray* are noted. Dorsiflexion and plantar flexion should be free and nonpainful. *Motion of the first metatarsophalangeal joint* should be free and without pain. Note should be made of *excessive callus formation* on the plantar aspect of the foot and toes or on the dorsum of the foot and toes.

David Drez, Jr., M.D.

Certain areas in the foot and ankle deserve special attention. The *peroneal tendons* as they course behind the lateral malleolus should be examined. Tenderness or synovitis in this area can be secondary to subluxation or dislocation of these tendons. Eversion of the foot against resistance will allow one to demonstrate subluxation or dislocation of the peroneal tendons. The area around the *anterior or posterior tibial tendons* is evaluated for tenderness as well. *Lateral ligamentous instability* of the ankle is checked by the anterior drawer and inversion stress test. Palpation of the *interdigital space,* especially the third and fourth, may indicate the presence of an *interdigital neuroma.* The *Achilles tendon* should be palpated along its entire course from its insertion to the musculotendinous junction. Tenderness and thickening may indicate abnormalities. The *inner border of the mid and distal tibia* should be palpated. Enlargement or tenderness in this area may be present and indicative of a stress reaction. The *undersurface of the foot* should be palpated. Tenderness over the metatarsal heads, the plantar fascia and anterior aspect of the os calcis should be sought.

Summary

The examination of the lower extremity outlined above emphasizes the importance of detecting minor anatomic abnormalities in runners. Such abnormalities may produce significant symptoms because of the tremendous loads imposed on the runner's musculoskeletal system.

References

1. Mann RA, et al: Running symposium. Foot and Ankle 1:199, 1981.
2. James SL: Examination of Runners, videotape. American Academy of Orthopedic Surgeons, 1981.
3. Inman VT: The Joints of the Ankle. Baltimore, Williams and Wilkins Co., 1976.
4. James SL, et al: Injuries to runners. Sports Med 6:43, 1978.
5. Wernick J, Langer S: A Practical Manual for a Basic Approach to Biomechanics, Vol 1. Deer Park, NY, Langer Acrylic Lab, 1972.
6. James SL, et al: Injuries to runners. Sports Med 5:40-42, 1978.
7. Drez D: Running footwear. Am J Sports Med 8:141, 1980.

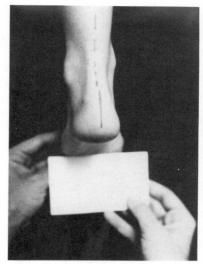

Fig. 2.10: Heel-forefoot alignment.

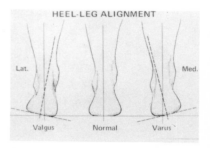

Fig. 2.11: Abnormalities of leg-heel alignment.

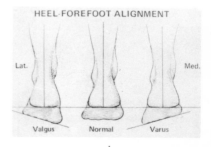

Fig. 2.12: Abnormalities of heel-forefoot alignment.

3

Stress Fractures in Runners

Angus M. McBryde, Jr.

One of the repetitive stress injuries of soft tissues and bone is stress fracture, which was first described in 1855 by Breithaupt and has since been identified by numerous appellations; eg, March fracture, fatigue fracture, overload fracture, exhaustion fracture, and runner's fracture.

During World War II, numerous reports detailed stress fracture of pelvic and lower extremity bones. These reports documented a broad clinical experience. The running-based military training activities provided experience pertinent to the modern-day runner,[1-3] but with definite clinical differences between the military stress fracture and those occurring in the athletic population.[4]

There are two excellent books on stress fractures. The Morris and Blickenstaff publication[5] is based primarily on a military population, but with selected examples of runner's stress fractures. Devas' book,[6] *not* military-based, serves as an excellent reference work and offers theory in certain areas.

Definition

Stress fracture is defined as a partial or complete fracture of bone due to its inability to withstand nonviolent stress that is applied in a rhythmic, repeated subthreshold manner. A distinct series of events—a process and not an occurrence—leads to stress fracture or, more accurately, stress syndrome of bone. Wolff's law, stating that "every change in the form and function of a bone or in its function alone is followed by a certain definite change in its external conformation," is constantly operative. As the end stage of this series of events, stress fracture is a fascinating, increasingly recognized, and increasingly common problem seen in the

Fig. 1: FW, a 15-year-old female distance runner showing the six-week evolution of a fibula stress fracture.

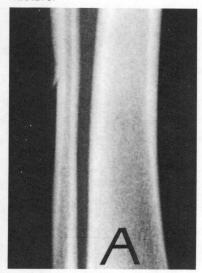

a. Two weeks after presentation.

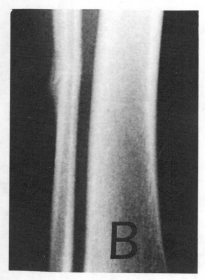

b. Three weeks after diagnosis.

Table 3.1
54 Clinical and Roentgenographic
Stress Fractures in Runners Examined in 1979

TIBIA		19
Upper Metaphysis	4	
Upper Shaft	7	
Midshaft	2	
Lower Tibia	6	
FIBULA		14
METATARSALS		10
Second	6	
Third	4	
FEMUR		8
Neck	4	
Upper Shaft	3	
Distal Shaft	1	
PELVIS		3
	TOTAL	54

athletic population in general and in the running population in particular. It occurs both in novice recreational and experienced competitive runners.[7]

Stress fractures in runners can be associated with toe-heel gait, hard-surface running, trunk and lower extremity malalignment, poor conditioning, and many other factors in the highly motivated runner/jogger.[8,9]

Because running is the common denominator for most sports, the "runner's fracture" of the fibula along with the metatarsal and tibia are most commonly involved (Table 3.1.)[7,10-12] The prototype fracture, using the fibula for example, occurs three to five centimeters proximal to the level of the ankle joint. Typically, symptoms occur with running and subside with rest. At two weeks, there is specific point localization to the distal fibula. Complete cessation of running is not necessary during healing (Fig. 3.1a-c), but running must be reduced below the level at which symptoms occur to permit ongoing remodeling and union of the fibular stress fracture, with confirmation by x-ray at the third to fourth week.

Cause and Pathology

Older military reports[13] and also more recent reports[14] suggest the cause of stress fractures to be repetitive stress due to the increased load after fatiguing of the supporting structures. Other older reports[15] and current reports[16,17] cite the muscle forces acting across and on the bone, which cause repetitive summation forces exceeding the stress-

Angus M. McBryde, Jr.

bearing capacity of that bone. In either case, progressive microfractures occur and function as the pathophysiologic precursor, terminating in a clinical fracture—a series of events analogous to what may occur in the femoral head.[18]

A simple hypothetical diagram explains the basic relationship between load repetition and bony injury[19] (Fig. 3.2). Time, and other unrelated and more general factors, such as the runner's pain threshhold, are important.

In metatarsal fractures specifically, a local temperature factor with reactive hyperemia occurs and can be measured with thermography.[20] The piezoelectric phenomenon is operative especially in long bones and is an integral basic electrical mechanism affecting cellular and structural activity in stress fractures. Research is ongoing in this area.[21]

What is this procession or continuum by which repetitive stress eventually causes a stress fracture (Fig. 3.3)? That cancellous bone as well as cortical bone has shock-absorption properties has long been hypothesized.[22] These and other properties mesh with the natural process of nonfracture-related osteoclastic and osteoblastic remodeling, which is ongoing and is increased with stress. The normal remodeling response to what becomes an abnormal stimulus with continued repetitive stress concentration in a certain osseous and juxta osseous area leads to trabecular microfractures. At this point, electron microscopy (EM) might show collagenous fragmentation with obliterated and narrowed canaliculi.[21] As is well known, mechanical properties of bone and its histological structure are correlated. Osteonal anatomy has been correlated with fracture from repetitive stress.[23] Cortical holes representing osteoclastic resorption occur rapidly at sites of accelerated normal cortical bone remodeling. This weakened cortex, including microfractures, leads to periosteal reinforcement until a refilling process has caught up and solidified the cortex.[24] So *if* the new bone (callous) at the site of these microfractures does not become functional and able to accept further stress, *if* the trabecular increase in cancellous bones is not prompt enough, *if* the numbers and alignment of the osteonal systems of cortical bone are not established quickly enough, and *if* the osteoclastic activity weakens the bone sufficiently, a certain threshhold is exceeded. The result is a peak bone loss occurring at 21 days.[25] It is at that point that clinical stress fracture can occur.

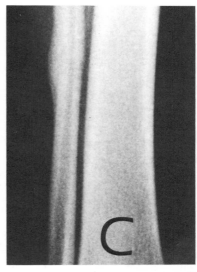

c. After having run track season competitively.

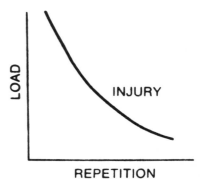

Fig. 3.2: Stress fractures lie along this hypothetical fatigue curve. When the repetitions reach a certain point, injury can occur even with small loads. From Frankel, Am J Sports Med 6:396, 1978.

RUNNING

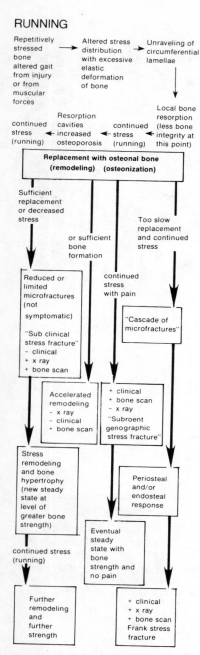

Fig. 3.3: A theoretical flow pattern of stress syndrome of bone (stress fracture) seen from the clinician's point of view. (Preparation aided by James A. McAlister, M.D.)

Table 3.2
Most Common Running Problems

Author's Rankings (376 Running Injuries)

A. Knee Pain	31.4%
B: Stress Fractures	14.4%
C. Hip Problems	12.0%
D. Plantar Fasciitis	10.7%
E. Shin Splints	8.3%
F. Back Problems	8.0%
G. Achilles Tendinitis	7.1%
H. Other	7.0%

Ranking by James et al[27] (164 of 232)

A. Knee Pain	29%
B. Posterior Tibial Syndrome (shin splints)	13%
C. Achilles Tendinitis	11%
D. Plantar Fasciitis	7%
E. Stress Fractures	6%
F. Iliotibial Tibial Tract Tendinitis	5%

(Fatigue infraction, defined as the "incomplete stress fracture,"[26] is not a useful concept.)

An important clinical corollary to the discussion is that many of the conditions now diagnosed as contusions, strains, posterior tibial syndrome, shin splints, or periostitis, would, if the inciting activity (running) were allowed to continue, progress to a clinical and roentgenographic stress fracture. Pain, however, causes most runners automatically to adjust their running schedule, thus preventing the end-stage bony structural change which can be identified as stress fracture.

Incidence and Correlating Factors

The lower extremities account for 95% of all stress fractures in athletes. That fact, of course, reflects running and the primary use of the lower extremity in sports.[10] Of the common runner's injuries, stress fractures have constituted roughly 6 to 10%.[27] Earlier reports[28] suggested a lower incidence. With increased awareness by runners and the general public of the preventive methods for more common soft-tissue running injuries, stress fractures can be expected to comprise a larger percentage. Our own recent running clinic statistics reflect this higher percentage (Table 3.2) of stress fractures, but perhaps that finding may be partly because of the clinic's function as a referral source from other orthopedists and physicians in

24

Angus M. McBryde, Jr.

the area for more intractable running injury problems. The numbers of stress fractures quoted in studies do not reflect subclinical and subroentgenographic stress reaction to bone—only those with roentgenographic *and* clinical evidence of stress fracture (Fig. 3.4). The relative incidence will also vary with the age and type of patient population; eg, university, retirement community, competitiveness, strength of running organizations.

Women seem more susceptible to stress fracture,[29] as well as to patellofemoral tracking problems. Their susceptibility may be because of the inherited sociocultural pattern requiring slower conditioning programs for women than for men. The known decreased bone density is a true anatomical difference, as is the width of the woman's child-bearing pelvis. The latter tends to produce a slightly different foot plant in running gait. These differences alone are relatively unimportant as a contributing factor to bony stress syndromes. The distribution of stress fractures and injury patterns in women parallel those in men.

Stress fractures can be multiple and bilateral (Fig. 3.5a and b), although they are usually single and unilateral. With bilateral fractures, the more symptomatic side usually keeps the running below the level that would cause pain contralaterally, thereby effectively masking the contralateral symptoms.

Stress fractures in Navy and Marine recruits vary in location because of the differing repetitive mechanical high-use activities (Navy/metatarsals vs Marine/os calcis).[30] Though the relationship is not delineated, the toe/heel, heel/toe and other gait variations must similarly play a part in the tendency for anatomical predisposition to certain stress fractures.

Stress fractures occur primarily in humans, race horses, and racing greyhounds[31-33]—those animals who train for maximum performance with pain (Fig. 3.6). Children, whose tibias and fibulas are primarily involved, are not exceptions to this.[34]

In 1935, Dr. Dudley Morton wrote *The Human Foot*, in which he described the "Morton's Foot."[35] Morton's foot is term abused by lay personnel, runners, and physicians. This condition (short first metatarsal, long second metatarsal, hypermobility of first metatarsal, posteriorly displaced sesamoids) has been linked with many runner's leg and foot problems in general and with stress fracture of the metatarsals in particular. It is also

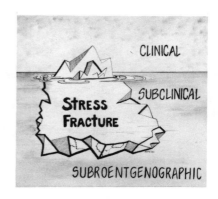

Fig. 3.4: Many stress fractures do not become diagnosed clinical entities.

Fig. 3.5: LM, a 34 year old man training at 50 miles per week, premarathon with persistent bilateral tibial symptoms.

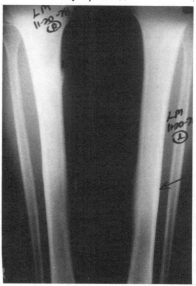

a. Anteroposterior roentgenogram, right and left tibia.

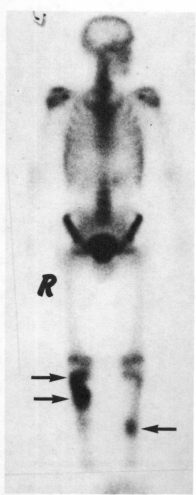

b. Corresponding bone scan with right upper tibia and left mid tibial fractures. Biking as a substitute sport for six weeks allowed a gradual return to full training with no further problems.

described as aggravating pronation and predisposing to degenerative changes at the junction of the first and second metatarsal bases.[36] Drez[37] found no statistical difference in relative roentgenographic first and second metatarsal length as it relates to metatarsal stress fractures and to a controlled group. He has defined a short first metatarsal as less than 73% of the length of the second metatarsal. Other studies[38] have not found a positive correlation with specific foot anatomy.

Diagnosis

Stress fracture diagnosis can be difficult clinically and radiographically. The index of suspicion must be high. Laboratory techniques can be used for local delineation and verification. On physical examination, local warmth, swelling, and tenderness of juxta osseous soft tissue localizes stress syndrome of bone or soft tissue. Further findings of periosteal thickening in subcutaneous bony areas indicate stress fracture as the most likely diagnosis.

Stress fracture of the proximal femur and other deeper bony parts may provide few positive findings on physical examination. The increase or occurrence of pain with active range of motion, but with appropriate painless passive range of motion in addition to relatively painless weight bearing, would imply that the stress reaction has not involved bone.

The clinical differential diagnosis includes shin splints[39] (posterior tibial stress syndrome), tendinitis (musculotendinous inflammation), muscle strain (musculotendinous tear), compartment syndrome, fascial hernia, sprained interosseous membrane, and muscle insertional tears.

The term, shin splints should be discarded entirely, used in a broader definition of musculotendinous inflammation plus the anatomic description of the pain, or limited to the definition of posterior tibial stress syndrome. Bone pain with bone scan localization to the posterior medial tibia is a stress of bone involving the posterior medial tibia. Though it does not present as a more classical stress fracture, these findings with or without roentgenographic changes should not be termed shin splints.[40]

Clement[41] suggests de-emphasis of the radiographic findings and increased emphasis on early detection, treatment, and rehabilitation. This more balanced clinical approach can keep the runner functional and injury at a grade I or II

Angus M. McBryde, Jr.

level, and will usually abort a full clinical and roentgenographic stress fracture. Traditional roentgenograms of necessary high quality continue to provide the proper tool for diagnosis, differential diagnosis, and follow-up. No other technique is as readily available in private offices.

Differential diagnosis roentgenographically includes malignancy,[42] usually osteogenic sarcoma (Fig. 3.7a-c), osteomyelitis, and osteoid osteoma. Ill-advised biopsies and even amputations have been done for stress fractures. An occasional biopsy in an atypical or questionable lesion should be considered. Seven documented stress fractures or stress syndromes of bone underwent biopsy at the Orthopaedic Hospital of Charlotte during 1978-1979. All of these problems were misdiagnosed preoperatively and corrected retrospectively with appropriate histopathlogy and a more detailed history. On the other hand, with the increased number of stress fractures seen, the physician should not become complacent with the diagnosis.

Radionuclide bone scanning (we used technetium 99M-labelled Medronate sodium) can provide the diagnosis as early as two to eight days after the onset of symptoms.[43,44] In this two- to three-week period before roentgenographic visualization, the bone scan evidence can become positive, and such early diagnosis may prevent a full clinical and radiographic syndrome.[45] Early diagnosis, early recognition of at risk stress fractures, and more confident treatment of stress syndromes of soft tissue[46-48] make scanning appropriate in selected and questionable cases.

Scintigraphic characterisitics may assume more importance in the future. Mid and distal third tibial stress syndromes tend to involve the posterior medidal cortex and be longitudinally oriented, whereas the proximal tibial fractures exhibit a transverse pattern or imaging.[49] Clinical applicability will remain questionable. Physical stress alone, even at high levels or with repetition, will not usually cause abnormal imaging. Already positive results on scans of continually stressed bones, however, may persist for up to 12 months. There is a 10 to 20% false-positive bone scan result with stress fractures because of accelerated bone remodeling. The false-positive finding indicates high sensitivity and low specificity. False-negative scans are extremely rare and essentially exclude the diagnosis of stress fracture.[46,50] In adolescents, positive imaging occurs at the epiphysis and can

Fig. 3.6: That stress fractures are related in normal bone to training and high repetitive stress is underscored by its occurrence in only three athletic animals: race dogs, race horses, and humans

Fig. 3.7: SD, a 19 year old with running-related upper tibial lesion.

a. Preoperative lateral view showing periosteal new bone and cortico-cancellous condensation of bone. Interpretation was "compatible with osteogenic sarcoma."

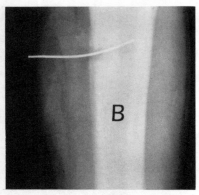

b. Open biopsy and localization.

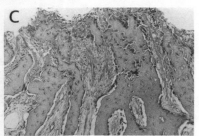

c. Fracture callous and new bone. Cellularity can cause confusion.

Fig. 3.8: AS, a 38 year old woman with left upper tibial pain for two months.

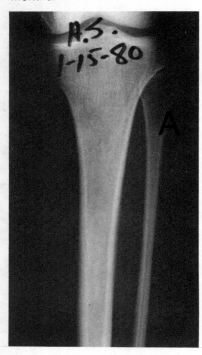

cause diagnostic confusion.[51] Subroentgenographic stress fractures (Fig. 3.8a-c) are responsible for much bone pain in the training athlete.[52]

Computerized tomography, xerography, and thermography can be of occasional differential help, especially with osteoid osteoma and nidus identification. Other techniques such as ultrasonic emission may be useful in the future.

Clinical Considerations

Training mistakes,[53] anatomic or malalignment asymmetries or asynchronies, and sudden changes in shoe type or surface contribute to stress fractures. Frequently, a relatively minor soft-tissue injury is allowed to progress with continuation of training at the same or higher level, and a frank stress fracture results. Similarly, a minor injury can cause a significant change in running gait, initiating mechanisms for stress fractures elsewhere.

Runners incur stress fracture of bony elements in the pelvis as well as in the lower extremities. The fractures may be proximal or distal in the long bone or characteristic in the pelvis and tarsal bones and can involve both cortical and cancellous areas. Numerous classification attempts exist.[54] Trabecular condensation of bone visible on x-ray film typifies metaphyseal long bone or short bone (tarsal) fractures. Cortical break/periosteal reaction typifies primarily cortical bone stress fractures.[55] Beyond this simple classification, there can be little of practical value. The individual's musculoskeletal anatomy, the skeletal maturity, and the point where stress is or is not stopped are the deciding variables and cannot be classified.

Each bone has its own clinical presentation and tendencies. The pelvis fracture causes symptoms of perineal, groin and adductor pain and usually occurs in the inferior pubic arch.[56] Stress avulsion can also occur and is common in shorter distance runners at the hamstring attachment to the ischium and at the subacetabular level (Fig. 3.9a and b). Tibial tubercle and lower pole patella stress avulsions are also seen in the skeletally immature runner.[11] Stress fractures of ossified spikes into the patella tendon insertion can occur.

The more proximal stress fracture in the lower extremity occurs after jumping and more violent leg activities; eg, hurdling, steeple-chase, European cross-country. Long distance running-related stress fractures are more common distally than proximally. Pars interarticularis stress frac-

Angus M. McBryde, Jr.

tures do occur with repetitive loading,[57,58] but are unusual in runners.

Running or stress fractures are unlikely to play a significant role in the development of osteoarthritis.[59] Of course, any displaced stress fracture that causes angulation, torsion, or other malalignment can affect the proximo-distal joints negatively and predispose them to future or stress-related problems. Likewise, metaphyseal stress fractures with components extending to the articular surfaces can create permanent problems. Stress fracture of the femoral neck with displacement may lead to avascular necrosis of the femoral head, although I personally have not seen this complication in a runner. Mechanics of bone hypertrophy and cartilage nutrition and regeneration have not been worked out in regard to repetitive loading in runners.[22,60]

An increasingly important question is the subjection of major weight-bearing joints—the hip, knee and ankle—with known abnormality to the repetitive stresses of running. Many joggers and mid-career runners have early clinical and roentgenographic findings of mild osteoarthritis at the tibiofemoral and patellofemoral joints. Postmeniscectomy compartment symptoms and sequelae of old adolescent hip disease (Legg-Perthes or slipped capital femoral epiphysis) are two commonly seen sequelae. A general rule for clinicians to follow is that permanently reduced mileage or permanent substitution is indicated if: 1) roentgenographic changes advance more quickly than anticipated;[61] 2) chronic local intra-articular painful symptoms persist; or 3) chronic effusion or synovitis persists.

Treatment

Clinically, it is important, relevant, and practical to emphasize and categorize stress fracture treatment patterns and not simply the roentgenographic patterns (Table 3.3). Stress fractures in runners have varying clinical significance depending on the location, nature of the stress syndrome, and duration of symptoms. Obviously, a clearly visible fracture line in the femoral neck indicating predisplacement demands immediate internal fixation.[62] Femoral neck and proximal tibial metaphysis fractures may both progress to displacement and serious complications in spite of cessation of the inciting activity. In these two cases in particular and to a lesser extent in all major long-bone stress fractures, close follow-up is

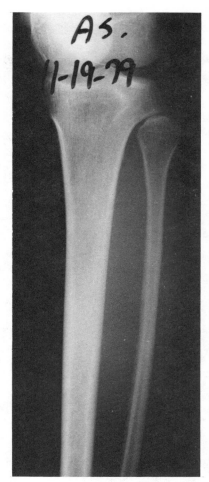

a. and b. Negative findings on x-ray film over a six-week period and no relief with local therapy, aspirin, and reduced mileage.

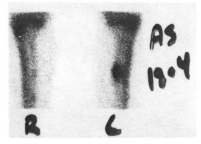

c. Positive bone scan indicating a subroentgenographic stress fracture. Substitute activity allowed her symptoms to subside. By April,

Fig. 3.9: MT, an 18 year old 440-yard-dash competitor with:

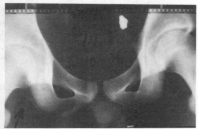

a. Partial avulsion of the hamstrings (semitendinosis)

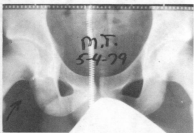

b. Irregularity of involved area one year later.

Fig. 3.10: CS, a 49 year old marathoner training at 70 miles weekly.

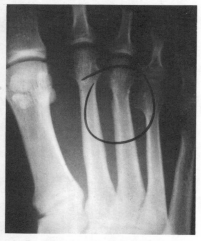

a. Presenting 10 days after pain onset with stress fracture involving the distal diaphysis of the third metatarsal.

Table 3.3
Stress Fractures-Relative Importanc;e in Clinical Treatment

Critical	
	Upper Tibial and Femoral Neck
	At Risk
Less Critical	
	Femoral Shaft, I, II, III
	Mid Tibial
Noncritical	
	Fibula
	Metastarsal
	Os Calcis
	Pelvis

indicated. A general guide is that if pain does not subside with unloading of the injured part within a few days total immobilization or, in the case of the femoral neck fracture, operative internal fixation is indicated.

The known subclinical or otherwise atypical stress fracture must be followed closely, particularly if an apparently healed fracture involves the entire circumference of the bone.

If "running through" or "running around" the stress fracture symptoms is not possible or advisable, then substitute sports are necessary. Race walking, cross-country skiing, swimming, biking, and selective strengthening activities serve as good substitutes. Especially with those fractures of bones that are not at risk, such as the fibula, techniques to permit painless running can be used. Calf sleeves, ice massage, anti-inflammatory drugs (usually aspirin), and gentler training should be tried.

The role of orthotics in stress fracture treatment or the role of any customized sports appliance built into or within running shoes to better distribute weight to all parts of the foot is still uncertain. Standard prevention and treatment requires modification of training, isometric rehabilitation,[41] and gradual monotered return to running. Electrical stimulation currently has no therapeutic role in treating stress fractures.

Specific Stress Fractures

Metatarsals

Metatarsal stress fractures are common. All metatarsals can be involved. The second and third are involved most often and the fourth, first, and fifth less often (Fig. 3.10a-c). The proximal shaft is involved about 5% of the time. Significant

Angus M. McBryde, Jr.

displacement or comminution of the metatarsal fracture is rare. Fracture of the base of the fifth metatarsal fracture is also rare.

Stress fractures may seem to be acute due to sudden overload of repetitively stressed bone. Figure 3.11a and b shows consecutive metatarsal fractures from an intra-marathon injury. Before acute injury, this case may have been a sub-clinical stress fracture or stress syndrome of bone.

Tarsal Bone

Tarsal stress fractures are most common in the os calcis and occasionally occur in the talus or cuneiform. Condensation of bone roughly parallel to the subtalar joint in the os calcis and parallel to the talonavicular joint in the talus is the usual finding on roentgenogram. In 1944, os calcis stress fractures, usually bilateral, were frequently noted in military training after cross-country runs consisting of the two-mile intermittent walk/run period.[63] With close clinical examination, Achilles tendinitis and retrocalcaneal bursitis can be easily differientiated from stress fractures. Plantar fasciitis can create confusion. Medial lateral compression pain and positive roentgenographic findings at three weeks confirm os calcis stress fracture. Treatment is not critical and symptoms usually permit resumption of a full running schedule at three weeks. Stress symptoms at the os calcis apophysis can occur and may be similar to those that occur at the tibial tubercle.

Fibula

Fibular stress fractures (Fig. 3.12a and b) cause lateral leg and ankle pain and are common in both runners and other athletes.[64] It is not an at risk fracture and its limited weight-bearing function[65] effectively allows "running through" the injury by simply reducing mileage temporarily. Drilling[66] is not recommended. Many persons with fibular stress fractures never reach the physician's office and those who do frequently fail to be examined roentgenographically. Proximal fibular stress fractures are uncommon.

Tibia

Tibial stress fractures are common. They vary in their at risk potential. It is roentgenographically difficult to diagnose a tibial stress fracture. Multiple oblique and marked injury site views can be necessary for accurate identification.

Though medial tibial plateau stress fractures are reportedly benign,[67] complications can occur.

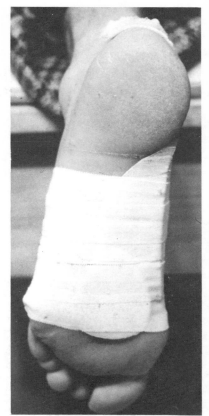

b. Low dye strapping with return to running three weeks after injury.

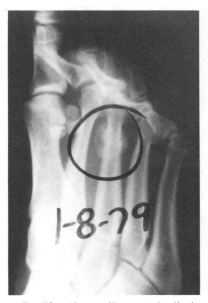

c. Proliferation callous and a limited running program.

Fig. 3.11. DH, a 35 year old marathoner without premarathon foot symptoms. Acute pain at the 15th and 18th miles of the marathon. He finished the marathon.

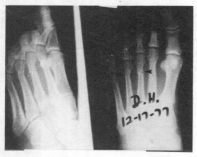

a. Fractures of necks of third and fourth metatarsals on the day of injury.

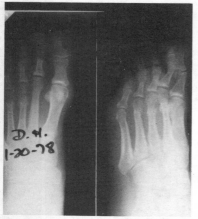

b. Early union four weeks later. Short leg walking cast used for one week with biking for three weeks. He ran the Boston Marathon successfully four months later.

Intra-articular extension and displacement can be a particular problem (Fig. 3.13a-d). These proximal subplateau stress fractures frequently appear to be pes anserine bursitis, medial strain, or patellofemoral problems. Minor condensation of bone can easily be missed, especially in the younger, but skeletally mature, runner with bony changes of recently closed physes. The proximity of the tibial collateral ligament attachment may be a significant factor.[68]

Often the patient seeks medical aid several weeks after forced mileage reduction, which allows union with minimal symptoms in spite of continued, but lessened stress. It is rare for tibial shaft stress fractures to completely displace, but persistent high mileage or running with pain can cause problems (Fig. 3.14a-e). The atypical fracture may occur in any athlete[69] or runner. Distal tibial fractures are less common and are metaphysical (Fig 3.15a and b).

The time of temporary disability and morbidity can be increased by not observing the principle of, "keep the level of running below that which causes pain." The principle implies not only reduced running mileage, but total abstinence and substitution at times. Plaster is rarely necessary if this principle is followed.[70]

With tibial stress fractures, it is generally necessary to stop running completely for a four- to eight-week period with substitute swimming or biking followed by reinstitution of a more gradual training program. The causative factors in the running history, running style or anatomic makeup should be identified and eliminated or corrected.

Femur

Femoral shaft stress fractures are of three types.[71] Proximal third shaft fractures at the medial subtrochanteric level are the most common and are typical (Fig. 3.16a and b).[5] Midshaft cortical fractures are less common in runners. The distal femur fractures are often metaphyseal and involve the condensation of bone (Fig. 3.17a-c).

Femoral Neck

In 1966 Morris and Blickenstaff described femoral-neck stress fractures.[72] Though not running-based, the apparently first-reported displaced femoral-neck stress fracture was an 18 year old Indian youth who was forced to crawl excessively on his elbows and toes.[73]

The so-called "transverse" or "compression" stress fractures of the femoral neck[74] do indeed need treatment. The different roentgenographic appearances, however, generally reflect the same pathophysiologic process at different times in the continuum. The variables of continued or lessened stress per unit time determine the roentgenographic appearance. Overinterpretation of the roentgenogram must be avoided, but it can establish the diagnosis, help possible displacement to be judged, and verify union. The clinical status, eg, pain, limp, patient cooperation, remain important in determing treatment. Unexplained pelvic, hip, or thigh pain even with negative findings on films should be watched closely.[75] In the femoral neck, roentgenograms may not show changes for up to five or six weeks.[63] Figure 3.18a-f illustrates the typical roentgenographic presentation and progression of the femoral neck stress fracture in a runner resistant to initial appropriate treatment. Figure 3.19a-d illustrates an undiagnosed femoral neck stress fracture with acute completion and subsequent nonunion. *If femoral neck stress fractures do not immediately become pain-free with cessation of running, with or without crutches, Knowles pinning is indicated.*

Pelvis

Pelvic stress fractures are seen in the anterior pelvis usually in the ischiopubic ramus and are more common in women (Fig 3.20). The predominant site may depend in part on the differential pull of the adductors medially and the hamstrings laterally.

Summary

Stress fractures in runners are common; their incidence is increasing. Causes are similar to those leading to other repetitive stress problems of soft tissue and bone. Treatment varies, but the level of running or nonrunning substitution must be kept below that which causes pain. Treatment of the at risk fractures demands special attention. The femoral neck fracture can require internal fixation. The tibial fracture rarely requires plaster. Patient understanding and cooperation are extremely important. Without this cooperation, major complications can occur.

References

1. Wolfe HRI, Robertson JM: Fatigue Fracture of Femur and Tibia. Lancet 11-13, July, 1945.

Fig. 3.12: SM, a 13 year old boy with an inversion-associated painful ankle for two weeks from running.

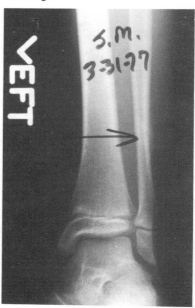

a. Periosteal reaction and typical "runner's fracture"

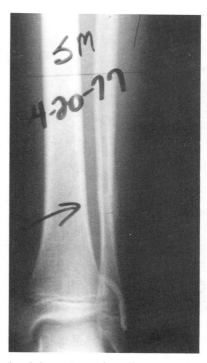

b. Adequate union three weeks later. Minimal interruption of running program.

Fig. 3.13: HM, a 51 year old sedentary printer began jogging with a quick mileage increase from five to 15 miles.

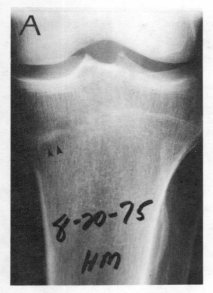

a. One week after symptoms appeared. Limits of bony change are hard to define.

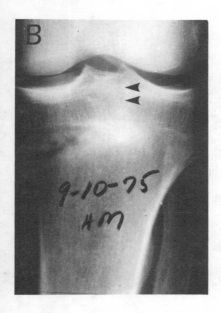

b. Limited weight bearing but extension to the interspinous articular surface effectively completing the medial tibial plateau fracture.

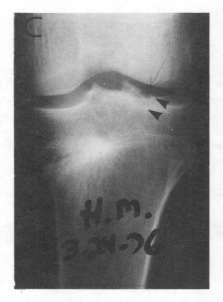

c. Union but with clinical mild varus of the upper tibia.

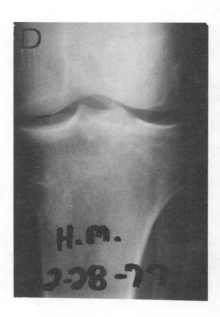

d. Union and remodeling. More permanent problems would have occurred if the intra-articular components had violated the medial or lateral compartment.

34

Angus M. McBryde, Jr.

Fig. 3.14: CM, a 38 year old man, ran 50 miles per week for two weeks after having been at 30 miles per week for the prior three months.

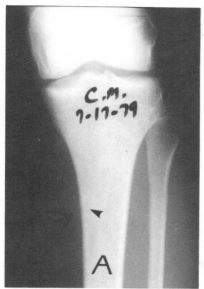

a. Cortical defect.

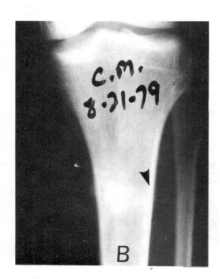

b. Extension of the fracture to the lateral cortex even with decreased stress. Also impressive condensation of bone.

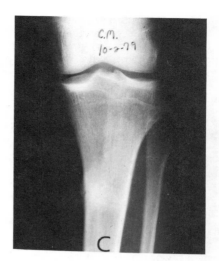

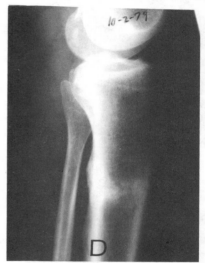

c. and d. Anteroposterior and lateral views still symptomatic three months after onset of symptoms but running with mild pain against instructions.

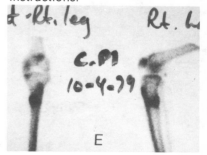

e. Bone scan hotly positive over a wide area.
Late remodeling, with miminal varus resulted.

Stress Fractures in Runners

Fig. 3.15: SM, a 25 year old woman who, after one month of running at 20 miles per week, had pain involving the ankle joint. Note the dual transverse areas of bone condensation in this metaphyseal fracture.

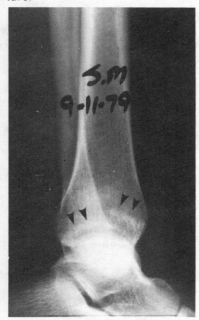

a. Anteroposterior roentgenogram

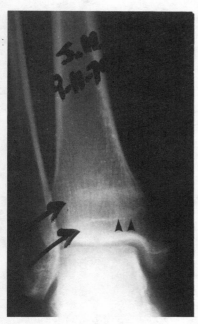

b. Lateral roentgenogram

Fig. 3.16: MP, an 18 year old cross-country runner with upper thigh pain one month before being seen. The onset of symptoms was at the last cross-country meet. Abstinence caused loss of symptoms.

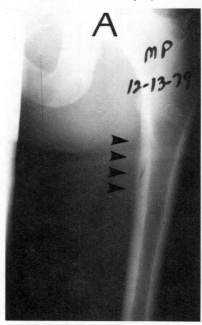

a. Roentgenogram taken at first examination.

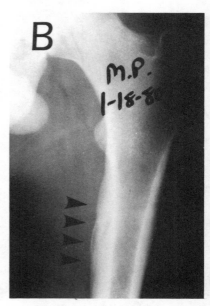

b. Full activity (basketball guard) without symptoms one month later. Quicker return because of substitute activity.

36

Angus M. McBryde, Jr.

Fig. 3.17: JD, a 16 year old distance runner.

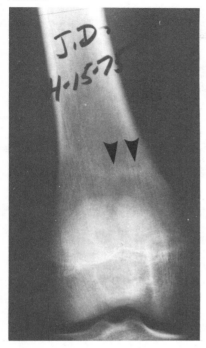

a. Two weeks after onset of right knee pain

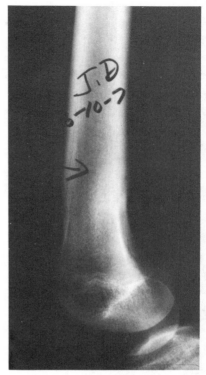

b. and c. Swimming as substitute activity and no symptoms after seven weeks.

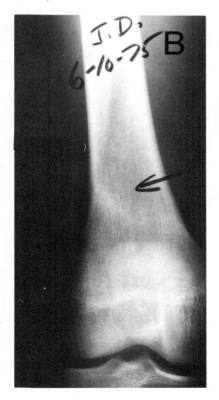

Fig. 3.18: TT, a 36 year old marathoner at 50 miles per week with a three-week history of right hip pain worse with running and better with rest.

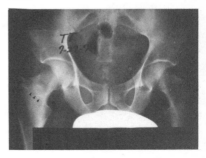

a. Initial roentgenograms show sclerosis across the distal neck.

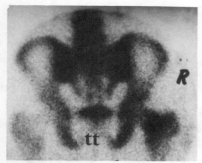

b. Bone scan strongly positive.

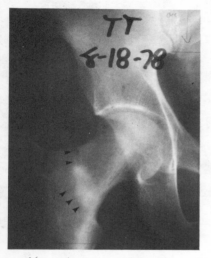

c. More bone condensation. A lucent line to the superior neck is present.

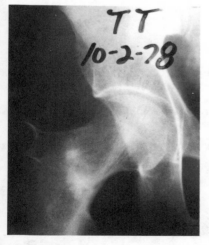

d. Continued stress after three months of symptoms. Surgery not done. Extension of the process is obvious with potential displacement.

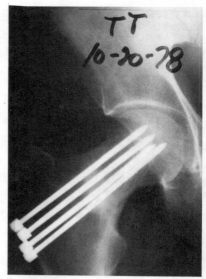

e. Knowles pinning carried out with immediate relief of hip pain.

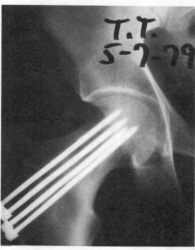

f. Again running at 50 miles per week with a healed femoral neck. The pins will remain unless bursal symptoms develop. He completed a marathon within eighteen months of his fracture.

38

Angus M. McBryde, Jr.

Fig. 3.19: JL a 37 year old with right hip pain four to six weeks after novice jogging. No diagnosis made. Forced to stop jogging but had continued pain with continued activity.

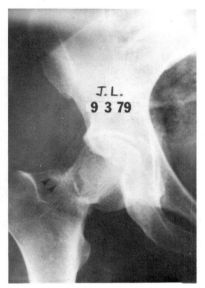

a. Acute hip pain at settling into the water after water skiing. No acute injury. Note sclerosis at the fracture site. Internally fixed.

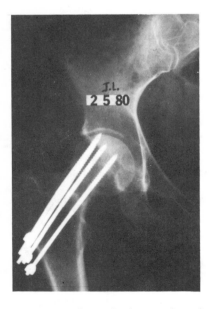

b. Appropriate pinning and position five months postinjury.

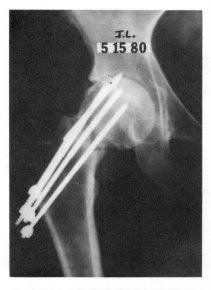

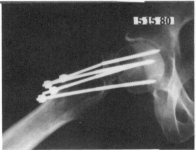

c. and d. Eight months postinjury with non-union, collapse with pin fracture and protrusion. Bone grafting, osteotomy, and internal fixation planned.

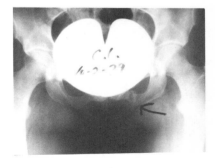

Fig. 3.20: CL, a 25 year old woman running at 35 miles per week without a change in training or shoes. Groin pain persisted for three weeks until findings on roentgenograms became positive.

Stress Fractures in Runners

2. Mann TP: Fatigue Fracture of Tibia. Lancet 2:8-10, 1945.
3. Leveton L: March (Fatigue) Fracture of the Long Bones of the Lower Extremity and Pelvis. Am J Surg 71:222-232, 1946.
4. McBryde AM: Stress Fractures in Athletes. J Sports Med 3:212-217, 1975.
5. Morris JM, Blickenstaff LD: Fatigue Fractures: A clinical study. Springfield, IL, Charles C Thomas, 1967.
6. Devas MB: Stress Fractures. Edinburgh, Churchill Livingston, 1975.
7. Blazina ME, Watanabe RS, et al: Fatigue Fractures in Track Athletes. Calif Med 97:61-63, 1962.
8. James SL, Brubaker E: Biomechanical and Neuromuscular Aspects of Running. Exercise and Sports Science Reviews. New York, Academic Press 1:189-214, 1973.
9. Corrigan AB, Fitch KD: Complications of Jogging. Med J Australia 2:363-368, 1972.
10. Orava PJ. Ala-Ketola L, et al: Stress Fractures Caused by Physical Exercise. Acta Orthop Scand 49:19-27, 1978.
11. Devas MB: Stress Fractures in Athletes. Nurs Times 76:227-232, 1971.
12. McBryde AM, Basset FH: Stress Fractures of the Fibula. GP 38:120-123, 1968.
13. Bernstein A, Stone JR: March Fracture, A Report of Three Hundred and Seven Cases and a New Method of Treatment. J Bone Joint Surg 26:743-750, 1944.
14. Baker J, Frankel VH, et al: Fatigue Fractures: Biomechanical Considerations. Proceedings. J Bone Joint Surg 54-A:1345, 1972.
15. Nickerson SH: March Fracture or Insufficiency Fracture Am J Surg 62:154-164, 1943.
16. Stanitski CL, et al: On the Nature of Stress Fractures. Am J Sports Med 6:391-396, 1978.
17. Walter NE, Wolf D: Stress Fractures in Young Athletes. Am J Sports Med 5:165-170, 1977.
18. Urovitz EPM, Fornasier VL, et al: Etiological Factors in the Pathogenesis of Femoral Trabecular Fatigue Fractures. Clin Orthop 127:275-280, 1977.
19. Frankel VH: Editorial Comment. Am J Sports Med 6:396, 1978.
20. Brand PW: The Cycle of Repetitive Stress on Insensitive Feet: Scientific Exhibit. Am Acad Orthop Surgeons, March, 1975.
21. Chamay A, Tschantz P: Mechanical Influences in Bone Remodeling. Experimental Research on Wolff's Law. J Biomechanics 5:170-180, 1972.
22. Radin EL, Parker HG, Pugh JW: Response of Joints to Impact Loading-III. J Biomechanics 6:51-57, 1973.
23. Evans FG, Riolo ML: Relations Between the Fatigue Life and History of Adult Human Cortical Bone. J Bone Joint Surg 52A:1579-1589, 1970.
24. Johnson LK: The Kinetics of Skeletal Remodeling Symposia, Structural Organization of the Skeleton, Bergsma, and Milch. Birth Defects. Original Article Series, National Foundation, II:66-142, 1966.
25. Johnson LC, Stratford HT, Geis RW, et al: Histogenesis of Stress Fractures. J Bone Joint Surg 45A:1542, 1963.
26. Burrows H: Fatigue Infraction of the Middle of the Tibia in Ballet Dancers. J Bone Joint Surg 38B:83-84, 1956.
27. James SL, Bates BT, Osternig LR: Injuries to Runners. Am J Sports Med 6:40-50, 1978.
28. Glick JM, Katch VL: Musculoskeletal Injuries in

Angus M. McBryde, Jr.

Jogging. Arch Phys Med 51:123-126, 1970.

29. Micheli LJ: Injuries to Female Athletes. Rurgical Rounds 44-52, May, 1979.

30. Gilbert RS, Johnson HA: Stress Fractures in Military Recruits. A Review of Twelve Years Experience. Military Med 131:716-621, 1966.

31. Bateman JK: Broken Hock in the Greyhound: Repair Methods and the Plastic Scaphoid. Vet Record 70:621-623, 1958.

32. Devas MB: Compression Stress Fractures in Man and the Greyhound. J Bone Joint Surg 43B:540-551, 1961.

33. Devas MB: Shin Splints or Stress Fractures in the Metacarpal Bone In Horses and Shin Soreness or Stress Fractures of the Tibia in Man. J Bone Joint Surg 49B:310-313, 1967.

34. Devas MB: Stress Fractures in Children. J Bone Joint Surg 45B:528-541, 1963.

35. Morton DJ: The Human Foot: The Evolution, Physiology and Functional Disorders. New York, Colombia Univ Press, 1935, p 257.

36. Moseley HF: Static Disorders of the Ankle and Foot. Clin Symp 9:85, 1957.

37. Drez D, Young JC, Johnson RD, et al: Metatarsal Stress Fractures. Am J Sports Med 8:123-125, 1980.

38. Kernodle HB, Jacobs JE: Metatarsal March Fracture. Southern Med J 37:579-582, 1944.

39. Andrish JT, Bergfeld JA, Walheim J: A Prospective Study on the Management of Shin Splints. J Bone Joint Surg 56A:1697-1700, 1974.

40. Jackson DW, Bailey D: Shin Splints in the Young Athlete. A Nonspecific Diagnosis. Phys Sports Med, 45-51, March 1975.

41. Clement DB: Tibial Stress Syndrome in Athletes. J Sports Med 2:81-85, 1974.

42. Newberg AH, Kalisher L: Case Reports: An Unusual Stress Fracture in a Jogger. J Trauma 181:816-817, 1978.

43. Siddiqui AR: Bone Scans for Early Detection of Stress Fractures. N Engl J Med 298:1033, 1978.

44. Garrick JG: Early Diagnosis of Stress Fractures and Their Precursors. Presented at New Orleans, American Academy of Orthopedic Surgeons, Feb 2, 1976.

45. Prather JL, Nusynowitz ML, Snowdy HA, et al: Scintigraphic Findings in Stress Fractures. J Bone Joint Surg 59A:896-874, 1977.

46. Strait JL: Early Diagnosis of Stress Fractures by Bone Scintography. Presented at Dallas, American Academy of Orthopedic Surgeons, Feb 27, 1978.

47. Norfray JF, Schlacter L, Kernahan WT Jr, et al: Early Confirmation of Stress Fractures in Joggers. JAMA 243:1647-1649, 1980.

48. Saunders AJS, Sayed TF, Hilson AJW, et al: Stress Lesions of the Lower Leg and Foot. Clin Radiol 30:649-651, 1979.

49. Roub LW, Gumerman LW, Hanley EN Jr, et al: Bone Stress: A Radionuclide Imaging Perspective. Radiology 132:431-438, 1979.

50. Wilcox, JR, Moniot AL, et al: Bone Scanning in the Evaluation of Exercise-Related Stress Injuries. Radiology 123:699-703, 1977.

51. Cahill BR: Stress Fracture of the Proximal Tibial Epiphysis: A Case Report. Am J Sports Med 5:186-187, 1977.

52. Jackson DW: Shin Splints: An Update. Phys Sports Med, 51-62, Oct 1978.
53. Graham CE: Stress Fractures in Joggers. Texas Med 66:68-73, 1970.
54. Kroening PM, Shelton ML: Stress Fractures. Am J Roentgen 89:1281-1286, 1963.
55. Savoca CJ: Stress Fractures. Radiology 100:519-524, 1971.
56. Selakovich W, Love L: Stress Fractures of the Pubic Ramus. J Bone Joint Surg 36a:573-576, 1954.
57. Wiltse LL, Widell EH Jr, Jackson DW: Fatigue Fractures: The Basic Lesion in Isthmic Spondylolisthesis. J Bone Joint Surg 57A:17-22, 1975.
58. Hutton WC, Stott JRR, Cyron BM: Is Spondylolysis a Fatigue Fracture. Spine 2:202-209, 1977.
59. Puranen J, Alaketola L, Peltokallio P, et al: Running and Primary Osteoarthritis of the Hip. Br Med J 2:424-425, 1975.
60. Cameron HR, Fornasier VL: Trabicular Stress Fractures. Clin Orthop 111:266-268, 1975.
61. Hunder GG: Harmful Effect of Jogging. Am Intern Med 71:664-665, 1969.
62. Ernst JR: Stress Fractures of the Neck of the Femur. J Trauma 4:71-83, 1964.
63. Hullinger CW: Insufficiency Fracture of the Calcaneus, Similar to March Fracture of the Metatarsal. J Bone Joint Surg 26:751-757, 1944.
64. Devas BM, Sweetman R: Stress Fractures of the Fibula. J Bone Joint Surg 38B:818-829, 1956.
65. Lambert KL: The Weight Bearing Function of the Fibula. J Bone Joint Surg 53A:507-513, 1971.
66. Williams JGP: Recalcitrant Stress Fracture, A Case Managed by Drilling. Br J Sports Med 13:84-85, 1979.
67. Engber WD: Stress Fractures of the Medial Tibial Plateau. J Bone Joint Surg 59A:767-768, 1977.
68. Protzman RR, Griffis CG: Stress Fractures in Men and Women Undergoing Military Training. J Bone Joint Surg 59A:825, 1977.
69. Brahms MA, Fumich RM, et al: Atypical Stress Fracture of the Tibia in a Professional Athlete. Am J Sports Med 8:131-132, 1980.
70. Kimball PR, Savastano AA: Fatigue Fractures of the Proximal Tibia. Clin Orthop 70:170-173, 1970.
71. Provost RA, Morris JM: Fatigue Fracture of the Femoral Shaft. J Bone Joint Surg 51A:487-498, 1969.
72. Blickenstaff LD, Morris JM: Fatigue Fracture of the Femoral Neck. J Bone Joint Surg 48A:1031-1047, 1966.
73. Bingham J: Stress Fracture of Femoral Neck. Lancet 2:13, July 7, 1945.
74. Devas MB: Stress Fractures of the Femoral Neck. J Bone Joint Surg 47B:728-738, 1965.
75. Bargren JH, Tilson DH, et al: Prevention of Displaced Fatigue Fractures of the Femur. J Bone Surg 53A:1115-1117, 1971.

Angus M. McBryde, Jr.

4

Spine Problems in the Runner

Douglas W. Jackson, M.D.

Symptoms related to the spine, restricting running and other strenuous activities, occur most commonly in runners between the ages of 30 and 50. They are often a manifestation of an underlying degenerative process and are similar to those seen in the general population. The onset of the spinal disability may develop in relation to running, or it may develop in an unrelated activity and be accentuated and prolonged by running. The mileage the runners can tolerate may be restricted when the spinal symptoms are present. Fortunately, most spine problems have a self-limited course, and the runner will be able to resume the desired mileage in time.

A period of low back pain is something that most adults experience sometime during their lives. The runner may find that running aggravates and tends to prolong the presence of what otherwise would be mild symptoms. Other spinal disorders are associated with more severe pain that may result in longer times in which the runner is unable to return to a desired mileage.

A prospective study of 1,000 consecutive adult runners having disabling musculoskeletal complaints showed only 11 (1.1%) of the complaints were related to the spine.[1] The incidence of spinal complaints varies significantly depending on the sampling of a given runner population and the average age of the runners being evaluated. For example, spinal complaints are infrequent in runners under age 25. Determining the exact incidence of spinal problems in the running population is further complicated, in that most spinal symptoms are of an aching nature and only intermittently increase in severity to the point that they restrict the runner's mileage. Athletes, or active people, often accept their spinal discomfort and never seek formal medical advice.

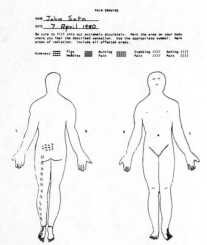

Fig. 4.2: The pain drawing is quite helpful in determining if the runner has a dermatomal distribution to their pain, or if it is localized.

Evaluation of the spinal disability of any runner should be detailed, and a diagnosis established so that a reasonable recommendation and prognosis may be given. The history and additional pertinent questions (Fig. 4.1), are of particular interest in the runner, who may also fill out a pain drawing (Fig. 4.2), which pictorially represents the pain location and aids the runner in characterizing the nature of the pain.[2,3] It also aids the physician in deciding whether the pain is localized and/or represents referred pain in a dermatomal or sclerotomal distribution. This assessment of the spinal pain, and its possible referred components, will help to determine which diagnostic tests are appropriate if conservative treatment measures fail. Runners with referred pain, particularly radicular pain, often require more aggressive restriction than those with more localized musculoskeletal complaints.

The physical examination of the runner with a spinal complaint is similar to an examination for any back problem, and includes documentation of

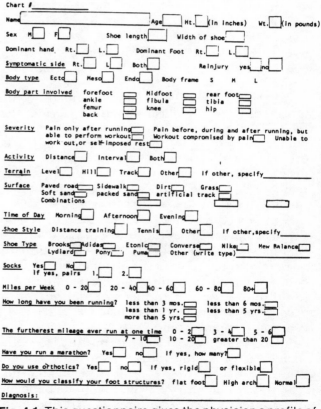

Fig. 4.1: This questionnaire gives the physician a profile of the runner's training and experience. This information can be integrated into the general history obtained for spinal disability.

Douglas W. Jackson, M.D.

any restriction in the range of motion of the spine and lower extremities, paraspinous muscle spasm, tenderness, reflex changes, sensory changes, motor weakness, and signs of nerve root irritation.

Leg-length discrepancies become more important in distance runners than in the general population. They can be evaluated by many different methods. A film of the pelvis with the patient standing takes into account the entire lower extremity, including the feet bearing weight. Measurements from the antero-superior iliac crest to the medial malleoli do not take into account foot structure. For example, when one foot is more pronated than the other it contributes to a relative leg-length discrepancy while weightbearing. In the runner complaining of nonspecific spinal discomfort, a discrepancy of greater than one centimeter should be empirically treated in an attempt to see whether such correction will be of some benefit. The question of which leg-length descrepancies are contributing factors is a multivariable problem to try to evaluate. A lift is an innocuous treatment and can be tried empirically as it does not represent much of a cost and seldom aggravates the underlying problem.

Roentgenographic evaluation of the area of the spine in which the runner is complaining of pain is usually of little help diagnostically in the management or prognosis of the spinal problem. In a series of roentgenograms of the lumbar spine in 90 asymptomatic marathon runners, we found that their incidence of degenerative changes was similar to that of the general population.[4] Many of those with mild roentogenographic changes did not seem to be having any more symptomatic spinal problems than those without changes at the time of their roentgenograms. The presence of changes in the lumbar spine does not preclude a runner from returning to unlimited mileage, and may or may not be associated with the patient's particular pain complex.

Supplemental diagnositic tests beyond the routine roentgenographic survey of the spine in the runner are seldom necessary. The use of electromyogram, myelogram, spinal fluid analysis, venography, bone scan, computerized axial tomography, segmental nerve blocks, Pentothal (thiopental) examinations, and psychometric evaluations are part of the armamentarium directed to those not responding once the initial impression has been made and program started.

As a rule, the distance runner does not have the

conflicting secondary gains and psychological overlay that interferes with recovery as often seen in other similarly aged adult patients with spinal complaints. Nevertheless, the psychological aspects of not being able to run cannot be ignored. To advise the runner to give up running as a solution for the spinal discomfort is seldom necessary. Controlled or restricted mileage is often part of the initial treatment program, which should be carefully outlined with the runner. Most runners, however, eventually return to unrestricted running, and telling the patient that fact on the initial evaluation will provide him with a source of relief.

Cervical Spine

The cervical spine infrequently presents symptoms that restrict running programs, but when cervical disc symptoms develop with associated radicular and paracervical pain and muscle spasm, it may curtail running for a significant period of time. The runner who sustains a whiplash injury may prolong the acute phase by continuing to run. Attention to the acute phase of a cervical disc injury, or injury to soft tissue of the cervical spine, may prevent chronic symptoms and headaches. The aggressive restriction of running during the acute phase of a cervical injury is often beneficial. Shoulder movement and motion of the upper extremity, and the muscle interaction with the cervical spine may increase the pain and lengthen the recovery time. Running in a cervical collar with restricted upper extremity motion is not enjoyable.

The stationary bicycle is an excellent alternative to maintain conditioning and usually will not aggravate the cervical spine during the acute symptoms. Most cervical symptoms will subside with a period of rest, and selected patients may require additional treatment such as cervical traction, immobilization, heat, massage, and other modalities. Acute symptoms may merit a short period of bedrest, with or without cervical traction. A short course of parenteral steroids, or other anti-inflammatory medication, analgesics, and muscle relaxants may be beneficial and could hasten the resolution of nerve root irritation symptoms. These treatments will vary and must be individualized with each case. Surgery usually is not necessary for cervical problems in the runner.

In the older runner, cervical disc disease and associated degenerative boney changes can be

Douglas W. Jackson, M.D.

associated with neurologic findings in the lower extremities as well as in the upper extremities. The neurologic status of both the upper and the lower extremities should be thoroughly evaluated in runners who have cervical spine complaints. Careful examination of the long tract signs, including clonus and spasticity, should be evaluated in cervical spine problems.

Occasionally, runners will develop symptoms of an acute "wryneck" in which the runner awakens in the morning with, or gradually develops, stiffness in the neck that is associated with some discomfort. These symptoms usually diminish as the runner warms up related to his running activity, and the cervical discomfort disappears during the workout. The symptoms return after the workout is completed and the runner cools down. This condition is usually a self-limited process unrelated to running and is seen frequently in the general adult population as well as in the runner. It is not associated with a long-term disability and usually the running program is disrupted for only seven to ten days.

In terms of returning the runner to the sport, nearly all cervical spine symptoms resolve readily with conservative measures. Cervical problems in runners are less difficult to manage than those in participants of some other sports in which more head and neck motion is required. Even if surgery is necessary; ie, disc removal and/or fusion, running usually remains an excellent fitness activity after recovery from the surgery.

Thoracic Spine

Pain and disability in the thoracic spine is seldom related exclusively to running. It can be associated with paraspinous muscle spasm, local pain, and radicular pain around the rib cage. The runner who notes an increased sensitivity in the skin in a thoracic dermatomal distribution and who develops radiating pain may be describing the prodromal of shingles, which is something that will become obvious when the skin rash occurs. The amount of pain and irritation that the runner has related to this virus varies significantly. The amount of restriction is essentially symptomatic and highly individualized. Occasionally, but rarely, an especially irritating postherpetic neuritis can develop.

Persistent localized thoracic pain is rare in the runner. If the tenderness is confined to a spinous process, or is reasonably well-localized, it should raise the suspicion of the possibility of an underlying malignancy or metastatic lesion in the middle-aged and older runner. Often careful scrutiny of the anteroposterior and lateral roentgenograms of the thoracic spine, as well as a complete medical examination, will suggest whether further studies are needed. If the pain does not resolve in a reasonable period, a bone scan and tomography of the area may be indicated. Just as metastatic disease and primary tumor involvement in the thoracic spine are infrequent occurrences, and are rare in the runner as well as in the general population, so is unexplained thoracic pain. Suspicion should be aroused. Fortunately such problems are unusual and unrelated to running, but they may develop in the runner and early symptoms should not be neglected.

Spondylitis confined to the thoracic spine also is a remote possibility. Signs and symptoms in other joints should alert the clinician to the appropriate diagnostic studies. Degenerative changes in the thoracic spine and old traumatic compression fractures usually do not restrict the running program, but do need individual assessment.

For those who have irritation with motion of the thoracic spine related to running, once again a stationary bicycle or rollerskating during the recovery period may be an alternative.

Lumbar Spine

The lumbar spine, by far, is the area of greatest disability related directly to running. In all of us as we grow older, our intravertebral discs alter. Usually this aging process of the disc is not associated with pain and there is gradual and rather uniform narrowing in the disc space. Those who have symptomatic pain with a disc, with or without associated radicular symptoms, may find their running curtailed for a significant period.

In running, as the hind leg trails, it is associated with hyperextension of the lumbar spine.[5] This hyperextension greatly aggravates most causes of lumbar pain and radicular symptoms. The degree of repetitive motion in the lumbar spine during distance running is unparalleled in other sports in the age group between 30 to 50 years. It is primarily the repetitive hyperextension of the lumbar spine that makes running so unique. The low back moves from the flat-backed position as the foot strikes to an extended lordotic position as

Douglas W. Jackson, M.D.

the trailing leg leaves the ground. Often the more competitive and faster runners will have more extension in the lumbar spine.

The more degenerative arthritic changes seen in the lumbar spine roentgenograms, associated with nerve foramina encroachment and spinal stenosis, may result in actual development of a mild cauda equina syndrome in the older runner. Their presentation may be one of pain and fatigability in the lower extremities with prolonged running. This condition should not be confused with a vascular problem and is related to neural element impingement with manifestations in the lower extremity. This problem is infrequent, as most people with this advanced degree of degenerative lumbar changes have enough associated pain that they are unable to carry out prolonged running.

Spondylolysis, defects of the pars interarticularis, that are present on lumbar films in skeletally mature runners are usually incidental findings (Fig. 4.3). The incidence of lumbar pars interarticularis defects among male runners is in the range of 5%, although the percentage may be higher in certain athletic populations.[6-8] Most lumbar pars interarticularis defects develop during childhood or early adolescence and are unrelated to the particular pain pattern in the adult. If localized vertebral instability or associated vertebral slippage is present, however, they may be associated with pain (Fig. 4.4a and b). Often, accelerated disc space narrowing at the level of the instability has been present for some time. Frequently, the symptomatic disc that causes these patients to complain is at the level above the obvious roentgenographic changes and instability.

Pars interarticularis defects in themselves usually will not permanently restrict running. Runners with vertebral slippage often are unaware of their spondylolisthesis until their first x-ray films are obtained in relationship to their new lumbar spine complaints (Fig. 4.5). They most often will be able to return to running after a conservative treatment program. Spondylolysis and spondylolisthesis are not the result of running, but when increased demands are placed on the lumbar spine, particularly the repetitive extension of the lumbar spine associated with running, the entire area may be more symptomatic and restricting. Although most of those types of low back problems will resolve through a period of rest, some surgical intervention may be

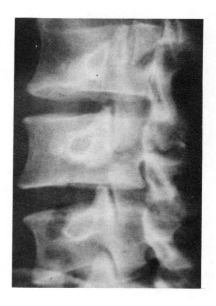

Fig. 4.3: This pars interarticularis defect was an incidental finding in a marathon runner. The runner was unaware of its' presence and denied any spine complaints.

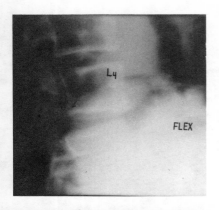

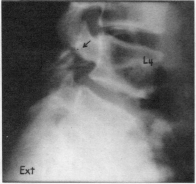

Fig. 4.4a and b: This segmental instability is associated with altered intervertebral disc motion between the 4th and 5th lumbar vertebrae. This runner complained of persistent discomfort with vigorous running.

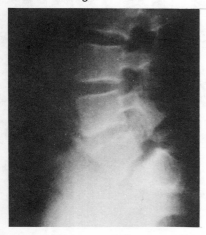

Fig. 4.5: Low grade spondylolisthesis is not inconsistent with distance running and a few internationally known runners have had this entity. They often have intervertebral narrowing at the level of instability.

necessary, and the possibility that the runners will have some permanent disability related to their running does exist.

Structural changes in the spine such as scoliosis, thoracic kyphosis and congenital abnormalities, may alter flexibility and restrict range of motion. They may be associated with degenerative changes that become more symptomatic as a result of the aging process, and are aggravated by running. Treatment must be individualized, but most affected patients can return to some type of satisfying fitness program if running is not tolerated. Attention to leg length discrepancies has already been alluded to and is something that needs to be watched for in this group.

Manifestations of inflammatory connective tissue disease in the spine and/or sacroiliac joints may present in the runner. These seronegative spondylo-arthropathies can be overlooked, particularly in the younger adult age group. The early presentation of spondylitis and its variants should be suspected in young runners complaining of lower spine and sacral discomfort. The tissue typing of HLA-B27 in these runners with unusual low back pain may be particularly worthwhile. A positive HLA-B27 can be obtained in about 7% or more of the normal male population, so it, in itself, is not diagnostic, but when coupled with a dramatic response to an anti-inflammatory medication or a positive bone scan, the diagnosis becomes more apparent.

Pain in the area of the sacroiliac joints in the lower lumbar spine should raise the question of ankylosing spondylitis, as well as variants of Reiter's syndrome. Details related to other joint involvement, arthritis, urethritis, conjunctivitis and mucous membrane lesions should be obtained appropriately. The bone scan is particularly helpful in those problems involving early sacroiliac joint inflammatory change. The roentgenograms may show no abnormality, and the increased boney activity can often be detected only by increased uptake on the technetium 99 bone scan. If it is part of a self-limited process, these early changes may never be detected on routine roentgenograms, or may develop years later. These processes may be associated with periods of disability that respond to rest and anti-inflammatory medication, and usually the athletes are able to continue with their running if that is their desire.

Douglas W. Jackson, M.D.

Nonspecific urethritis in the runner associated with discomfort in the sacroiliac joints is often associated with a period of disability, and evaluation of this entity may require an extensive rheumatologic or urologic workup.

Treatment of Lumbar Spine Problems

Most conservative programs related to treating acute disc problems associated with radicular pain have as the basis of their treatment, rest, antilordotic exercises, and positioning. Because runners are subjected to repetitive hyper-extension, those interested in the fastest recovery should consider a period of bedrest at the onset of intense acute low back pain. This rest may be associated with traction and analgesics if necessary. The role of the anti-inflammatory medication and muscle relaxers should be individualized. Runners as a group do not respond favorably to the suggestion of bedrest, although they may pay considerably more attention if they understand its potential role in the ultimate return to their running. Runners tend to be highly activity-oriented people, and often the milder problems can be controlled by limiting their exercise and running program.[9] A period of *controlled rest* with restriction in running and other activities can be tried in the milder cases for a trial period in the treatment program. Abdominal exercises and antilordotic positioning for the lumbar spine should be included as well as significant reduction in mileage. This rest may be supplemented by the simple use of heat and relaxation techniques as necessary.

In those runners who have radicular symptoms that persist two to three weeks or longer and do not respond to rest, a lumbar epidural cortisone injection may hasten the resolution of the more chronic symptoms (Fig. 4.6). It may significantly reduce the runner's radicular pain and hasten the ability to resume running after just one injection. The lumbar epidural cortisone injection, coupled with restricted mileage, flexion exercises, and gradual resumption of their running program, has succeeded in about 40% of the athletes on whom we have used it.[10,11] The longer-lasting epidural effects of DepoMedrol have been preferred to the shorter-acting water soluble suspensions.

The intradiscal cortisone injection has not been beneficial in any of our runners, and my

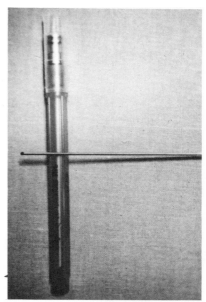

Fig. 4.6: The epidural needle facilitates the placement in the epidural space without penetrating the dura. The short beveled needle helps prevent dural leaks at the time of the epidural injection.

experience with the lumbar facet injection has been limited. Lumbar facet syndrome is difficult to diagnose. Some runners are believed to have symptoms related to impingement of the facets from repetitive hyperextension of the lumbar spine during the running gait. If a facet injection is believed to be indicated, localizing the position of the needle in the facet joint usually requires image intensification control, and may even be aided with the use of a facet arthrogram before the injection. It has been reported to be beneficial in some population groups, but has not been reported as a source of success in runners.

Mobilization (manipulation) of the lumbar spine, both actively and passively, is reasonable in localized lumbar spine problems in distance runners. It can be done by the physician, by a therapist, or by other persons trained in mobilization techniques. Often the runner finds that the treatment relieves symptoms for two to three hours only. On occasion, some treatments may result in dramatic relief. Usually, however, the mobilization techniques are coupled with additional treatments.

The efficiency of transelectrical nerve stimulation (TENS) in the distance runner is limited. It may give temporary noninvasive analgesia while the underlying process proceeds to heal. It should not be used to increase the pain tolerance for prolonged training. Most runners respond to rest with or without TENS.

Corsets and antilordotic braces in the runners are of little value unless used during the acute phase to aid in positioning and restricting activity for a short time. In the milder cases of low back discomfort, wet-suit lumbar binders that increase the local skin temperature may give symptomatic relief while the patient is running.

Some lumbar pain syndromes are aggravated by activities other than running. The running only accounts for a portion of the disability. For example, a person may have a job requiring prolonged sitting, and repeated bending, lifting, and stooping. These activities keep the back aggravated and yet it is during running that the greatest disability is present. Often an effective solution requires altering the entire requirements placed on the back if the runner is to continue running. Time is well spent in reviewing lifting habits, bending techniques, ways of getting into and out of chairs and automobiles, and sleeping

Douglas W. Jackson, M.D.

positions and surfaces; placing a foot on a short stool if prolonged standing is necessary can be helpful.

The prevention of spinal symptoms in the runner is a goal, and proper stretching, good muscle balance, and proper lifting and posture habits are important in an effective preventive program. To minimize the episodes of difficulty, a runner should stretch regularly, preferably before and after running. Allotting enough time is always difficult, but a runner with a back problem should definitely make a priority of having a stretching program before and after running. Although most runners will spend time stretching the Achilles tendon and the hamstrings, they usually do not specifically work on the spine. A full range of motion of the spine is maintained by stretching. Almost all beneficial stretching avoids hyperextension of the lumbar spine. This factor is particularly important in doing the sit-ups and other calisthenics that some runners do as part of their warm up and cooling down period.

Lumbar surgery in the runner can be highly successful and I am aware of several runners who have returned to marathon running after one level, and multiple level, disc surgery, and lumbar spine fusions (Fig. 4.7). The ability to run a marathon after lumbar spine surgery remains a possibility, but not in all cases. If recovery is incomplete or the pain is only partially resolved after surgery, and the patient has associated chronic changes related to the neural elements, he may not be able to continue with his running program. For these persons swimming and bicycling may become substitutes for running. That choice is an individual matter. That someone who has had lumbar spine surgery is precluded from future running is a popular misconception. As yet there is no conclusive evidence that a postsurgical, pain-free spine more rapidly degenerates with running than does the spine that has never had surgery. The runner who has had a disabling back condition of long duration, with or without surgery, is likely to have recurrent episodes of back disability, whether that person runs or not. Controlled studies have not been done to support positions for or against running in patients with lumbar spine problems. My experience is that if the spine can be maintained pain-free, running has not proved to be that detrimental.

Fortunately for the runner, the spine is in an

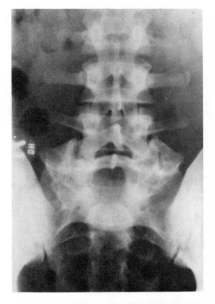

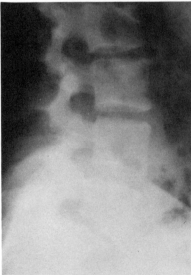

Fig. 4.7: This young runner that had a spinal fusion 7 years prior to these roentgenograms, for a low grade spondylolisthesis, showing essentially no symptoms associated with running. The spine above the level of the fusion is remarkably free of degenerative changes at the time of the roentgenograms.

area that does not present a great deal of disability and usually responds to conservative treatment, enabling the runner to return to unlimited mileage. To minimize spinal problems, each runner should maintain flexibility of the spine, use good lifting habits, and respect warning pains if they should develop. For those few who have a significant problem in spite of their efforts, the prognosis is usually good. Running with its demands of repetitive range of motion of the lumbar spine, particularly the increasing lordosis related to the trailing leg, may be more than certain spines can tolerate. Tolerance is highly individualized and each patient needs an evaluation and interpretation of his particular case. Many chronic lumbar spine patients do well only in the antilordotic position. It may even mean a certain percentage of runners will need to switch to alternate fitness programs of cycling or swimming. Fortunately, few patients must give up running altogether. Runners should take good care of their spines because the spine is one of the areas in which a chronic disabling condition, if allowed to develop, will significantly limit running.

References

1. Jackson DW, Pagliano J: The ultimate study of running injuries. Runners World Nov:42-50, 1980.
2. Palmer H: Pain maps in differential diagnosis of psychosomatic disorders. Med Press, May 25, 1960, p 454.
3. Ransford AO, Cairns D, Mooney V: The pain drawing as an aid to psychologic evaluation of the patient with low back pain. Spine 1:127, 1976.
4. Sutker A, Jackson DW: Roentgenographic changes in the lumbar spine in marathon runners. (publication pending)
5. Slocum DB, James SL: Biomechanics of running. JAMA 205:721-728, 1968.
6. Jackson DW, Wiltse LL, Cirincione RJ: Spondylolysis in the female gymnast. Clin Orthop 117:68-73, 1976.
7. Wiltse LL, Widell EH, Jackson W: Fatigue fracture: The basic lesion in isthmic spondylolisthesis. J Bone Joint Surg 57A:17-22, 1975.
8. Jackson DW, Wiltse LL, Dingeman R, Hayes M: Stress reactions involving the pars intaricularis in young athletes. Am J Sports Med 9(5):304-312, 1981.
9. Guten G: Herniated lumbar disc associated with running: A review of 10 cases. Am J Sports Med 9(3):155-159, 1981.
10. Jackson DW, Rettig A, Wiltse LL: Epidural cortisone injections in the young athletic adult. Am J Sports Med 8:239-243, 1980.
11. Rettig A, Jackson DW, Wiltse LL, Secrist L: The epidural venogram as a diagnostic procedure in the young athlete with symptoms of lumbar disc disease. Am J Sports Med 5:158-162, 1977.

Douglas W. Jackson, M.D.

5

Running Injuries of the Knee

Robert Leach, M.D.

When an orthopedic surgeon writes about sports injuries of the knee, he usually is primarily concerned with ligamentous instability or meniscal tears. Those injuries, however, play a minor role in runners unless the runner has had these problems before, and they resurface to cause him trouble again. Most running problems that cause knee pain are due to chronic stress, and not to one single injury.[1,2]

When examining a runner who presents with knee pain, the physician must recognize that the foot, ankle, leg, and hip all may contribute to certain problems.[3,4] The physical examination of a runner with knee pain includes looking at the runner's standing position and his gait (Fig. 5.1a and b). Leg length, tibia varus or valgus, and internal and external tibial torsion, must be observed, while retroversion and anteversion of the femur should be tested. A complete foot examination and evaluation of the wear pattern on the runner's shoes must be done, because abnormal foot mechanics may have a direct bearing on a number of knee problems. One must look for foot pronation (Fig. 5.2), or supination, cavus or pes planus, and heel varus or valgus. A number of these abnormalities of the lower extremities combine to form syndrome patterns that produce knee pain.

After a general examination of the lower extremity has been done, turn to the knee itself. A systematic examination of the knee includes the usual tests for pathological menisci and ligamentous derangements[5] (Fig. 5.3). The knee must be checked for an effusion, joint-line tenderness, McMurray's sign, varus or valgus instability, anterior posterior instability, and rotatory insta-

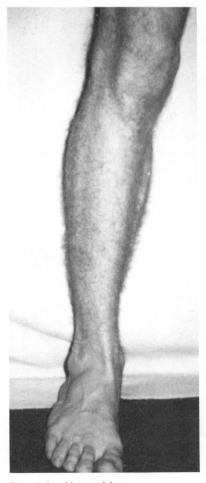

Fig. 5.1a: Normal leg.

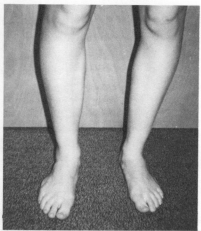

b. Tibia vara with foot pronation.

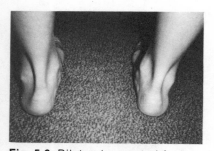

Fig. 5.2: Bilateral pronated feet.

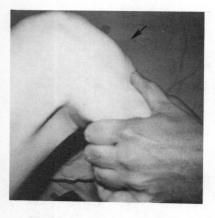

Fig. 5.3: Arrow points to tibial tubercle pulled forward in positive anterior drawer sign.

bility. Particular attention must be paid to the quadriceps and hamstrings. Look for atrophy of any of the muscle groups of the thigh, and test for muscle strength. Is there any abnormal tightness of the hamstrings or flexors, or external rotators of the hip? Tightness of these muscle groups or of the gastro-soleus complex may have a bearing on some knee problems. All painful areas must be examined carefully and point tenderness will help to distinguish certain specific syndromes.

I do not take x-rays of the knee of all runners who have knee pain. If intra-articular pathology is suspected, however, routine AP, lateral, and tunnel view roentgenograms should be made. In patients with patellar pain or in whom extensor malalignment is a problem, one must have a view of the patellofemoral groove such as the Hughston[6] view (Fig. 5.4), or the ones described by Labelle and Laurin[7] or Merchant and associates.[8]

Dealing with runners with knee pain is different from handling other athletes with knee pain. With a chronically unstable ligament or meniscal tear, most athletes in other sports will not be able to perform. Many runners will have a problem that produces less disability. The problem may produce pain that, while allowing the runner to run, may keep him from functioning optimally or from running for as long a period as he desires. It may be difficult for a physician to understand why a patient would worry if he can run three miles but not six miles. The tendency is to tell the runner to stop after three miles. This may not be the goal of the runner,nor should it be the goal of the physician. Our aim should be to allow each runner to achieve his or her own potential and goals, however difficult it may prove.

Let me make several comments on taking a runner's history. When dealing with knee problems, physicians are usually concerned with dealing with the acute onset of a knee injury and the subsequent events. Many times runners do not have an acute injury but a series of events or running days in which pain gradually begins. Still, the physician should try to pin the runner down as to the precise time that pain began. Was there a change in the training pattern, increased mileage, more hills, or interval workouts suddenly started? When does the pain occur? Is it present at the beginning of a run or near the end? Does the pain persist or increase with running and how is it the next day? Is this pain present only with

Robert Leach

running or is it associated with normal activities? What happens when going up and down stairs or ramps? What physical manifestations has the runner noticed? Swelling? Does the runner detect any noises in the knee, such as popping or grinding? Finally, the physician must know what treatment the runner has previously had. Has there been a shoe change? Orthotics? Medications? Injections? Have exercises been prescribed and if so, which ones? What has been their effect?

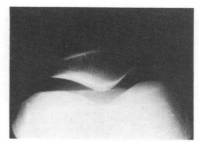

Fig. 5.4: Normal Hughston view of patella.

Intra-Articular Pathology

Meniscal Injuries

Except for chondromalacia, intra-articular pathology is not a common form of disability in runners. Although a runner with a misstep could tear the medial or lateral cartilage, acute meniscal injuries are uncommon. The symptoms and findings on physical examination of such a patient will be no different from other athletes with a meniscal tear. There is usually the history of an acute injury followed by pain. The runner may have felt something giving way within the knee, and swelling occurs within the first 12 hours. If the patient's knee appears to recover from this first episode, then the history of the knee locking or giving way with repeated minor episodes of swelling begins. The usual physical signs include a small-joint effusion, joint-line tenderness, localized pain with full extension of the knee (with the examiner's thumb putting pressure on the affected joint line), and a positive McMurray test in about half of the cases. An arthrogram can be helpful, although I prefer an arthroscopy. If the arthroscope shows a tear of the meniscus, the offending portion must be removed either totally or partially, depending on the tear and the surgeon's philosophy. Both sides of the joint must be examined arthroscopically, because there may be a relatively silent tear on one side that is a potential source of trouble, with a more major tear on the symptomatic side. I personally believe that partial meniscectomy in a runner is a reasonable way to handle certain specific tears.

The postoperative rehabilitation, even if the surgery is done via the arthroscope, is important. Many runners have tight hamstrings, and while directing much of our attention to strengthening the quadriceps muscle, we must also work on stretching out the hamstrings. To send a runner

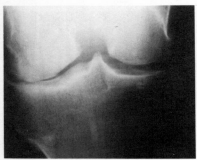

Fig. 5.5: Degenerative joint disease on lateral side secondary to early menisectomy.

out on the road before he or she has completely rehabilitated the quadriceps and the hamstring muscle groups is asking for recurrent difficulty and synovitis.

Old Truama

Many runners are more likely to have trouble because of a previous sports injury (Fig. 5.5) and subsequent intra-articular pathology than because of an acute running injury. Typical of these are people who have played other sports and have had a previous menisectomy, osteochondritic defect, or ligamentous injury. While the old history is important and the diagnosis frequently obvious, how well the runner will do depends on the present integrity of the articular cartilage. With a relatively intact articular cartilage, which sometimes can be determined only by arthroscopy, and with a willingness to work to strengthen the quadriceps and hamstring muscles, many patients are able to continue running despite previous knee injuries. They may have to decrease the total mileage or cut down or stop certain workouts such as running hills or interval training. Many people who have had previous injuries such as an anterior cruciate tear and do have laxity, are still able to run, provided that they do not have to cut or run on uneven ground. With rotatory instability, a derotation brace can be especially helpful.

Some patients with a history of an old injury and a synovitis produced by running will do well by taking anti-inflammatory agents, decreasing mileage, and increasing the strength of the thigh muscles. If a runner has synovitis after relatively short runs, he may be unable to continue to participate in running and might be better advised to do other sports such as bicycling, swimming, and cross-country skiing. I do not believe it is reasonable to suppress a synovitis continuously with anti-inflammatory medications and to continue running. For the short-term measure, the oral anti-inflammatory agents are excellent, but if the synovitis continues, either an offending agent must be found or the runner would be better off in another sport.

A few patients with long-term symptoms and synovitis may have minor degenerative changes of the meniscus that should be able to be seen by arthroscopy. If these meniscal injuries are minor, a partial menisectomy may cure the problem. I examine by arthroscopy such patients who continue to have intermittent synovitis, to ascertain the

Robert Leach

status of the joint and see whether anything can be done operatively of a relatively minor nature that would enable the runner to continue. Major meniscal pathology may be handled by total meniscectomy and obviously is done only if needed.

Loose Bodies

Loose bodies are a relatively uncommon cause of knee pain in a runner. The usual history is that of an occasional catching or giving way of the knee joint. The athlete may say he can feel something moving around, and even feel the loose body. Each episode of pain or transient locking is followed by a period of brief effusion and reduced activity that allows the knee to return to nearly normal. On physical examination, the examiner may or may not feel the loose body. X-rays should include a tunnel view and may show an old osteochondritic defect or, in the younger person, a relatively new defect. If the loose body is ossified, it may be seen on x-ray. If there are chances of degenerative arthritis, the loose body may be a fragment from a fractured osteophyte. If a loose body is suspected, arthroscopy is helpful for visualization, and a loose body can be removed either through the arthroscope or by open arthrotomy. I think that if a loose body is known to be causing symptoms, it is better to remove it, because it will be a source of potential difficulty over the years.

One other source of loose bodies is an osteochondral fracture off either the patella or the femur (Fig. 5.6) as result of an acute dislocation of the patella. The patient will usually be aware of what has happened but in some instances, does not realize the patella has dislocated. A bloody effusion and tenderness on the medial aspect of the patella will point to the diagnosis. A small osteochondral fragment may not be visible on x-ray film because there is little bone attached to the articular cartilage. Again, the arthroscope helps either by locating the loose fragment or showing the defect in the patella or femur so that the examiner knows that there is a loose fragment.

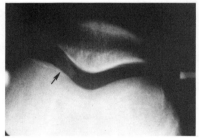

Fig. 5.6: Arrow points to osteochondral fragment between patella and femur.

Baker's Cyst

A Baker's cyst, despite its extra-articular location, usually occurs in response to an intra-articular problem. Frequently, a torn cartilage causes the synovitis and a secondary effusion that fills the Baker's cyst. When a patient presents with a Baker's cyst, always look for intra-articular pathology. The Baker's cyst can usually be confirmed either by an arthrogram or by ultra-sound studies. I do not operate on Baker's cysts initially, but try to deal with the intra-articular pathology, and the cyst usually will then recede. If a large Baker's cyst starts to dissect into the soft tissues of the leg, it may have to be removed. One must be careful to differentiate a large popliteus muscle belly, which can easily be palpated in a thin runner, from a true Baker's cyst.

Overuse Synovitis

Some runners may have a chronic knee synovitis without apparent intra-articular pathology and with no history suggesting possible injury other than that of increased running. Be sure that no intra-articular pathology is producing the synovitis. In such patients, we usually find a history of increased mileage or more vigorous workouts. An oral anti-inflammatory medication for several weeks combined with decreased mileage and less strenuous workouts plus applying ice packs to the knee after running may decrease the synovitis. If the synovitis persists, I believe that runner should stop running completely until the knee stays dry for several weeks. Then a gradual resumption of running can be tried.

Should intra-articular steroids be used? I dislike using them because of the deleterious effect on articular cartilage. In an occasional instance, it may be reasonable to try an intra-articular steroid injection for a synvotis that is secondary to overuse and has not quieted down with rest. The runner should not run for the next 14 days to allow the synovium and the articular cartilage to recover. Then the running program should be reinitiated slowly.

Intra-Articular Plica

An intra-articular plica, as a source of disabling knee pain in runners, has become a popular diagnosis in recent years.[9] Certain physicians seem to see, diagnose, and treat the condition more than others do. Although the condition has received much notice, I believe that the diagnosis of synovial plica as a common cause of knee pain is overemphasized.

The medial synovial plica is a fibrotic band extending from the supero-medial part of the suprapatellar pouch adjacent to the medial pole of the patella, going laterally to insert on the medial aspect of the infrapatellar fat pad. This tissue is present in many patients but is pathological in

Robert Leach

only a few. If it becomes thickened, it can snap over the medical femoral condyle and cause local chondromalacic changes in some patients. Most patients will complain of a snapping sensation, whereas others feel an aching pain produced particularly by running or going up and down stairs. Tenderness is found over the medial femoral condyle or the medial aspect of the patella. The diagnosis can be confirmed by arthroscopy, which may show changes on the condyle and the plica. Some patients respond to conservative measures including decreased activity, quadriceps progressive resistance exercises, ice applied after running, and aspirin. In others, the plica must be excised, usually through the arthroscope but sometimes by open arthrotomy.

From the number of patients whom I have seen who have had a plica previously operated on but who continue to have knee pain, I believe this diagnosis must be carefully studied before we can say it is a common cause of pain in runners.

Patella Problems

In a runner's clinic conducted by James and his associates, knee problems were the most common cause of pain in runners, and the most common causes of knee pain were conditions of the patellofemoral joint.[10] In this section, I will divide some of the patella problems into subdivisions. However, some of these diagnostic entities fade into each other and may be stages of the same condition.

First, let me state that I have no idea what the term "runner's knee" describes. To some physicians this means pain occurring on the lateral aspect of the patella. To others, it represents chondromalacia of the patella or a nonspecific tendinitis. To runners, it is any pain around the knee. I consider it a wastebasket term. Physicians dealing with runners should make an accurate diagnosis to determine the cause of pain, and thus treat their patients reasonably.

Lateral Compression Syndrome

The lateral compresssion syndrome[11,12] is characterized by pain on the lateral aspect of the knee at the patellofemoral joint. Increased mileage, hard surfaces, interval workouts, and hills all may contribute to the problem. Runners describe the pain as being deep and aching, and relieved by rest. Sometimes the runners feel uncomfortable

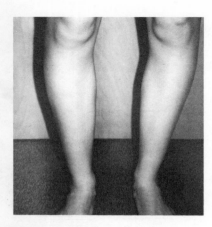

Fig. 5.7: Miserable malalignment with tibia vara, pronated feet, and "squinting in" patellae.

when sitting for a long time and say their knees feel tight or creaky.

On physical examination, no effusion and no patellar crepitus will be present. The Q angle is usually normal with little tendency to lateral subluxation of the patella, particularly when the patella is compressed against the femoral joint surface. If the patella is examined with an arthroscope, the articular surface looks normal.

Perhaps the lateral compression syndrome is a precursor to chondromalacia. Perhaps it is not. This pain on the lateral aspect of the knee may be caused by static deformities, such as foot pronation or tibia varum, which causes pressure of the lateral facet of the patella. Some patients have the miserable malalignment syndrome (Fig. 5.7) described by James et al,[10] and Kennedy,[11] which includes internal rotation of the hips, medial squinting patella, external tibial torsion, tibia vara, and excessive foot pronation, all of which cause altered patellofemoral mechanics.

We direct treatment toward proper alignment of the whole lower extremity and do a careful check on the runner's training program. During the painful phase, we ask runners to decrease their mileage, run on soft surfaces, stay off hills, and stop interval workouts. At the same time, we try to correct any static foot or lower leg faults. For a pronated foot we prescribe a proper foot orthotic to help with foot strike. Many of these runners have tight posterior heel cords, and stretching of the gastro-soleus Achilles tendon complex is mandatory. We demand that the patient strengthen the quadriceps muscles of the thigh, usually beginning with isometric resistance exercises. After several weeks of these exercises, he progresses to limited isotonics, working only from 35° of flexion to full extension. Generally, runners start with low weights and a large number of repetitions and gradually work up in weights. Adolescent runners may be helped with a patella-stabilizing device. Aspirin is the only medication I have recommended. Some stronger anti-inflammatory agents may be used, but I have not found them necessary. I would not inject an intra-articular steroid, because I can see no physiologic reason for doing so.

Chondromalacia

Chondromalacia implies physical damage to the articular surface of the patella (Fig. 5.8), and possibly to the opposing femoral surface. It is a

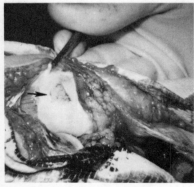

Fig. 5.8: Arrow points to severe chondromalacic changes on patella.

Robert Leach

common cause of knee pain in runners, and the physical complaints are similar to those of the lateral compression syndrome. With chondromalacia, the pain is usually more severe and of longer duration. The runner will frequently complain of a noisy knee. Hill running, downhill in particular, increases the pain, and increased mileage may cause not only pain but swelling of the knee joint.

On physical examination, there is audible crepitus as the knee moves in flexion and extension. The examiner will find tenderness on the undersurface of the patella either medially (Fig. 5.9) or laterally, and compressing the patella against the femur causes intense pain. I cause patellofemoral compression by having the knee flexed to 20° and anchoring the patella with my hand. The patient then attempts to extend the knee, which causes intense pain if he has chondromalacia. An effusion indicates synovial irritation and probable severe chondromalacic changes. Some patients will have an increased Q angle (Fig. 5.10) and lateral subluxation of the patella. Some will have the same lower extremity findings seen in the lateral compression syndrome, such as excessive foot pronation, tibia varum, external tibial torsion, and femoral anteversion. A number of runners will have none of these findings.

The treatment of chondromalacia is similar to that for the lateral compression syndrome, except that it may take longer for results, and some patients will not respond to conservative measures. I ask the runners to decrease their mileage, stay off hills, and stop interval workouts. I ask if they have been running on a particular surface that seems to bother them. Sometimes running on a particular track or the crown of a road will put stress on one leg and force the foot into pronation or the knee into valgus, which would cause lateral tracking of the patella. Static defects of the lower extremity must be corrected. Not all patients with chondromalacia need orthotics, but some do and respond well to them.

The major treatment is directed at increasing quadriceps strength and stretching out the hamstrings. This includes isometric progressive resistance exercises coupled with an active hamstring stretching program. If the patient has an effusion, I stop his running completely and put him on a regimen of progressive resistance exercises and aspirin. During this period, I ask him to keep his cardiorespiratory system in tone by swimming or

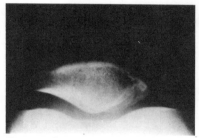

Fig. 5.9: Damage to medial facet of patella secondary to dislocation.

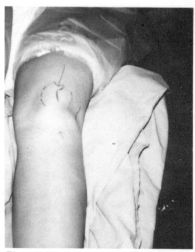

Fig. 5.10: Increased Q angle in patellar subluxer.

sometimes by bicycling. Bicycling, however, does bother some patients with chondromalacia. Once the effusion has quieted down, they may then return to running, but the exercise program must be continued, with a gradual progression to an isotonic program.

In those patients with a loose patella, a patellar stabilization device helps. These devices can be made by cutting out a horseshoe-shaped piece of felt that is held in position with an elastic wrap or neoprene sleeve. Other devices, such as the patellar alignment control brace of Marshall or Palumbo, can be equally helpful.

If, after following conservative measures, the runner continues to have difficulty and cannot run, arthroscopy is the next step. This procedure gives the physician a precise idea of the amount of damage to the undersurface of the patella, and he can observe any tendency to lateral subluxation of the patella as the knee moves. With significant damage and pain, surgery may be indicated. A variety of procedures, such as lateral retinacular release and arthroscopic shaving, lateral retinacular release alone, soft tissue or bony extensor realignment procedures, and even the tibial tubercle osteotomy of Maquet, may help some runners return to full-time running.

Patellar Subluxation and Dislocation

Some patients with patellar chondromalacia have patellar subluxations or dislocations.[6,13] If the runner's complaint is less of pain and more of sudden knee collapse and the physical findings show that the patella can easily be subluxed, the diagnosis is easy (Fig. 5.11). Such patients usually have a Q angle of over 20°, valgus of the lower leg, and often an undeveloped vastus medialis muscle, plus the findings of chondromalacia.

In those patients who have recurrent patellar subluxations or dislocations and major physical findings but who want to continue to run, a brief try can be made to strengthen the quadriceps muscle. One of the patellar realignment braces may help. If, however, little or no progress has been made after two months, particularly in those with a poor vastus medialis or those in whom the vastus medialis attaches high on the patella, I believe an extensor realignment procedure should be done. A variety of operations are available. In those patients having a Q angle less than 20° and no significant valgus of the lower extremity, I perform a release of the extensor retinaculum

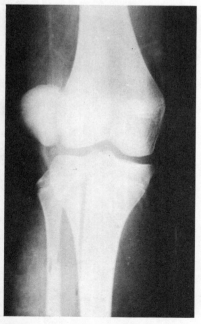

Fig. 5.11: Acute patellar dislocation

Robert Leach

laterally and a vastus medialis advancement and capsular imbrication medially. If the Q angle is 20° or greater or there is significant valgus of the lower leg, I do either a lateral release plus a Trillat advancement of the tibial tubercle, or a lateral release, vastus medialis advancement, capsular imbrication medially, and medial transfer of half of the patellar ligament (Fig. 5.12). The vastus medialis muscle must be strengthened after all surgery. Unfortunately, not all patients subjected to this surgery will be able to return to running. Some may find they are better off going to another type of physical activity.

In those few patients who have severe patello-femoral arthrosis and who cannot be helped by other procedures, the tibial tubercle osteotomy described by Kaufer[14] may be beneficial (Fig. 5.13). This procedure should be reserved for those patients who do not respond to conservative treatment or to other operative procedures. It is risky to tell any runner who has severe patello-femoral arthrosis that any surgery can get him back to normal activity, but the Maquet offers at least the possibility of doing so.

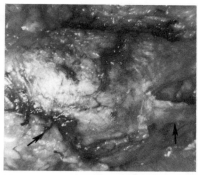

Fig. 5.12: Vastus medialis advancement (top arrow) and medial placement (distal arrow) of part of patellar ligament.

Quadriceps Tendinitis

The quadriceps muscle itself is not a common source of disabling pain. Some newly devoted joggers may go out more strongly than they should, and these muscles will ache afterwards for the first several days. This aching usually passes quickly as the muscles become accustomed to the increased activity. Ruptures of the quadriceps muscle are uncommon except in more violent physical activity, as in football. A rupture could occur if a runner who was going downhill misstepped and the lower leg went into flexion while there was a sudden violent contracture of the quadriceps. The runner would be unable to fully extend the knee and would have extreme weakness on attempted extension. There would be local tenderness, and a defect should be palpated in the quadriceps muscle. Because this defect may fill with blood initially, the presence of local tenderness is a diagnostic help. A quadriceps rupture could be treated either conservatively with six weeks of rest, or by operative repair if the defect is major.

More common than quadriceps muscle pain is the chronic pain from quadriceps tendinitis. The quadriceps tendon has a broad insertion into the upper pole of the patella, and this apparently

Fig. 5.13: Bone graft (arrow) in Maquet tibial tuberosity advancement.

dissipates the muscle power. No one other area is inclined to break down as quickly as the patellar ligament where it attaches to the lower pole of the patella. Quadriceps tendinitis is characterized by pain at the upper pole of the patella, usually more common laterally than medially. It is increased by more mileage and particularly by going up and down hills.

Most runners can decrease symptoms by lowering their mileage and changing their running route, plus applying ice to the area after activity. If the symptoms are severe, anti-inflammatory agents such as aspirin, ibuprofen, sulindac (Clinoril), or even phenylbutazone (Butazolidin) can be particularly helpful. I have usually found that aspirin and ice applications are enough to control pain. The quadriceps muscle must be kept strong, and isometric progressive resistance exercise are advised. If the knee is in the fully extended position with weights applied, pain does not seem to increase. I ask runners to increase endurance by concentrating on repetitions and low weights rather than working up to very high weights. It is particularly important to be sure that the runners do their stretching exercises, which include stretching of the hamstrings and the quadriceps before and after running. A local steroid injection into an area of tenderness is seldom needed by these patients.

Tendinitis of the Patellar Ligament

Jumper's knee is the euphemism for the condition characterized by tenderness where the patellar ligament attaches to the lower pole of the patella.[15] It is particularly common in basketball players and in certain track athletes such as high jumpers and hurdlers, but less common in distance runners. The condition results from chronic stress put on the patellar ligament as the athletes do major physical activity, particularly running and jumping. The pain is felt below the knee; usually both patient and physician can delineate it as being acutely localized to the attachment of the patellar ligament to the lower pole of the patella. There is evidence of soft tissue swelling. Pain increases with physical activity and decreases with rest. Many runners have a long history of difficulty, extending over several years (Fig. 5.14).

Conservative measures include a slow warm-up and ice application after activity. I frequently prescribe oral anti-inflammatory agents, starting

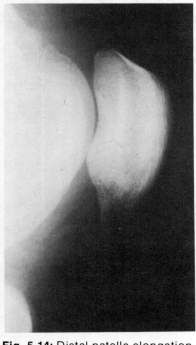

Fig. 5.14: Distal patella elongation in patellar tendinitis.

Robert Leach

with aspirin and progressing to some of the stronger agents if the aspirin does not work. Sometimes a centering device for the patella, such as a neoprene sleeve with a patella hole, will help. Rest frequently improves the condition, but a return to normal activity may be accompanied by a return of pain. In my experience, conservative measures have not always worked and some people continue to have pain when they run or jump. It is particularly difficult to treat high jumpers and hurdlers because of the force generated by the take off. Putting an athlete into a cast will cause quadriceps muscle atrophy, but I have sometimes used a knee immobilizer for a week to decrease pain while anti-inflammatory agents are being used.

Rarely, I have given a one-time injection of a steroid preparation into the locally tender area. The more acute the tenderness, the more likely the steroid injection will help. Along with the steroid injection, I have used multiple punctures with the injecting needle at the attachment of the patellar ligament to the distal pole of the patella. After a steroid injection, the athlete must refrain from activities for a minimum of two weeks.

Rarely, a patient is unable to continue running and surgery may be performed. An incision is made directly over the tender area and the patellar tendon split. There is usually an area of mucinous degeneration, which may be only a few millimeters in diameter but must be curetted. The base of the patella is also curetted and the tendon reattached to the bone. Do not hasten the athlete into action too quickly after surgery. It takes about three months before everything quiets down and allows the athlete to return to normal activity.

Osgood-Schlatter Disease

Osgood-Schlatter disease is confined to young athletes, some of whom are runners. Pain presents at the attachment of the patellar ligament to the tibial tuberosity and is due to chronic stress. Osgood-Schlatter disease is characterized by a bony abnormality (Fig. 5.15) plus soft tissue inflammation. If the physical findings are consistent with Osgood-Schlatter disease, I ask the patient to decrease running by about 50% and to stay on even surfaces and off banked tracks or hills. Ice applied to the knee for 15 minutes after activity helps, and in young patients, several aspirin taken a half hour before running will help them get through a workout. If the aspirin does not help,

Fig. 5.15: Osgood-Schlatter disease with loose ossicle.

another mild oral anti-inflammatory agent may be needed. I rarely inject steroids into the locally tender area because the condition is self-limited, and I have found that with rest, ice packs, and aspirin, the condition improves. If the runner has acute tenderness due to Osgood-Schlatter disease, immobilization in a knee splint for several weeks can be helpful. I do not like to put such a knee into a cast, which will induce marked atrophy and occasional minor knee stiffness. If all else fails, sometimes the younger runner will have to stop running for a while. Surgery is seldom indicated. If a loose ossicle is present in later adolescent years, it can be removed. Otherwise, having to operate on someone because of symptomatic Osgood-Schlatter disease is a rarity.

One occasionally sees an older patient with a fused tibial apophysis and a bony bump, typical of an earlier Osgood-Schlatter disease. There may be tenderness where the patellar ligament attaches. At this point, it should be called a patellar ligament tendonitis rather than Osgood-Schlatter disease. I find it useful to explain to the person what the bump comes from and that it is not the cause of pain itself. In most instances, conservative measures such as decreased running and application of ice packs are enough to allow people to continue sports. If the small bursa underneath the patellar ligament distally is inflamed, a steroid can be injected into this area with expected good results. In this instance, we inject underneath the patellar ligament where it attaches to the bone, rather than into the ligament itself.

Pre-Pattelar Bursitis

Pre-pattelar bursitis, while uncommon in runners, is occasionally seen. The runner feels pain in front of the patella in the soft tissues. It may be induced by chronic stress or more likely by a blow to the knee. Pre-patellar bursitis must be differentiated from patellar or quadriceps tendinitis. The soft tissue swelling occurs in the pre-patellar area, and there may be fluids in the bursa. Application of ice packs several times a day, combined with compression, may be enough to control symptoms. If the bursa is enlarged, however, I sometimes aspirate the bursa and advise rest and compression to quiet it down. If that treatment is not enough, a steriod injection into the bursa helps. Rarely, excision of the bursa is needed.

Ligamentous Injuries

Sprains or major tears of the ligamentous

Robert Leach

structures of the knee, such as the medial collateral, lateral collateral, anterior and posterior cruciate ligaments, are uncommon in runners. If, however, the runner slips or has a misstep and puts appropriate stress on the knee, sprains or tears may occur. This kind of stress might happen in cross-country events where the runners are often on uneven surfaces. A runner could land awkwardly on his leg and apply a valgus stress, which could produce pain and soft tissue swelling around the medial collateral ligament. In such an instance, on examination, the knee would almost always be stable, and I would treat this type of sprain by keeping a knee splint on it for 14 to 21 days. I use removable splints rather than casts in these injuries when I think the ligament is intact.

Another rare ligamentous injury for a runner would occur if he landed on the extended knee and felt a popping sensation. If this event were followed by an effusion, it would likely be caused by a tear of the anterior cruciate ligament. An aspiration of the knee would show gross blood, which would necessitate a careful physical examination and possibly even arthroscopic examination. It is sometimes difficult to detect an anterior cruciate tear, for in an otherwise undamaged knee the Lachman test and the drawer sign may be negative. Arthroscopic examination should be directed at both the cruciate and the postero-medial and postero-lateral corners of the menisci to see whether there is a peripheral tear. A hemarthrosis of the knee is a frequent sign of an anterior cruciate ligament tear and warrants careful follow-up. Although it depends on the surgeon's experience and his philosophy, in most instances, I perform a primary repair of an acute tear of the anterior cruciate.

Ligamentous injuries may play a major role for runners when the athlete has had old ligamentous injuries and turns to running as his new sport. Many people with previous knee injuries are able to run without significant difficulty as long as there is no articular cartilage damage. Running straight ahead is not difficult, but when one starts to pivot or cut, the knee instability syndromes are a problem. In some patients with old ligamentous injuries causing instability, the increased activity causes synovitis. We must be careful to see whether the patient is injuring himself by continuing to run. Major muscle rehabilitation programs of both the quadriceps and hamstrings may allow such a person to run. In other instances, a derotation brace may be enough to help.

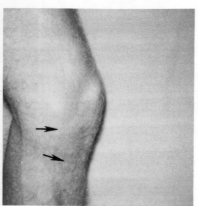

Fig. 5.16. Proximal arrow points to joint line. Distal arrow points to area of pes anserinus bursitis.

Pes Anserinus Bursitis

One interesting condition occurring primarily in runners is characterized by pain on the medial aspect of the knee below the joint line in the area of the pes anserinus bursa (Fig. 5.16). In all runners, the hamstring muscles are constantly acting because of the need for deceleration, which is controlled by the hamstrings. These muscles act as knee flexors and internal rotators of the tibia and must act to counterbalance the external rotation and pronation of the foot, which occurs after heel strike during running. The large pes bursa is between the medial collateral ligament and the three tendons as they cross to attach to the medial aspect of the tibia. Characteristically, pain occurs in both distance runners and intermediate sprinters, with less trouble for people who run dashes.

Physical examination shows local tenderness over the pes anserinus bursa with soft tissue swelling and even local crepitus. If the examination is done with the knee extended, the pain may appear to be nearer the joint line, but if the knee is flexed, the tenderness will be detected over the pes anserinus bursa, a fact that easily distinguishes it from a tear of the medial meniscus.

Treatment is directed toward decreasing the inflammatory response. If there are obvious static foot abnormalities, shoe orthotics may be of some help in trying to decrease the tendency towards external rotation or pronation of the foot. As with so many of the other conditions around the knee, decreasing mileage and interval workouts, and applying ice after running is helpful. Some runners have found that wrapping the upper leg with an elastic bandage or an elastic neoprene sleeve is sometimes helpful. Oral anti-inflammatory agents are especially effective, with Butazolidin seemingly most helpful in the acute cases. If pain persists and the runner is unable to continue, this is one time that I believe that a local injection of a steroid will not harm the runner. After receiving the injection, the runner should rest for at least 14 days.

Pes anserinus bursitis is a condition that I have seen particularly in runners who are running on indoor tracks that have tight or heavily banked corners. As they go around the corner, they must drive off hard on the outside foot, causing a tendency for the muscles on the inner aspect of the leg to tightly contract, and sometimes this chronic stress causes irritation. It is difficult to have

Robert Leach

runners reverse their direction on the track during workouts but occasionally that maneuver will help. Usually, however the conservative measures mentioned will suffice.

Iliotibial Band Syndrome

The iliotibial tract is an important lateral stabilizer of the knee and is very active in running. Before and during foot strike, it helps to externally rotate the leg and stabilize it during the early phase. As the knee goes from flexion to extension and back, the iliotibial tract passes from behind the lateral epicondyle to in front of it, and the repeated excursion may cause irritation of the iliotibial tract[16] against the lateral epicondyle, and inflame the areolar tissue in this area (Fig. 5.17). Characteristically, such an injury is seen in long-distance runners and is particularly painful when running downhill. The longer the distance the runner goes, the more pain he has. Keeping the knee still when walking usually relieves the pain.

On physical examination, the only positive finding is local tenderness at the lateral epicondyle where the iliotibial band crosses. At 30° of flexion as the iliotibial band goes over the lateral epicondyle, tenderness is maximal. There may be some swelling and occasionally thickening of the tissue in this area.

Initial treatment is directed toward decreasing mileage, improving foot strike, and protecting against any excessive wear on the lateral aspect of the heel that might tend to cause more foot pronation. Decreased mileage with application of ice packs after activity and the taking of oral anti-inflammatory agents will help a number of patients. Some, however, will need a steroid injection into the locally tender area, followed by two weeks of rest. The steroid is injected into the areolar tissue just under the iliotibial tract. These measures should help most runners, although Noble[17] has reported doing a partial release of the iliotibial band surgically in a few recalcitrant cases.

Popliteus Tendinitis

Mayfield[18] describes this syndrome, caused by popliteus tendon tenosynovitis, which is characterized by pain on the lateral aspect of the knee just above the joint line and anterior to the lateral collateral ligament. The pain is aggravated by weight bearing, is felt particularly when the knee

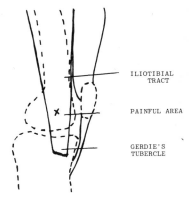

ILIOTIBIAL TRACT

PAINFUL AREA

GERDIE'S TUBERCLE

Fig. 5.17: The painful area (x) in iliotibial tract syndrome.

is flexed from 15 to 30°, and is increased with downhill running. Because of the intra-articular position of the popliteus tendon, this pain penetrates more deeply than does the pain in some of the other syndromes we have been talking about.

Tenderness is felt usually just anterior and just posterior to the lateral collateral ligament and just above the joint line. We test the popliteal pain by flexing the affected knee to 90° and putting the lateral malleolus of the affected leg on the opposite leg. This positioning produces stress on the popliteus tendon and most patients have pain in that area. Occasionally, one sees small radio-densities in the area of the popliteus tendon, but this is uncommon.

Again, the general management of this condition includes proper foot positioning by whatever means is needed, and decreasing activity. Oral anti-inflammatory agents and ice application after running are usually enough to handle the condition. If the pain persists, the condition may be confused with a peripheral tear of the lateral meniscus, and arthroscopy may be indicated in some instances. If the arthroscopy is negative except for inflammation around the popliteus tendon, which can usually be seen, a local injection of steroid into that area is reasonable. The runner would then have to rest for at least two weeks. Conservative measures usually suffice.

Medial Collateral Ligament Bursitis

Brantigan and Voshell[19] described the "no name, no fame bursa," which is located between the superficial and deep portions of the medial collateral ligament at the medial joint line (Fig. 5.18). Occasionally, runners have pain in this area that may be difficult to distinguish from the pain of a peripheral meniscal tear or even of inflammation of the pes anserinus bursa. With inflammation of Voshell's bursa, the runner will often have pain even when sitting, particularly if he is in cramped quarters and is forced to keep his knees at 80 to 100° of flexion. There should be no effusion, and tenderness would be localized to the area just below the joint line and at the medial collateral ligament.

Occasionally, injecting a small amount of local anesthetic just to the medial collateral ligament, being careful not to put it in the joint, will cause the pain to disappear, and thus help to make the diagnosis.

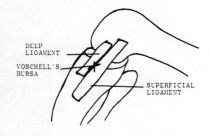

Fig. 5.18: The Voshell's bursa (x) between deep and superficial medial collateral ligament.

Robert Leach

The hallmarks of treatment are rest and oral anti-inflammatory agents plus ice application after running. If the pain does not disappear after a suitable period, a local injection of steroid into the area may rapidly relieve symptoms, but again, the runner should not run for about 14 days to allow the full effect of the steroid and reparation of the damaged tissues. Generally, this bursitis can be well controlled by conservative measures.

Stress Fracture of The Proximal Tibial

Although stress fractures are common in runners, such fractures are rarely located at the medial aspect of the proximal tibia.[20] With a fracture in that location, the runner usually complains of localized tenderness that is increased by running and helped somewhat by rest. Ordinary walking does not seem to be painful. The diagnosis may be difficult because of the other anatomical entities in the area, such as the pes anserinus bursa, which may confuse the issue.

Findings on early x-ray may be negative, but x-ray film taken four to six weeks after the onset of pain should show some sclerosis around the medial cortex. If the history and the physical examination are suggestive and x-rays are negative, a bone scan can be taken, which would usually show a hot spot and provide the diagnosis.

The only treatment for stress fractures is rest. It is my practice to tell the runners to stay off the road completely until localized tenderness is gone. If they return before the localized tenderness disappears, the pain recurs and the symptoms are drawn out over a long period.

Hamstring Injuries

Injuries to the hamstring muscles and tendons are common in a variety of running sports. The most common injury is a strain, which seems to occur more often near the origin or the insertion than the middle of the muscle belly. Total rupture of a hamstring muscle or tendon is unusual but is occasionally seen in sprinters or hurdlers. More common is the partial tear of the muscles. After an acute episode, there is usually localized swelling, which is probably deep hemorrhage, and pain with palpation or any attempted stretching of the hamstrings. Full extension of the knee or a long stride causes pain.

The acute treatment should be directed at complete rest plus applying ice packs to the affected area. After the acute pain has quieted down, I start the patients on a regimen of gradual stretching exercises, but have them keep their exercises within the limits of pain. An anti-inflammatory agent may be helpful in relieving some pain and spasm, but I have found that the combination of ice application and gentle stretching seems to be the most efficacious method of handling the problem. As the pain and spasm recede, I ask the runners to begin to stretch more and finally to go on doing a full series of stretching exercises. At the same time, they start on mild resistance exercise.

The major problem with runners having hamstring pulls is that they return to action too quickly, which makes them subject to recurrent injuries. I try to keep them out of training until the hamstring tenderness is completely gone and they are able to stretch as well as they could before injury. The runner and his coach may have to recognize that missing part or all of a season is necessary to prevent the runner from sustaining permanent damage. Once the injury seems to be healed, the runner must be assiduous in stretching his hamstring muscles. It is important for both the quadriceps and the hamstring muscles to be strengthened so that there is no imbalance of the muscle tendon units around the knee.

References

1. Apple DF: Knee pain in runners. South Med J: 1377-1379, 1979.
2. Brubaker CE, Jones SL: Injuries to runners. J Sports Med 2:189-198, 1974.
3. Baugher WH, Balady GJ, Warren RF, Marshall JL: Injuries of the musculoskeletal system in runners. CORR, Vol 5, Oct, 1979.
4. Buchbinder MR: The relationship of abnormal pronation to chondromalacia of the patella in distance runners. J Am Podiatry Assoc 69:159-162,
5. Ellison AE: Skiing Injuries. Clinical symposium. CIBA, 29:18-37, 1977.
6. Hughston JC: Subluxation of the patella. J Bone Joint Surg 50A:1003-1026, 1968.
7. Labelle H, Laurin CA: Radiological investigation of normal and abnormal patellae. J Bone Joint Surg 57B:530, 1975.
8. Merchant AC, Mercer RL, Jacobson RH, Cool CR: Roentgenographic analysis of patellofemoral congruence. J Bone Joint Surg 56A:1391-1396, Oct 1974.
9. Brouklin B, Foy JM, Blazina, ME, Del Pizzo W, Hirsh L: The synovial shelf syndrome. Clin Orth Related Res 142:135-138, 1979.
10. James SL, Bates BT, Ostering LR: Injuries to runners. Am J Sports Med 6:40-50, 1978.
11. Kennedy JC: The Injured Adolescent Knee. Williams & Wilkins Co., Baltimore, 1979.

Robert Leach

12. Larson RL, Cabaud HE, Slocum DB, James SL Keenan T, Hutchinson T: The patellar compression syndrome: Surgical treatment by lateral retinacular release. Clin Orthop 134:158-167, 1978.

13. Slocum DB, James SL, Larson RL: Surgical treatment of the dislocating patella in athletes. Presented at the Annual Meeting of the American Orthopedic Association, Hot Springs, VA, 1973.

14. Kaufer H: Mechanical function of the patella. J Bone Joint Surg 53A:1551-1560, 1971.

15. Blazina ME, Kerlan RK, Jobe RW, Carter VS, Carlson GJ, Orthop Clin North Am 4:665-678, 1973.

16. Renne JW: The iliotibial band friction syndrome. J Bone Joint Surg 57A:1110-1111, 1975.

17. Noble CA: Iliotibial band friction syndrome in runners. Am J Sports Med 8:232-234, 1980.

18. Mayfield GW: Popliteus tendon tenosynovitis. Am J Sports Med. 5:31-36, 1977.

19. Brantigan OC, Voshell AF: The mechanics of the ligaments and menisci of the knee joint. J Bone Joint Surg 23:43-66, 1941.

20. Colt EW, Spyropoulos E: Running and stress fractures. Br Med J 2(6192):706, 1979.

6

Tendinitis and Plantar Fasciitis in Runners

William G. Clancy, Jr., M.D.

Tendinitis

The term *tendinitis* appears to be confusing and perplexing. It is frequently used incorrectly to describe inflammatory reaction involving either the tendon and/or the tendon sheath. Dorland's Medical Dictionary defines *tendinitis* as an inflammation of the tendon, and *tenosynovitis* and *tenovaginitis* as an inflammation of the tendon sheath.[1] Blakiston's New Gould Medical Dictionary defines *tendinitis* as an inflammation of the tendon usually at the point of its attachment to bone, *tenovaginitis* as an inflammation of the tendon and its sheath, and *tenosynovitis* as inflammation of the sheath of a tendon.[2]

For the various injuries to the tendon and its surrounding tissue to be adequately diagnosed and treated, a consistent and accurate classification system based on documented pathologic findings is imperative. The literature is presently deficient on documentation of the various pathological entities. To date, Puddu's classification of tendon injuries appears the most complete.[3] Our operative and clinical findings, however, as well as those found in a review of the literature, suggest that a more detailed classification than that presented by Puddu, et al, should be developed.[3-12]

The classification system presented in this chapter is intended to be simplistic, functional, and to correspond to the pathologic findings noted by the author and those reported in the literature (Table 6.1.).

Tenosynovitis and tenovaginitis refer to an inflammation involving the paratenon or tendon sheath without any involvement of the tendon itself. The primary causes are either from tissue friction or from an external mechanical irritation.

Table 6.1
Classification of Tendon Injury

I. Tenosynovitis and tenovaginitis—an inflammation of only the paratenon, either lined by synovium or not.

II. Tendinitis—an injury or symptomatic degeneration of the tendon with a resultant inflammatory reaction of the surrounding paratenon.
  1. acute—symptoms present less than two weeks.
  2. subacute—symptoms present longer than two weeks but less than six weeks.
  3. chronic—symptoms present six weeks or longer.
    a. interstitial microscopic failure
    b. central necrosis
    c. frank partial rupture
    d. acute complete rupture

III. Tendinosis—asymptomatic tendon degeneration due to either aging, accumulated microtrauma, or both.
  1. interstitial
  2. partial rupture
  3. acute rupture

We have seen several cases of pes tenosynovitis secondary to repetitive motion over an enchondroma on the proximal tibia, Achilles tenovaginitis from an exostosis on the posterior tibia, and flexor hallucis tenosynovitis from an enchondroma on the talus. All were relieved by excision of the bony prominence. External causes of tenosynovitis are not common but do occur. Extensor tenosynovitis of the dorsum of the foot is not uncommon in runners and basketball players who tie their shoelaces too tightly, thus trapping the extensor sheaths. Achilles tenovaginitis is not infrequently seen when an inexperienced person mechanically crimps the Achilles tendon sheath while taping an ankle.

Friction between the tendon and tendon sheath and/or the tendon sheath and the surrounding tissue may lead to an inflammatory reaction within the tendon sheath and surrounding tissue. Snook[12] noted this entity at surgery in the Achilles tendon in several runners. If this inflammatory reaction becomes chronic, the secondary vascular changes in the paratenon could possibly lead to tendon degeneration, because the tendon receives its blood supply almost exclusively on a segmental basis through the mesotenon or vascular septa of the paratenon.[13-16]

Tendinitis in this classification refers to a primary injury or symptomatic degeneration within the tendon, or a combination of both with a secondary symptomatic inflammatory reaction occurring within the paratenon (R Ljungqvist,

William G. Clancey, Jr., M.D.

personal communication). There are two potential causes. As is well documented, repeated loading of the musculotendinous unit leads to fatigue of the muscle, shortening, and decreased flexibility, which may result in passive increased loading of the tendon during the state of relaxation. For example, the gastro-soleus muscles in distance runners must be relaxed to allow for heel strike. If this muscle group is tight from fatigue, then theoretically the Achilles tendon is subjected to increased loading. It is of interest that patients with acute and chronic Achilles tendinitis are more often symptomatic not on heel-off, but at heel strike, and the symptoms are diminished if they run with elastic tape extending from their heel to their calf.

The second cause is that of repetitive active loading of the musculotendinous unit, leading to collagen failure. This fatigue, or stress failure of the tendon, could be considered analogous to stress fractures of bones as seen in runners. Peacock,[14] and Peacock and Van Wenkle[17] showed that tenocytes are essentially end stage cells and that they are capable of only a highly limited repair potential. That fact may explain why many cases of chronic Achilles tendinitis treated adequately may still take up to six months of rest to become asymptomatic. Environmental factors as well as variations of normal anatomy leading to increased loading of the musculotendinous unit may predispose to the development of tendinitis.

Tendinitis can be classified as acute, subacute, and chronic. *Acute* tendinitis includes those in which the patient is symptomatic for less than two weeks; *subacute* cases include those in which the patient has had symptoms less than six weeks; and those in which the patient has had symptoms longer than six weeks would be termed *chronic*. The terminology is based both on the expected inflammatory response of tissue in general and on the expected clinical prognosis based on the length of symptoms.

The subclassification of chronic tendinitis is based on the changes found at surgery in 27 athletes with chronic tendinitis involving the Achilles tendon (21), the posterior tibial tendon (3), the anterior tibial tendon (1), and the peroneal tendons (2). The subclassifications are:

1. interstitial microscopic failures
2. central necrosis
3. partial rupture

Tendinitis and Plantar Fasciitis

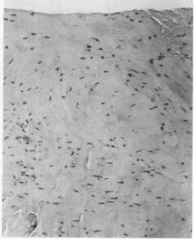

Fig. 6.1 and **Fig. 6.2:** Photomicrograph of biopsies from two cases of chronic Achilles tendinitis, demonstrating areas of collagen degeneration containing splaying of fibers and loss of cellularity.

Of those patients with interstitial failure, about one-third had a definite nodular deformity palpable on examination. The pathologic findings covered the gamut of collagen degeneration, including mucoid degeneration, splaying of fibers with acellularity and perivascular as well as interstitial infiltration, fibrocartilage metaplasia, calcification, and bone metaplasia (Figs. 6.1-6.3).

In two patients, central necrosis[6] was found in which the outer tendon appeared completely normal. In one patient a large partial rupture was found, and in the other there was complete disruption without any tissue filling the defect (Figs. 6.4 and 6.5). The partial ruptures were obvious when the tendon sheath was incised (Fig. 6.6).

Tendinosis, a term first described by Puddu, et al,[3] refers to degenerative lesions of tendon tissue without any alteration of the paratenon, and without clinical symptoms. This finding has been noted by many authors.[4,5,8] The changes may consist of either mucoid, fatty hyaline, and/or fibrinoid degeneration, cartilage metaplasia, calcification, and bone metaplasia. These changes were initially noted when biopsies were taken of acute ruptures of the Achilles tendon in previously asymptomatic patients.[4,8] It is uncertain whether these changes were purely due to aging, accelerated aging, accumulated microtrauma, or a combination of those factors. With time and repetitive loading, these patients may develop clinical symptoms, and the condition would then be termed *tendinitis*. As previously noted, a number of patients with Achilles tendinosis may develop acute spontaneous subcutaneous ruptures of the Achilles tendon.

Treatment

In general, those patients with acute tenosynovitis and tenovaginitis respond readily within ten days to rest, local heat application or contrast baths, and oral anti-inflammatory medication. One must look for internal or external mechanical causative factors. In those cases that have not resolved within a reasonable amount of time, the judicious use of a local steroid injection about the sheath, but not directly into the tendon, may be considered. One must be sure that the entity is definitely tenosynovitis and not a true tendinitis, because the risk of potential rupture from masking the symptoms of the underlying tendon problem, or the direct effect of cortisone on diminishing the

William G. Clancey, Jr., M.D.

tensile strength of the tendon may lead to rupture.

Those with acute tendinitis usually will be totally asymptomatic within two weeks with a program of rest, localized heat application or contrast baths, and stretching. The role of oral anti-inflammatory agents has not been well documented in this entity. When the involved area is no longer tender to palpation, the athlete may resume his training program on a graduated basis. To prevent recurrence, one must try to evaluate any predisposing factors such as errors in the training program, any adverse environmental factors, and any significant variations of anatomy.

Subacute tendinitis, in which symptoms are present for up to six weeks, usually takes about six weeks to resolve on the above program. Patients recovering from subacute tendinitis should not return to training until the area is no longer tender to palpation.

Patients with chronic tendinitis, whose symptoms are present for six weeks or longer, will usually need at least six weeks and frequently much longer for their symptoms to abate so that they can resume training without recurrence. Those with obvious tendon deformity should still be treated conservatively for at least three to six months before surgery is recommended. Surgery is generally not recommended in those with chronic symptoms and without tendon deformity unless they are still symptomatic after six months of a good conservative program.

Surgery consists of incising the tendon sheath and examining the tendon by palpation. In the normal-appearing tendon, several longitudinal incisions are made into the tendon in the area of previously noted tenderness. If there are no gross pathologic changes, a biopsy is taken and the subcutaneous tissue and skin are closed over drains. The longitudinal incisions are used for a two-fold purpose: first, to see if there is any area of central necrosis or rupture; and second, to stimulate a healing reaction. If a significant area of degeneration is found, it is excised. If the deficit is not too large, the tendon is closed. If the defect is significant, the plantaris tendon is resected as proximally as possible, and then interwoven through the defect (Fig. 6.7). If an exceptionally large area of calcification is present or an area of multiple ruptures are found, as occasionally seen in the Achilles tendon, then the entire area of the tendon is resected, even if this procedure necessitates resecting a segment of tendon. A Bosworth

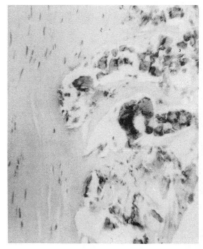

Fig. 6.3: Photomicrograph of a biopsy of a case of chronic Achilles tendinitis showing calcific replacement of an area of collagen degeneration.

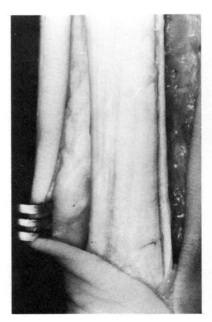

Fig. 6.4: Apparently normal-appearing Achilles tendon in a patient with chronic Achilles tendinitis.

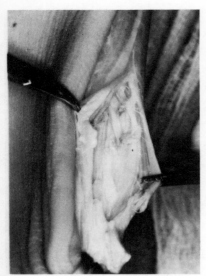

Fig. 6.5: A longitudinal incision of an Achilles tendon in a patient with chronic Achilles tendinitis.

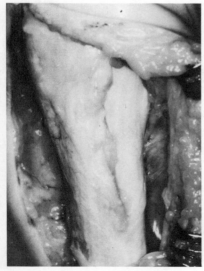

Fig. 6.6: An obvious partial rupture of an Achilles tendon within which there is significant calcific replacement.

turndown flap then is done (Fig. 6.8).

Those who have had only an incision placed in the tendon, or had a small defect resected and closed, are placed in a short leg cast for two weeks. If the Achilles tendon was the site of surgery, the cast is maintained for three to four weeks to allow for healing of the poorly vascularized skin and subcutaneous tissue. Early controlled motion is the desired goal where possible.

Achilles tendinitis is by far the most common tendinitis seen. The athlete usually notes the onset of pain with crepitance just above the heel counter usually several hours after a run. The pain is usually most noticeable on climbing stairs and perhaps on normal walking for the first two to three days, then the symptoms are present only on running, usually just at heel strike. On examination, some crepitance may be present to active motion. Only one small painful area will be present to palpation, and it will be only the size of the breadth of the examining finger tips. It is usually about two to three centimeters above the superior lip of the calcaneus. Examination of the opposite normal Achilles will demonstrate a distinct difference in pain.

A thorough history should be taken to determine whether there has been any change in the surface or in training patterns that may be predisposed to the injury. The most common errors are a significant increase in mileage over a short time, a significant increase in an interval program, an increase in hill running, or a recent layoff from running with a too rapid return to the previous level of running. During the physical examination, one should look for predisposing factors that are highly associated with Achilles tendinitis, such as heel valgus, pronation, femoral anteversion, or a tight gastro-soleus muscle group.

Retrocalcaneal bursitis is frequently misdiagnosed as Achilles tendinitis or insertional tendinitis. Rarely, if ever, is there any pathologic involvement of the Achilles tendon fibers as they insert into the calcaneus. Although the athlete may complain of pain at the insertion of the Achilles tendon into the calcaneus, careful pressure on both sides of the calcaneus should reduplicate his symptoms. Local injection of steroid and xylocaine into this area between the upper one-third of the calcaneus and the Achilles tendon should temporarily alleviate all symptoms. It is important to note that the Achilles tendon inserts

William G. Clancey, Jr., M.D.

far inferiorly on the calcaneus. In general, a significant number of our patients with retrocalcaneal bursitis have a cavus foot deformity with or without an exostosis of the superior lip of the calcaneus. Repeated episodes of retrocalcaneal bursitis dictate an osteotomy of the superior lip, which has been performed in eight runners with excellent results. Posterior tibial tendinitis, like peroneal tendinitis, is fortunately only infrequently encountered in the runner. Those with posterior tibial will present with pain located at the posterior inferior edge of the medial malleolous. Occasionally, they may have some tenderness more proximally. This is often misdiagnosed as shin splints, but one should note that no muscle is attached to the posterior tibial tendon at this point.

Posterior tibial tendinitis is usually seen early in the beginning of a training program and is highly associated with running on asphalt or concrete surfaces. Foot pronation is the most common anatomic variation seen with this entity. Treatment is essentially the same as that for Achilles tendinitis. If symptoms have been present for four weeks, roentgenograms should be obtained to make sure it is not a stress fracture of the distal tibia or medial malleolus. If significant foot pronation is present, flexible foot orthotics with a medial heel wedge can be beneficial.

Peroneal tendinitis is even more uncommon than Achilles or posterior tibial tendinitis and is usually seen early in a training program. The area of maximum tenderness is generally just distal to the lateral malleolus but not as far as the base of the fifth metatarsal. If the symptoms are present just behind the lateral malleolus, be sure it is not a stress fracture of the distal fibula, which is the second most common site of a this condition in runners. The periosteal inflammatory reaction of a distal fibula stress fracture may cause an inflammatory reaction of the peroneal sheath. Roentgenograms at four weeks will document a stress fracture, if present. Treatment is essentially the same as that for Achilles and posterior tibial tendinitis.

In my opinion, the above tendinitides in most cases represent a primary injury to the tendon with a secondary inflammatory reaction of the paratenon, causing the symptoms of pain and crepitance. The use of steroids is rarely if ever indicated in these conditions, because it can mask the

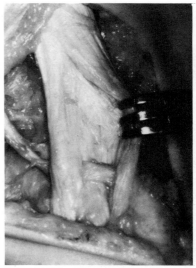

Fig. 6.7: After the area of degeneration was resected, the plantaris was interwoven through the tear.

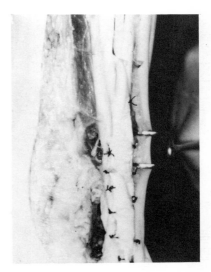

Fig. 6.8: A Bosworth turndown procedure is used as replacement for a segmental resection of an area of complete degeneration in case of chronic Achilles tendinitis.

symptoms, directly decrease the tendon's tensile strength, and inhibit the tendon's healing response.

Extensor tenosynovitis, which presents as a swollen forefoot with crepitance on extension and flexion of the toes, represents a tenosynovitis of the extensor tendons usually secondary to tying the shoelaces too tightly. With localized heat or contrast baths, and oral anti-inflammatory agents, the symptoms should subside significantly within several days. A soft spongy pad, along with an application of vasoline to the forefoot, should enable the runner to resume running in a few days, even if some discomfort is still present.

It must be remembered that a stress fracture of one of the metatarsals can cause the same symptoms and edema of the dorsum of the foot. Careful palpation of each metatarsal shaft should render the correct diagnosis almost immediately, long before an x-ray would be positive—generally three to four weeks after onset of symptoms.

Plantar Fasciitis

Plantar fasciitis is a term used to describe a painful condition located about the posterior medial surface of the foot just distal to the attachment of the plantar fascia to the calcaneus. This extremely disabling entity is seen far more commonly in distance runners than sprinters or middle-distance runners.

Initially, the symptoms are of gradual onset, and of extremely low intensity. The athlete is usually able to carry on with his training program for several weeks to several months without alteration in intensity or distance. With time, though, the pain becomes more noticeable and the athlete is forced to change his gait pattern by keeping the foot in a rather supinated or inverted posture from foot strike through to toe off. That position appears to minimize the symptoms. The athlete may be able to continue his level of training for several more weeks or months before the pain becomes so severe that he can no longer train. The pain is generally most severe after running, and early in the morning after rising. It is not uncommon for the athlete to feel or complain of a nodularity in the proximal medial plantar fascia.

Physical examination will usually reveal that the maximal area of tenderness is located over the medial edge of the plantar fascia just distal to the insertion of the calcaneus. In some, the maximal

William G. Clancey, Jr., M.D.

area of tenderness may be present just at the plantar fascia insertion into the calcaneus. These patients almost always have pain to palpation of the posterior inferior origin of the abductor hallucis muscle, possibly, as has been theorized, as a result of the overuse of the abductor hallucis muscle in its role to aid in producing forefoot supination to decrease the loading on the plantar fascia.

I believe that plantar fasciitis is an inflammatory reaction that is the result of a fatigue failure in the plantar fascia, somewhat analogous to the pathological concept of chronic tendinitis. This belief is based on the results of tissue biopsies in six cases of chronic plantar fasciitis in runners who were surgically treated. All specimens demonstrated the typical findings of collagen degeneration, as previously described.

This injury must be differentiated from the much rarer entity of tarsal tunnel or plantar nerve entrapment syndrome. Those with tarsal tunnel syndrome may also complain of a burning pain with paresthesias of the heel. They will usually have a positive Tinel sign on palpation of the distal posterior tibial nerve and over the fibrous tunnel within the abductor hallicus muscle. Unfortunately, electrodiagnostic studies are not as diagnostic as reported. They are frequently negative except in those with long-standing nerve entrapment. These patients can be distinguished from those with plantar fasciitis in that they do not have pain to direct palpation of the plantar fascia.

Treatment

Once the diagnosis is made, the athlete is removed from running, but is allowed to bike or swim to maintain his cardiovascular conditioning. He is fitted with an orthotic device with a one-eighth inch medial heel wedge to decrease the loading of the plantar fascia. The patient is seen at six-week intervals. When there is no longer any pain to palpation of the plantar fascia, and no noticeable symptoms in the morning, a graduated running prescription is given. The orthosis is kept in the running shoe for the next several months.

In general, if the patient is seen within several weeks after the onset of symptoms, it usually takes a minimum of six weeks of rest before his foot is no longer tender to palpation and running can be resumed. Many cases may take as long as three months to resolve. In those who have had symptoms for several months, and who have

Fig. 6.9: The medial plantar incision for release of the plantar fascia.

Fig. 6.10: Isolation of the fascia overlying the abductor hallucis and the extension of the plantar fascia.

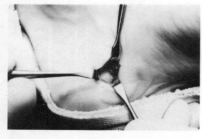

Fig. 6.11: Utilization of a meniscotome for release of the plantar fascia.

continued to train, it will take at least three months, and often six months, for the symptoms to resolve.

Those who are still symptomatic after four to six months of appropriate treatment should be considered for surgical release of their plantar fascia. The surgery can be done as an outpatient procedure under Bier block. It consists of a one-inch longitudinal incision made along the medial aspect of the plantar fascia insertion (Fig. 6.9). The abductor hallicus fascia (Fig. 6.10) and the plantar fascia are completely released with a meniscotome (Fig. 6.11). A bulky dressing with or without a posterior mold is applied and worn for ten days. The patient is then started on a gentle static stretching program and allowed to start swimming At three weeks he is allowed to start biking. At four weeks, five minutes of continuous jump roping is begun and is increased to ten minutes at the fifth week. At six weeks, he is allowed to start a graduated running program every third day. At eight weeks, he can resume a daily running program.

This surgical procedure has been done on ten runners with chronic resistant plantar fasciitis with excellent results. All returned to running within eight weeks, and have had no recurrences.

Tendinitis and plantar fasciitis are significant disabling problems that unfortunately require a significant rest from the patient's desired activity. To achieve a good result, the physician must understand the underlying pathology and investigate any predisposing factors. Because significant time is required for these entities to resolve, the physician and the athlete must have good communication so that the athlete will adhere to the recomended programs.

References

1. Dorland's Illustrated Medical Dictionary, Twenty-fifth Edition. Philadelphia, WB Saunders Co, 1974.
2. Blackiston's New Gould Medical Dictionary, Fourth Edition. New York, McGraw-Hill Co, 1979.
3. Puddu G, Ippolito E, Postacchini F: A classification of Achilles tendon disease. Am J Sports Med 4:145-150, 1976.
4. Arner O, Londholm A, Orell S: Histological changes in subcutaneous rupture Achilles tendon. Acta Chir Scand 116:484-490, 1958.
5. Arner O, Lindholm A: Subcutaneous rupture of the Achilles tendon. Acta Chir Scand (Suppl) 239, 1959.
6. Burry HC, Pool CJ: Central degeneration of the Achilles tendon. Rheumatol Rehabil 12:177-181, 1973.
7. Clancy WG, Neidhart D, Brand RL: Achilles tendinitis

William G. Clancey, Jr., M.D.

in runners: a report of five cases. Am J Sports Med 4:46-57, 1976.

8. Davidsson L, Solo M: Pathogenesis of subcutaneous tendon rupture. Acta Chir Scand 135:209-212, 1969.

9. Denstad TF, Roassa A: Surgical treatment of partial Achilles tendon rupture. Am J Sports Med 7:15-17, 1979.

10. Fox JM, Blazina ME, Jobe FW, et al: Degeneration and rupture of the Achilles tendon. Clin Orthop 107:221-224, 1975.

11. Ljungqvist R: Subcutaneous partial rupture of the Achilles tendon. Acta Orthop Scand (Suppl) 113:1-86, 1968.

12. Snook GA: Achilles tendon tenosynovitis in long-distance runners. Med Sci Sports 4:155-157, 1972.

13. Lagergren C, Lindholm A: Vascular distribution in the Achilles tendon. Acta Chir Scand 116:491-495, 1958.

14. Peacock EE: A study of the circulation in normal tendons and healing grafts. Ann Surg 149:415, 1959.

15. Schatzker MD, Branemark PI: Intravital observation on the microvascular anatomy and microcirculation of the tendon. Acta Orthop Scand (Suppl) 126, 1969.

16. Smith JW: Blood supply of tendons. Am J Surg 109:272-276, 1965.

17. Peacock EE, Van Wenkle W: Surgery and Biology of Wound Repair. Philadelphia, WB Saunders Co, 1970.

7

Exertional Compartment Syndromes

Scott J. Mubarak, M.D.

A compartment syndrome is due to increased tissue fluid pressure in a closed fascial space compromising the circulation to the nerves and muscles within the involved compartment. The initial insult causes hemorrhage, edema, or both, to accumulate in the closed fascial compartments of the extremities. The noncompliance of the compartment's fascial boundaries causes an increase in intracompartment fluid pressure that, in turn, produces ischemia. Without immediate decompression of the compartment, the indwelling muscles and nerves may be permanently damaged, resulting in a Volkmann's contracture (Fig. 7.1). The syndrome is most commonly caused by fracture, severe contusion, drug overdose with limb compression, or postischemic swelling. Rarely, intense use of muscles, as during strenuous exercise, may initiate compartment syndromes.

The exercise-initiated compartment syndromes are divided, by clinical findings and reversibility, into two forms. An acute syndrome exists when intramuscular pressure is elevated to such a level and is of such a duration, that immediate decompression is necessary to prevent intracompartmental necrosis. The clinical findings and course are the same as a compartment syndrome initiated by a fracture or contusion, except the event occurs after strenuous activities without external trauma. The second form, a chronic compartment syndrome, exists when exercise raises intracompartmental pressure sufficiently to produce small-vessel compromise and therefore ischemia, pain, and, on rare occasions, neurologic deficit. These symptoms disappear when the

Supported by USPMS Grant AM-18824 and Veterans Administration

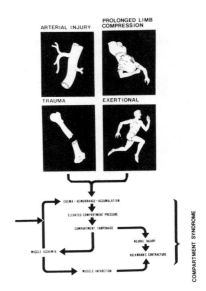

Fig. 7.1: Pathophysiology of a compartment syndrome. Multiple causes may initiate a compartment syndrome: untreated, a Volkmann's contracture will result. Immediate surgical intervention is necessary to break this cycle. Strenuous exercise may initiate an acute compartment syndrome. (From Mubarak SJ, Hargens AR: Diagnosis and Management of compartment syndromes. AAOS: Symposium on Trauma to the Leg and its Sequelae. St Louis, CV Mosby, 1981).

activity is stopped and reappear during the next period of exercise. If, however, the exercise is continued despite pain (ie, with continued ischemia), a chronic compartment syndrome may proceed to an acute form that requires decompression. An example of the latter is when a military recruit exercises under duress beyond his own limits of pain tolerance.

History

Anterior compartment syndrome initiated by exertion was probably first described by Dr. Edward Wilson, the medical officer on Captain R. R. Scott's illfated race to the South Pole[1] (Fig. 7.2). Scott, Wilson, and three others lost in their attempt to reach the South Pole before the Norwegian, Roald Amundson. On the return trip from the pole, Dr. Wilson had severe pain and swelling in the area of the anterior compartment, which he accurately described in his diary. The following, dated January 30, 1912, is an excerpt from his dairy:

> My left leg exceedingly painful all day so I gave Birdie my ski and hobbled along side the sledge on foot. The whole of the tibialis anticus is swollen and tight, and full of tenosynovitis, and the skin red and oedematous over the shin.

Over the ensuing days his leg gradually became less painful as his general medical condition deteriorated. Dr. Wilson perished along with Scott and the others in the expedition on their return trip from the South Pole.

Thirty years passed before exertional anterior compartment syndromes of the leg became recognized as an entity. In a lecture in 1943, Vogt[2] described a case of ischemic muscle necrosis after marching (Table 7.1). In 1944, Horn[3] added two more cases, one involving the anterior and lateral compartments, and an isolated one of the anterior compartment. That same year, Sirbu, et al,[4] described a case of the anterior compartment syndrome resulting from a long march. He performed a fasciotomy and termed the disorder "march synovitis." Over the next 15 years, many isolated cases of acute anterior compartment syndromes of the leg resulting from exertion were reported.[5-10] Only two cases of the acute syndrome with lateral compartment involvement[11] and one case involving the superficial posterior compartment have been reported.[12]

Fig. 7.2: Dr. Edward Wilson (fourth from left) and Capt. R.R. Scott (third from left) pose by the Norwegian flag at the South Pole in early January, 1912. These explorers perished on the return trip from the South Pole. Dr. Edward Wilson was hobbled by the effects of an anterior compartment syndrome. With permission from Peter Brent: *Captain Scott,* Sat Review Press, New York, 1974.

Scott J. Mubarak, M.D.

Table 7.1

Historical Description of Exertional Compartment
Syndromes of the Leg

Compartment	Acute Form	Chronic Form
Anterior	Wilson, 1912 Vogt, 1943 Horn, 1944 Siru, et al, 1944	Mavor, 1956
Lateral	Blandy & Fuller, 1957	Reneman, 1968
Superficial Posterior	Mubarak, et al, 1978	Kirby, 1970
Deep Posterior	—	—

Mavor,[13] in 1956, was probably the first to report a chronic form of the anterior exertional compartment syndrome. His affected patient had recurring pain in his anterior compartment associated with numbness and a muscle hernia. Fasciotomy relieved him of his problem. The existence of a chronic syndrome was questioned by Griffith[14] and later by Grunwald and Silberman.[15] Nevertheless, subsequent reports by various authors and the pressure studies of French and Price[16] confirmed the existence of this entity. In his monograph on this subject, Reneman reported on more than 61 chronic cases, also with pressure documentation.[17]

A chronic form involving other compartments of the leg has been described, although tissue pressure documentation is lacking. Reneman reported on seven cases of the chronic syndrome involving both the lateral and anterior compartments.[17] Kirby reported on a patient with bilateral chronic superficial posterior compartment syndromes; his patient's symptoms were relieved by fasciotomies.[18] Three additional cases of chronic syndromes in the superficial posterior compartment were reported by Snook.[19] Eleven cases of exertional syndromes involving the deep posterior tibial compartment were reported by Puranen.[20]

Isolated chronic cases involving the second interosseous compartment of the hand[21] and the volar compartment of the forearm[22] have also been documented.

Pathogenesis

The exact pathogenesis of the exertional tibial compartment syndrome is unknown. Elevated compartment pressure is the immediate cause of

Table 7.2
Probable Factors in the Pathogenesis of the
Exertional Compartment Syndrome

A. Limited Compartment Size
  1) Thickened Fascia

B. Increased Volume of Compartment Contents
  1) Acutely—Muscle swelling due to increased capillary permeability and intracellular edema
  2) Acutely—Restricted venous of lymphatic outflow
  3) Acutely—Hemorrhage due to torn muscle fibers
  4) Chronically—Muscle hypertrophy

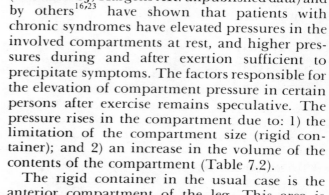

muscle and nerve ischemia in acute compartment syndromes. Furthermore, studies in our laboratory (Mubarak SJ, Hargens AR: unpublished data) and by others[16,23] have shown that patients with chronic syndromes have elevated pressures in the involved compartments at rest, and higher pressures during and after exertion sufficient to precipitate symptoms. The factors responsible for the elevation of compartment pressure in certain persons after exercise remains speculative. The pressure rises in the compartment due to: 1) the limitation of the compartment size (rigid container); and 2) an increase in the volume of the contents of the compartment (Table 7.2).

The rigid container in the usual case is the anterior compartment of the leg. This area is enclosed in a noncompliant osteofascial envelope made up of the anterior compartment fascia, the interosseous ligament, the tibia, and the fibula (Fig. 7.3). Because room for expansion is minimal, fluid accumulation in this space will cause a rise in pressure.

During exercise two interesting phenomena occur. First, during a strong isometric or isotonic contraction, intramuscular pressure rises sufficiently to render the muscle ischemic while the contraction is maintained. This fact has been noted by a number of authors using a variety of indirect methods of estimating tissue pressure,[24-30] but only recently was it confirmed by direct measurement of the muscle during contraction in our own laboratory, using the wick catheter.[31-33] The pressure rises acutely during a muscle contraction, probably both by a mechanical means and because of a cessation of blood flow out of the muscle.

Second, with prolonged exercise, muscle in-

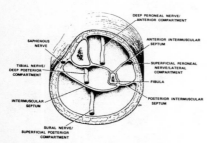

Fig. 7.3: The leg consists of four compartments. Each contains a peripheral nerve. The anterior compartment is most frequently involved with exertional compartment syndromes. With permission from Mubarak SJ, Owens CA: Double incision fasciotomy of the leg for decompression in compartment syndromes. J Bone Joint Surg 59A:184-187, 1977.

Scott J. Mubarak, M.D.

creases acutely in bulk by as much as 20%.[34] Linge[35] demonstrated acute hypertrophy in untrained rats after five hours of exercise. These findings are probably due to increased capillary permeability resulting in fluid accumulation in both the intracellular and extracellular spaces. Other possibilities have been suggested to account for the volume increase in the compartment of subjects under exercise conditions. Anomalies of venous or lymphatic return may exist in patients with the chronic syndrome.[17] Unaccustomed exercise may lead to hemorrhage from torn muscle fibers as an additive source of fluid accumulation.[5,36] Finally, in the chronic state, muscle hypertrophy occurs with repeated exercise or conditioning. Whatever the cause, the pressure rises and therefore, fluid must accumulate in the compartment interstitial spaces to cause either chronic and/or acute compartment syndromes after exertion.

Extertional Tibial Compartment Syndrome: Acute Form
Background and Clinical Presentation

Excessive use of muscles as a cause of an acute compartment syndrome is extremely uncommon. Less than 100 cases are documented in the literature, and during the past six years of our study of over 80 patients with acute syndromes, only two cases were initiated by exercise.

Most cases of the acute syndrome developed in patients performing tasks (forced marches or prolonged runs) to which they were unaccustomed. In some cases the patient had symptoms of a chronic compartment syndrome for months before the acute episode (17% in Reneman's experience).[23] The initial symptom of this acute compartment syndrome is severe pain over the involved compartment. The pain is initiated during the exercise, or develops within 12 hours after the exercise. As the pain increases, numbness and weakness are noted, and medical attention is sought.

The clinical findings in acute compartment syndromes initiated by exertion are identical to those of an acute syndrome of any cause (Fig. 7.4). There will be increased pressure and pain over the involved compartment or compartments. Stretching the involved muscles of that compartment will exacerbate this pain. Muscle weakness (paresis) and a neurologic deficit will be present. A careful

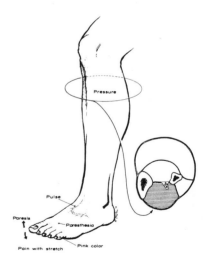

Fig. 7.4: Early findings of an acute compartment syndrome illustrated in the anterior compartment. Modified from Mubarak SJ, et al: Laboratory diagnosis of orthoeaedic diseases: Secion I—Muscle Pressure Measurement With The Wick Catheter. Practice of Surgery, Hagerstown, MD, Harper & Row, Inc, Chapter 20N, 1978.

Table 7.3

Typical Findings of Acute Compartment Syndromes of the Leg

	Anterior	Lateral	Superficial Posterior	Deep Posterior
Sensory Deficit	Deep Peroneal Nerve	Superficial and Deep Peroneal Nerves	Sural Nerve	Tibial Nerve
Muscle Weakness	Tibialis Anterior Toe Extensors	Peroneus Longus and Brevis	Gastrocnemius and Soleus	Tibialis Posterior Toe Flexors
Pain with Stretch	Foot and Toe Flexion	Foot Inversion	Foot Dorsiflexion	Toe Extension
Pedal Pulses	Intact	Intact	Intact	Intact

94

Scott J. Mubarak, M.D.

sensory examination using two-point discrimination can be helpful in documenting which compartments are involved. Capillary fill and pedal pulses (dorsalis pedis and posterior tibial) are routinely intact, though palpation may be difficult because of ankle and foot edema. A Doppler evaluation can be useful in this situation. This finding is true because even though intra-compartmental pressure may be high enough to cause ischemia to muscle and nerve, it is only rarely high enough to occlude a major artery.

The clinical findings for each of the isolated compartments of the leg are listed (Table 7.3). Note that a lateral compartment syndrome will usually involve both superficial and deep peroneal nerves that originate in this compartment.

Laboratory Investigations

Tissue pressure measurement: This is the best objective test for determining the need for fasciotomy. The wick catheter technique, which we have used over the past six years, provides an accurate and reproducible means of determining tissue pressure under equilibrium conditions.[31] Other techniques are available and have been found to be equally valuable in the diagnosis of acute compartment syndromes.[37-39]

If the intracompartmental pressures are greater than 30 mm Hg (normal 0-8 mm Hg) in association with the appropriate clinical findings, surgical decompression should be done immediately.[40-41]

Electromyography and nerve conduction: Matsen used electromyography and nerve conduction occasionally to serially monitor a decline in nerve function,[42] which is suggestive, but not diagnostic, of a compartment syndrome. We have not found this testing to be of much value in the acute syndrome. The problem by definition is increased pressure in the compartment, and the treatment is decompression. Thus, measurement of the pressure is the most direct means of diagnosing this pathologic state and evaluating the adequacy of surgical decompression. When a neurologic deficit is present postoperatively, electromyography may be helpful in establishing whether the patient is improving.[43,44]

Arteriography and doppler: These tests are only used to more fully evaluate the arterial supply to the limb. If a possible arterial injury coexistent with the compartment syndrome is suspected, these tests should be used. With only a compartment syndrome, the arteriographic finding may show small-vessel (arteriolar) cut-off created by the pressure elevation.

Differential Diagnosis

The acute compartment syndrome must be differentiated from a direct nerve contusion (neurapraxia) and an arterial injury. Because either of those two may coexist with a compartment syndrome, tissue pressure measurement and arteriography are extremely important diagnostically. Problems such as a large subcutaneous hematoma or an abscess present with swelling and often moderate pain; however, without neurologic deficit, these problems are usually easily differentiated from a compartment syndrome.

Treatment for Acute Compartment Syndrome

The treatment is the same as for any acute compartment syndrome—immediate surgical decompression. We use the double-incision technique, using one or both incisions as necessary to decompress the involved compartments. The details of this technique are described elsewhere.[45] The incisions are left open and the limb is splinted. At five to seven days, delayed primary closure or skin grafting is done.

Extertional Tibial Compartment Syndrome: Chronic Form

Background and Clinical Presentation

The chronic form of exertional tibial compartment syndrome is much more common than the acute form. Reneman[23] reported the largest series (61 cases) with nearly all involving only the anterior compartment. Symptoms were bilateral in 95% of his patients and in about 75% of our patients (Mubarak SJ, Hargens AR: unpublished data). Most of Reneman's patients were from the military, whereas our patients range from casual joggers to enthusiastic marathoners. Most of our patients are male.

In most cases, the patient notes recurrent pain over the anterior or lateral compartment area, which is initiated by exercise and has been present for several months. The exercise may vary from a prolonged walk or march, to a marathon run. For a given patient the onset of the pain is reproducible for a specific speed and distance. Usually the patient must discontinue his run and rest for a few minutes. Some persons, however, can continue the

Scott J. Mubarak, M.D.

run at a reduced speed, whereas others who discontinue their exercise immediately may be bothered by symptoms for hours.

The pain is described as a feeling of either pressure, aching, cramping, or a stabbing sensation over the anterior compartment. Occasionally, associated symptoms include numbness on the dorsum of the foot, weakness, or an acutal foot drop.

The findings on physical examination before exercise are few. Findings from neurocirculatory examinations are normal. Usually the muscles are well developed in all compartments. It is best to ask the patient to perform his or her usual run or exercise that initiates the problem. A postexercise sensation of increased fullness over the anterior compartment may be noted, but the neurocirculatory status will usually remain normal. Occasionally, hypesthesia on the dorsum of the foot will be documented. Changes in the pedal pulses after exercise require further workup of the vascular system.

Muscle hernias, noted in 60% of Reneman's cases,[23] may be clinically more obvious after exercise. We have encountered these fascial defects in only 20% of our patients (Mubarak SJ, Hargens AR: unpublished data). Most are located in the lower one third of the leg overlying the anterior intramuscular septum between the anterior and lateral compartments (Fig. 7.5). In this location the fascial defect may represent an enlargement of the orifice through which a branch of the superficial peroneal nerve (medial dorsal cutaneous nerve) exits the lateral compartment. We have encountered this situation on three occasions. The muscle herniation may cause superficial peroneal nerve irritation and even neuroma formation (Fig. 7.6).[17,46]

Laboratory Investigations

Tissue pressure measurement: The needle technique was first used by French and Price in 1962 to study chronic syndromes[16]. Reneman, using the same technique, investigated a large number of patients. He found that the intramuscular pressures at rest, immediately after exercise, and at six minutes after exercise, exceeded normal control subjects of comparable age.[17] He could not measure the pressures continuously during exercise with this technique.

Using the wick catheter technique, we observed similar changes in pressure between the two

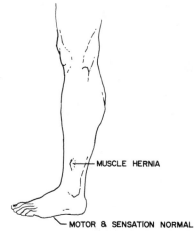

Fig. 7.5: Muscle hernias are commonly associated with chronic exertional compartment syndromes and neurologic examination is usually normal.

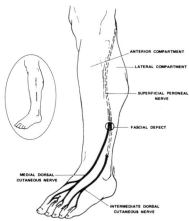

Fig. 7.6: Relationship of superficial peroneal nerve branches to the fascial defect commonly seen with chronic exertional compartment syndromes. With permission from Garfin S, et al: Exertional anterolateral compartment syndrome. J Bone Joint Surg 59A:404-405, 1977.

Fig. 7.7: The wick catheter has been inserted into the right anterior compartment of a patient with a suspected chronic compartment syndrome. The foot is attached to an isokinetic exerciser. Intracompartmental pressures are continuously recorded by the wick catheter connected to a pressure transducer and strip recorder.

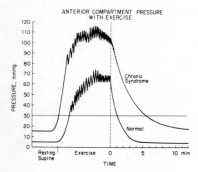

Fig. 7.8: Illustrative anterior compartment pressures recorded with the wick catheter during exercise of a normal subject and a patient afflicted with a chronic anterior compartment syndrome. The resting pressure of the chronic syndrome is elevated over that of the normal control. During exercise the pressure rises to greater than 75 mm Hg and remains greater than 30 mm Hg for more than five minutes in the patient with the chronic syndrome.

groups with the additional advantage of continuous monitoring during the exercise. The wick catheter is inserted into the involved compartment under sterile conditions and local anesthesia. It is taped into position, and pressure measurements are determined during complete rest in the supine position. The subject's foot is then attached to an isokinetic exerciser (Orthotron, Lumex Corporation) using the foot attachment apparatus (Fig. 7.7). A standard setting is used for all patients. The subject is instructed to dorsiflex and plantarflex the foot once every two seconds, until the activity must be stopped because of pain or fatigue. The pressures are continuously recorded by the wick catheter connected to a pressure transducer and strip recorder. We have found this method of exercise the most standard, although on occasion we have used a treadmill or had the patient run his usual distance to initiate the pain. Reinsertion of the wick in these circumstances must be rapid because the intramuscular pressures fall quickly.

In normal subjects, resting supine, the mean pressure of the anterior compartment is 4±4 mm Hg. During exercise, pressure rises to more than 50 mm Hg. Moreover, intramuscular pressure rises and falls with each muscular contracture and relaxation. When the patient stops the exercise because of fatigue or pain, intramuscular pressure begins to fall. In normal subjects the pressure will decline below 30 mm Hg immediately, and at five minutes pressure will be back to the pre-exercise rest levels. (Fig. 7.7).

Intramuscular pressure measured at rest is usually greater than 15 mm Hg in patients with the chronic syndrome. During exercise these pressures rise to greater than 75 mm Hg. At times the pressure during exercise may exceed 100 mm Hg. At completion of the exercise, intramuscular pressure will remain greater than 30 mm Hg for five minutes or longer and usually symptoms of pain and possibly paresthesia are present (Fig. 7.8). We have used these findings as our laboratory confirmation of the chronic compartment syndrome. In these patients we recommend fasciotomy which should normalize both resting and postexercise intramuscular pressure.

Venograms: These were used by Reneman in his study of the chronic syndrome. When neither of the anterior tibial veins filled at two or four minutes after exercise, he considered that circumstance diagnostic of a chronic syndrome. Although the investigation was interesting, the technique

Scott J. Mubarak, M.D.

has flaws, and is much more invasive than tissue pressure measurement.[17]

Electromyography and nerve conduction: Leach, et al,[43] reported on one patient who demonstrated denervation potentials in the anterior compartment. Reneman used electromyography and nerve conduction in five patients. He could find no abnormality either at rest or during exercise.[17] We agree that electromyography is of little value, although nerve conduction may be helpful if patients with a possible chronic compartment syndrome have a subjective neurologic deficit.

Sodium[28] chloride clearance: French and Price[16] and Kennelly and Blumberg[47] demonstrated reduced clearance of sodium[28] chloride after exercise, but no change at rest when compared with data on normal subjects. We have had no experience with this technique.

Differential Diagnosis

Intermittent claudication due to partial femoral artery obstruction: By history, this condition is identical to exertional tibial compartment syndrome, except that the patients tend to be a little older than the chronic syndrome patients. The diagnostic clue in this entity is that the pedal pulses present at rest disappear with exercise. An arteriogram will confirm this diagnosis.

Stress fractures of the tibia or fibula: This diagnosis can be made clinically by noting local tenderness over the bone at the fracture site. Although the radiographs will initially be negative, changes will usually be found ten to 14 days after the onset of pain. A bone scan will usually be positive at the onset and may be beneficial in the diagnosis.

Tenosynovitis: Tenosynovitis of the dorsiflexors of the foot is characterized by crepitus, erythema, and pain on movement of the tendons localized to the dorsum of the foot and ankle (see Chapter 6).

Infection: Cellulitis, pretibial fever,[48] and tropical diseases[49] may initially suggest a compartment syndrome. In most cases the patients will be febrile with the loss of function secondary to pain. Infections are rarely confused with the chronic syndrome.

Shin splints: These are usually defined as the pain associated with activity at the beginning of training, after a relatively inactive period.[50] The pain and tenderness are usually located over the anterior compartment, and clear in a couple of

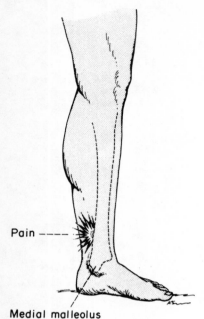

Pain - - - -

Medial malleolus

Fig. 7.9: Clinical findings of the medial tibial syndrome. There is a localized area of tenderness over the posteromedial edge of the distal one third of the tibia (arrow).

weeks as the athlete becomes conditioned. Reneman believes that shin splints may represent a mild form of the chronic compartment syndrome.[17]

Medial tibial syndrome: This has been classified by various authors as a stress fracture,[51] deep posterior compartment syndrome,[20] or a shin splint.[50,52,53] Because the cause is unknown, the terminology selected by Puranen is probably most appropriate for this affliction.

This syndrome is usually seen in runners, but has been noted in athletes participating in tennis, volleyball, basketball, and long jumping. The pain is recurrent and associated with repetitive strenuous exercise. It is located along the medial border of the distal tibia. It increases after running a given distance and decreases with rest. Pain is often present even without exericse when the posteromedial edge of the distal tibia is palpated.

The physical findings are highly specific. There is a localized area of tenderness over the posteromedial edge of the distal one third of the tibia (Fig. 7.9). This area is often endurated and exquisitely tender. The posterior compartment muscles are sometimes atrophied. No motor, sensory, or circulatory disturbances are found. On examination of the patient after exertion, the painful area will be more symptomatic. Injection of xylocaine into this area will relieve the pain and allow the patient to exercise without discomfort.

Initially, radiographs are always normal. If the duration of the pain exceeds three to four weeks, hypertrophy of the cortex and possibly some periosteal new bone formation may be noted. Devas[51] presented a series of patients with evidence of a stress fracture of the tibial cortex in this area. Bone scanning may show a mild uptake or have entirely normal results.[20] (Mubarak SJ, Hargens AR: unpublished data.) Even when positive, however, the bone scan uptake is not as increased as with a stress fracture.

Tissue pressure has been measured using the needle technique by D'Ambrosia, et al.[54] In their series, rest pressures in 14 athletes were all within normal limits. Eriksson and Wallensten also have noted "normal" pressure studies in patients with the medial tibial syndrome.[55] Similarly, in a series of 14 patients whom we have studied with this symptom complex, the rest and postexercise pressures have remained well within normal limits. Our mean rest pressure was 8 mm Hg, and immediately postexercise, the mean pressure was 9

Scott J. Mubarak, M.D.

mm Hg. During exercise, the pressure rose to an average of 55 mm Hg.

Devas was one of the first to report on patients with the medial tibial syndrome. He believed that this entity represented an incomplete fracture involving one cortex of the tibia.[51] Fourteen of his patients had radiographic changes in the lower one third of the tibia medially. In nine he was able to demonstrate an actual fracture line, and in five others, only periosteal reaction. Jackson and Bailey[53] supported the opinion of Devas that the medial tibial syndrome represented an atypical stress fracture. Although only one of their athletes had a fracture line, follow-up films on many others showed periosteal new bone formation and the cortical hypertrophy typical of this entity. Clement[56] believed that the syndrome represented a periostitis, and that with continued stress or overloading, a typical stress fracture could result.

Puranen,[20] without pressure measurement documentation, theorized that the medial tibial syndrome represented a deep posterior compartment syndrome. His rationale was primarily based on the mild uptake shown on strontium bone scans and negative radiographic findings in these patients. Puranen noted that the radiographs of typical stress fractures would be more obvious than with this syndrome. Furthermore, he had excellent results in all 11 patients in whom he had done deep posterior compartment fasciotomies. Nevertheless, since then, the intramuscular pressure studies of D'Ambrosia, et al,[54] Eriksson and Wallensten[55] and from our laboratory, refute the possibility that the medial tibial syndrome is a deep posterior compartment syndrome.

Biopsy material from two of our patients who underwent fasciotomies showed, on microscopic examination, inflammation and a vasculitis in the area of tenderness (Fig. 7.10). (Mubarak SJ, Hargens AR: unpublished data.) This finding, the mildly positive bone scan results, and the radiographic appearance lend support for periostitis as the cause. As Devas[51] noted, however, inflammation is a common finding in the region around a stress fracture. In summary, the available information on the medial tibial syndrome indicates that it most likely represents a stress reaction to the fascia, periostium, and bone at this location of the leg, and is not a compartment syndrome.

The treatment of this entity is in wide dispute. It is obviously highly resistant to the usual measures.

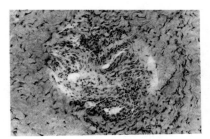

Fig. 7.10: Photomicrograph (200X) of fascia overlying deep posterior compartment of a patient with the medial tibial syndrome. This illustrates the inflammation and vasculitis noted in this entity.

Andrish, et al,[52] in a prospective study of shin splints, tried a variety of therapeutic measures. Most of their patients had the findings of the medial tibial syndrome. Aspirin, Phenobutazone, heel cord stretching, heel pads, and cast immobilization did not improve their overall results. Rest remained the treatment of choice for this particular entity. Jackson and Bailey[53] reported no success with taping or arch supports, and found that aspirin and local injection of steroids also were not beneficial. They found that a well-cushioned shoe was subjectively the most beneficial. Clement,[56] in a report of 20 patients, recommended a two-phase approach. First, he prescribed rest, including crutches and anti-inflammatory medication, then a graduated exercise program using isometric and isotonic exercise. The most divergent approach was that of Puranen.[20] He did posterior compartment fasciotomies in the 11 patients he reviewed, and reported satisfactory results in all patients.[20]

We have taken an approach of treating these patients conservatively. The common denominator with all treatment modalities is rest and then resumption of sporting activities in a graduated fashion. With time, most will improve. Taping, arch supports, and altering shoe wear may help. Two patients in our experience have undergone deep posterior compartment fasciotomies. Both persons had bilateral symptomatology; however, the surgery was done on only the most involved side. Both patients reported excellent improvement one year after their procedures, but neither returned for surgery on their contralateral sides. If fasciotomy can benefit the more recalcitrant cases of this syndrome, a large, well controlled study will be necessary to prove this point. At this time we do not recommend surgical intervention for treatment of this entity.

Treatment for Chronic Compartment Syndrome

Once the diagnosis of a chronic exertional compartment syndrome of the leg has been established by history, examination, and pressure measurements, fasciotomy is usually required. In many instances, however, when the diagnosis and treatment is outlined to the patients, they will prefer to limit running or alter their exercise program. With the chronic form, fasciotomy is not urgently needed as it is with an acute compartment syndrome. Reneman[23] noted ten patients who declined his recommended surgical decompres-

Scott J. Mubarak, M.D.

sion, and all were symptomatic at ten to 12 months follow-up. Most patients in our experience who desire to maintain a given level of jogging or running will require fasciotomy.

Mavor[13] was the first to successfully treat a chronic compartment syndrome with fasciotomy. Reneman,[17] who has the largest experience, uses a blind technique for decompression of the anterior compartment. He notes this technique is not useful in the lateral compartment because of the location of the superficial peroneal nerve. Reneman uses a diathermic wire to burn through the fascia to minimize the skin incision. We prefer a more direct approach and can accomplish a satisfactory fasciotomy of both the anterior and lateral compartments through a two-inch skin incision.

The necessary instruments for this procedure include right-ankle retractors (Army-Navy), a 12 inch Metzenbaum scissors, and/or a fasciotome. We have developed a commerically available fasciotome* that was modified from the instruments suggested by others.[57-59] The fasciotome is designed to incise the fascia without the need for a long skin incison.

For either anterior or lateral compartment involvement, both compartments are decompressed. The skin incision is in the mid portion of the leg halfway between the fibula and the anterior portion of the tibial crest. The usual length is two inches (Fig. 7.11). Muscle hernias are frequent in the lower one third of the leg in the area overlying the anterior intermuscular septum, which is the site of emergence through the fascia of one or both sensory branches of the superficial peroneal nerve. If such a muscle hernia is present, the skin incision should be located over the muscle hernia so that one can explore the fascial defect and identify the superficial peroneal nerve (Fig. 7.6). Through this approach one can easily decompress both the anterior and lateral compartments. Closure of this defect is never indicated because of the risk of precipitating an acute compartment syndrome.[4,43,60,61]

After making the skin incision, the edges are undermined proximally and distally to allow for wide exposure of the fascia. After such exposure, almost the full extent of the compartment fascia should be visible. This step is extremely important when a small incision is used. A transverse

Fig. 7.11: Skin incision used for decompression of the anterior and lateral compartments. With permission from Mubarak SJ, Owen CA: Double incision fasciotomy of the leg for decompression in compartment syndromes. J Bone Joint Surg 59A:184:187, 1977.

---

*Made by Down Surgical Company, Toronto, Ontario, Canada.

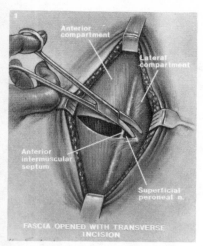

Fig. 7.12: Close-up anterolateral incision: Step 1. With permission from Mubarak SJ, Hargens AR: Diagnosis and Management of compartment syndromes. AAOS: Symposium on Trauma to the Leg and Its Sequelae. St. Louis, CV Mosby, 1981.

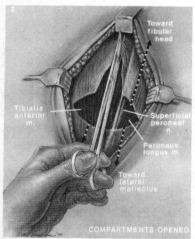

Fig. 7.13: Close-up of anterolateral incision: Step 2. With permission from Mubarak SJ, Hargens AR: Diagnosis and management of compartment syndromes. AAOS Symposium on Trauma to the Leg and Its Sequelae. St Louis, CV Mosby, 1981.

Table 7.4
Anterior Compartment Pressures in Patient with
Bilateral Chronic Exertional Compartment Syndromes:
Effect of Fasciotomy

	Resting Pressure	Postexercise*
	Right/Left	Right/Left
Preoperative	15/16 mm Hg	28/28 mm/Hg
Postfasciotomy (one year)	8/10 mm Hg	16/16 mm Hg

*5 minutes

incision is then made through the fascia, through which the anterior intermuscular septum that separates the anterior compartment from the lateral can be seen (Fig. 7.12). This septum must be identified to enable location of the superficial peroneal nerve, which lies in the lateral compartment next to the septum. Then by means of the long, Metzenbaum scissors or the fasciotome, the anterior compartment is opened (Fig. 7.13). Visualization is aided by retraction with the right angle retractors. The scissors are pushed under direct vision with the tips open slightly in the direction of the great toe distally, and proximally towards the patella. If the tip of the scissors is suspected to have strayed from the fascia, the instrument is left in place and a small incision is made over the scissors' tip. If the fasciotomy is incomplete, further release can be performed through an accessory incision.

The lateral compartment fasciotomy is made in line with the fibular shaft (Fig. 7.13). The scissors or fasciotome are directed proximally towards the fibular head and distally towards the lateral malleolus. In this way, the fascial incision is posterior to the superficial peroneal nerve. The incision is closed with an intradermal running stitch. A light dressing is applied.

The patient is usually discharged the following day. Light exercises are begun within ten days and are gradually increased according to the patient's abilities. Follow-up measurements on patients who have had surgical decompression show a more normal tissue pressure during exercise. In Reneman's experience, the pressure at rest and after exercise does not completely return to normal limits. In the few patients whom we have had an opportunity to study postfasciotomy, the tissue pressure measurements were essentially the same as those of normal runners (Table 7.4).

Scott J. Mubarak, M.D.

References

1. Freedman BJ: Dr Edward Wilson of the Antarctic: A biographical sketch, followed by an inquiry into the nature of his last illness. Proc Roy Soc Med 47:7-13, 1953.
2. Vogt PR: Ischemic muscular necrosis following marching. Read before Oregon State Med Soc, September 4, 1943.
3. Horn CE: Acute ischaemia of the anterior tibial muscle and the long extensor muscles of the toes. J Bone Joint Surg 27A:615-622, 1945.
4. Sirbu AB, Murphy MJ, White AS: Soft tissue complications of fracture of the leg. Calif West Med 60:53-56, 1944.
5. Carter AB, Richards RL, Zachary RB: The anterior tibial syndrome. Lancet 2:928-934, 1949.
6. Hughes JR: Ischaemic necrosis of the anterior tibial muscles due to fatigue. J Bone Joint Surg 30-B:581-594, 1948.
7. Kornstad L: Tibialis-anterior syndromet. Nord Med 53:694, 1955.
8. Kunkel MG, Lynn RB: The anterior tibial compartment syndrome. Can J Surg 1:212-217, 1958.
9. Severin E: Unwandlung des musculus tibialis anterior in Narbengewebe nach uberanstrengung. Acta Chir Scand 89:426, 1944.
10. Tilloston JF, Conventry MB: Spontaneous ischemic necrosis of the anterior tibial muscle; report of a case. Proc Mayo Clin 25:223, 1950.
11. Blandy JP, Fuller R: March gangrene. J Bone Joint Surg 39-B:670-693, 1957.
12. Mubarak SJ, Owen CA, Garfin SR, et al: Acute exertional superficial posterior compartment syndrome. Am J Sports Med 6:287-290, 1978.
13. Mavor GE: The anterior tibial syndrome. J Bone Joint Surg 38B:513-517, 1956.
14. Griffiths DL: The anterior tibial syndrome: A chronic form? J Bone Joint Surg 38B:438-439, 1956.
15. Grunwald A, Silberman Z: Anterior tibial syndrome. JAMA 171:132-2210, 1959.
16. French EB, Price WH: Anterior tibial pain. Br Med J 2:1290-1296, 1962.
17. Reneman RS: The Anterior and the Lateral Compartment Syndrome of the Leg. The Hague, Mouton, 1968.
18. Kirby NG: Exercise ischaemia in the fascial compartmen of the soleus. J Bone Joint Surg 52B:738-740, 1970.
19. Snook GA: Intermittent claudication in athletes. J Sports Med 3:71-75, 1975.
20. Puranen J: The medial tibial syndrome. Exercise ischaemia in the medial fascial compartment of the leg. J Bone Joint Surg 56B:712-715, 1974.
21. Reid RL, Travis RT: Acute necrosis of the second interosseous compartment of the hand. J Bone Joint Surg 55A:1095-1097, 1973.
22. Tompkins DG: Exercise myopathy of the extensor carpi ulnaris muscle. Report of a case. J Bone Joint Surg 59A:407-408, 1977.
23. Reneman RS: The anterior and the lateral compartmental syndrome of the leg due to intensive use of muscles. Clin Orthop 113:69-80, 1975.
24. Anrep GV, Blalock A, Samaan A: The effect of muscular contraction upon blood flow in skeletal muscle. Proc

Roy Soc London (Biol) 114:223-245, 1934.

25. Ashton H: The effect of increased tissue pressure on blood flow. Clin Orthop 113:15-26, 1975.

26. Barcroft H, Millen JLE: The blood flow through muscle during sustained contraction. J Physiol 97:17-31, 1939.

27. Grant RT: Observations on the blood circulation in voluntary muscle in man. Clin Sci 3:157-173, 1938.

28. Hill AV: The pressure developed in muscle during contraction. J Physiol 107:518-526, 1948.

29. Kjellmer I: An indirect method for estimating tissue pressure with special reference to tissue pressure in muscle during exercise. Acta Physiol Scand 62:31-40, 1964.

30. Wells HS, Youmans JB, Miller DG, Jr: Tissue pressure (intracutaneous, subcutaneous, and intramuscular) as related to venous pressure, capillary filtration, and other factors. J Clin Invest 17:489-499, 1938.

31. Mubarak SJ, Hargens AR, Owen CA, et al: The wick catheter technique for measurement of intramuscular pressure: A new research and clinical tool. J Bone Joint Surg 58A:1016-1020, 1976.

32. Owen CA, Schmidt DA, Hargens AR, et al: Intramuscular fluid pressure during isometric contraction. Am J Sports Med, submitted.

33. Schmidt DA, Owen CA Hargens AR, et al: An assessment of isometric quadricepts exercises. Am J Sports Med submitted, 1981.

34. Wright S: Applied Physiology, Tenth Edition. London, Oxford Univ Press, 1961.

35. Linge B Van: Experimentele Spierhypertrofie Bij de Rat. Van Garkum, Assen, 1959.

36. Pearson C, Adams RD, Denny-Brown D: Traumatic necrosis of pretibial muscles. New Engl J Med 231:213-217, 1948.

37. Brooker AR, Pezenshki C: Tissue pressure to evaluate compartmental syndrome. J Trauma 19:689-691, 1979.

38. Matsen FA, Mayo KA, Sheridan GW, et al: Monitoring of intramuscular pressure. Surg 79:702-709, 1976.

39. Whitesides TE, Haney TC, Morimoto K, et al: Tissue pressure measurements as a determinant for the need of fasciotomy. Clin Orthop 113:43-51, 1975.

40. Hargens AR, Romine JS, Sipe JC, et al: Peripheral nerve conduction block by high muscle compartment pressure. J Bone Joint Surg 61A:192-200, 1979.

41. Hargens AR, Ronnie JS, Sipe JC, et al: Peripheral nerve conduction block by high muscle compartment pressure. J Bone Joint Surg 61A:192-200, 1979.

42. Mubarak SJ, Owen CA, Hargens AR, et al: Acute compartment syndromes: Disagnosis and treatment with the aid of the wick catheter. J Bone Joint Surg 60A:1091-1095, 1978.

43. Leach RE, Hammon G, Stryker WS: Anterior tibial compartment syndrome: Acute and chronic. J Bone Joint Surg 49A:451-462, 1967.

44. Leach RE, Zohn DA, Stryker WS: Anterior tibial compartment syndrome. Arch Surg 88:187-192, 1964.

45. Mubarak SJ, Owen CA: Double incision fasciotomy of the leg for decompression in compartment syndromes. J Bone Joint Surg 59A:184-187, 1977.

46. Garfin SR, Mubarak SJ, Owen CA: Exertional anterolateral compartment syndrome. J Bone Joint Surg 59A:404-405, 1977.

Scott J. Mubarak, M.D.

47. Kennelly BM, Blumberg L: Bilateral anterior tibial claudication. JAMA 203:487-491, 1968.
48. Daniels BW, Grennan HA: Pretibial fever JAMA 122:361-365, 1943.
49. Browne SG: The anterior tibial compartment syndrome. Differential diagnosis in a nigerian leprosarium. Br J Surg 49:429, 1962.
50. Slocum DB: The shin splint syndrome: medical aspects and differential diagnosis. Am J Surg 114:875-881, 1967.
51. Devas MB: Stress fractures of the tibia in athletes or "shin soreness." J Bone Joint Surg 40B:227-239, 1958.
52. Andrish JT, Bergfeld JA, Walheim J: A prospective study on the management of shin splints. J Bone Joint Surg 56A:1697-1700, 1974.
53. Jackson DW, Bailey D: Shin splints in the young athlete: A nonspecific diagnosis. Physician Sports Med 3:45-51, 1975.
54. D'Ambrosia RD, Zelis RF, Chuinard RG, et al: Interstitial pressure measurements in the anterior and posterior compartments in athletes with shin splints. Am J Sports Med 5:127-131, 1977.
55. Eriksson E, Wallensten R: Can research into muscle morphology and muscle metabolism improve orthopaedic treatment? Presented at the Association Meeting, Western Orthopedics, Las Vegas, NV, October 16, 1979.
56. Clement DB: Tibial stress syndrome in athletes. J Sports Med 2:81-85, 1974.
57. Bate JT: A subcutaneous fasciotome. Clin Orthop 83:235-236, 1972.
58. Mozes M, Ramon Y, Jahr J: The anterior tibial syndrome. J Bone Joint Surg 44A:730, 1962.
59. Rosato FE, Barker CF, Roberts B, et al: Subcutaneous fasciotomy, description of a new technique and instrument. Surg 59:282, 1966.
60. Paton DF: The pathogenesis of anterior tibial syndrome. J Bone Joint Surg 50B:383-385, 1968.
61. Wolfort FG, Mogelvang LC, Filtzer HS: Anterior tibial compartment syndrome following muscle hernia repair. Arch Surg 106:97-99.

The author wishes to thank Debra Guthrie for her assistance in preparing this manuscript.

8

Heat Injury in Runners: Treatment and Prevention

Peter G. Hanson, M.S., M.D.

Heat injury has become a major medical problem in warm-weather road races. An estimated 25 million persons currently participate in fun runs and competitive road races in the United States each year. Many local events attract 500 to 1,000 runners, whereas major road races draw 5,000 to 26,000 participants. Recently, a class-action law suit was filed against road-race organizers by a group of heat-injury victims who participated in the 10km (6.2 mi) Atlanta Peachtree Roadrace in 1977.[1]

The incidence of clinically significant injury is estimated at 0.1 to 2.0% of race participants when ambient temperatures are 24 to 27°C* (75-80°F).[2-4] Even this seemingly small fraction could represent 50 to 200 heat casualties, and quickly overwhelm the medical facilities of a medium-sized city[5]. In addition, a much greater percentage of subclinal heat morbidity probably goes unreported. Therefore, medical personnel who provide care for participants in road races must develop plans to prevent and treat potential heat-injury cases.

This chapter summarizes the clinical physiology and initial management of heat injury in runners, and suggests some possible strategies for preventing heat injury in road races.

Temperature Regulation in Runners

Body Temperature

During steady-state exercise, body temperature in runners normally increases to a range of 38 to 40°C (100-104°F) (Fig. 8.1). The elevation in

*Wet Bulb-Globe Temperature index (see section on prevention).

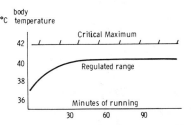

Fig. 8.1: Body temperature during running.

body temperature is actively regulated to maintain a state of "controlled hyperthermia," which is also compatible with optimum biochemical activity, blood flow, and oxygen transport for muscle contraction.

The runner is, however, also vulnerable to heat injury as a consequence of the complex interplay between increased heat production, dehydration, and circulatory and metabolic failure that may occur with substantial exercise. The *critical thermal maximum* core temperature for humans appears to be 42°C (107.6°F).[6] Sustained temperatures above this level result in thermal injury and clinical heat stroke. Surprisingly, some well-conditioned runners may attain rectal temperatures of 41.0 to 41.5°C (105.8-106.7°F) with no evidence of heat stroke.[3,7]

Rectal temperature in runners is strongly influenced by the higher temperatures of venous blood returning from active leg muscles (40.5-41.5°C; 104.9-106.7°F) and the visceral-hepatic temperatures (41.0-41.5°C).[8] These facts may explain the remarkable elevation in rectal temperatures measured in some runners. Esophageal temperature is probably a closer measure of core and brain temperature.[9] For clinical purposes, however, we must assume most runners will maintain body temperature within 1.5 to 2.0°C (2.7-3.6°F) of the critical level for heatstroke.

Heat Balance

Body-heat content (H) is determined by the balance between metabolic heat production (M), additional heat gain from solar radiation (R), heat gain or loss from convection and conduction (C), and heat loss from evaporation (E) of sweat and lung water. These factors are usually expressed as a heat-balance equation:

$$H = M + R + C - E$$

For the warm-weather runner this equation is dominated by heat gains from metabolism and solar radiation, and heat loss from evaporative cooling (Fig. 8.2).

Metabolic heat production is proportional to relative percent of maximal oxygen consumption (VO2 max). An average runner usually maintains a metabolic rate equal to 75-80% VO2 max during races greater than 10 km.[10] Oxygen consumption and corresponding heat production may be roughly estimated from running velocity and an assumed caloric equivalent for oxygen consump-

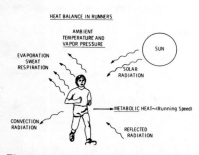

Fig. 8.2: Heat balance in runners

Peter G. Hanson, M.D.

tion summarized below:

$$VO_2 \text{ (ml/kg.min)} = 178 \text{ x (m/min - 150)} + 33$$
$$\text{Kcal/hr} = VO_2 \text{ (ml/kg. min)} \text{ x kg x 5 cal/}$$
$$\text{L x 60 min}$$

Estimated metabolic heat production for a 75-kg runner with an average velocity of 200 meters/min would approximate 1,000 Kcal/hr.

Radiant heat gain (R) is determined by the intensity of solar insolation (I), the surface area of exposure (A), and a radiant uptake constant (a):

$$R = a \text{ x } A \text{ x } I$$

Radiant insolation may exceed 1,000 watts/M^2 on a clear summer day. An average runner with 0.5 to 1.0 M^2 of exposed (shadow) surface could gain 150 to 200 Kcal of additional heat per hour.[1]

The combined heat gains from exercise metabolism and environmental radiation would produce a progressive rise in body temperature of 2.5°C every 10 minutes in the absence of efficient body-cooling mechanisms.

Heat Loss

Temperature regulation during steady-state running depends almost entirely on increased skin blood flow and the evaporation of sweat (95%) and pulmonary water (5%). Each liter of completely evaporated water provides 580 Kcal heat loss. Sweat production and pulmonary water excretion are also proportional to the relative work intensity. Water loss may range from 1.5 to 2.5 liters per hour, depending on body size. The net effect of cooling, however, may vary greatly, depending on environmental factors of ambient temperature, vapor pressure, and wind velocity. Even under ideal conditions, 20-30% of sweat is probably lost to physical runoff.

Fluid Loss

Fluid losses of 1.5 to 2.5 liters per hour impose an additional burden to temperature regulation. Voluntary fluid intake by runners seldom replaces more than 25-30% of these losses.[12,13] As a result, total body water depletion may approach 4-5% for events of one hour's duration, and 8-10% for marathons.

Sweat is a hypo-osmolar filtrate (50-150 mOsm/L) so that water loss greatly exceeds electrolyte loss. At high sweat rates the concentrations of sodium and chloride do increase, whereas potas-

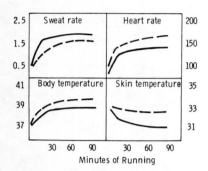

Fig. 8.3: Physiological responses to steady state exercise in acclimatized (——) and unacclimatized (- - -) runners. (compiled from multiple references)

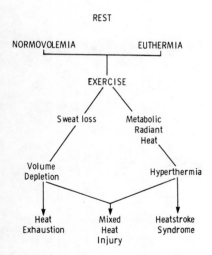

Fig. 8.4

sium concentration remains constant. Corresponding electrolyte losses in prolonged sweating may equal 5-10% of extracellular sodium and 1-2% of total body potassium.[12]

Volume depletion and electrolyte losses clearly potentiate the probability of heat injury in runners. Body temperature during exercise is significantly higher when dehydration exceeds 3% body weight.[10,14] In addition, reduced blood volume further decreases cardiovascular efficiency and cooling capacity.

Heat Acclimation

Temperature regulation and responses to exercise are dramatically improved with heat acclimation (Fig. 8.3). In the acclimatized runner, sweating and increased skin blood flow are initiated at lower core temperatures so that maximum rectal and skin temperatures are cooler for the same metabolic rate.[15]

Heart rate and cardiac output demands are also reduced in the heat-acclimatized runner. The improved cardiovascular responses are probably related to a reduction in peripheral venous volume and a corresponding increase in central blood volume secondary to cooler skin temperatures.

The apparent tolerance to higher body temperatures and efficient cooling capacity of elite athletes is reflected in the comparatively few reports of heat injury in international class runners. Highly trained runners appear to have superior cooling capacities during sustained exercise. Gisolfi found significantly lower values for rectal and skin temperatures in a group of highly trained distance runners compared with those of well-conditioned college athletes running at the same percent VO_2 max and equal sweat rates.[16]

Novice runners by comparison are more likely to be unacclimated and relatively untrained for warm-weather road races. In addition, they may attempt to complete distances that exceed their training level or run at an excessive rate to finish, possibly ignoring premonitory symptoms of impending heat injury.

Heat-Injury Syndromes

Heat injury in runners should be considered as a continuum of clinical states characterized by variable combinations or hyperthermia and volume depletion. The evolution of heat injury in runners is illustrated in a simplified format (Fig. 8.4).

Peter G. Hanson, M.D.

From a state of normal temperature and fluid volume, sustained exercise produces a combination of progressive dehydration and regulated hyperthermia. Excessive early fluid depletion leads to a predominate heat exhaustion syndrome with moderate hyperthermia. Progressive metabolic hyperthermia may produce heatstroke syndrome with mild dehydration. There is abundant opportunity for "mixed heat injury syndromes" with significant dehydration and hyperthermia. This condition should be considered in the initial evaluation and management of apparent heat injury in runners.[17] Table 8.1 summarizes the clinical findings, initial management, and potential complications of heat injury.

Heatstroke

Heatstroke is the most serious of heat injuries that may be encountered in runners. The mechanism of exertional heatstroke probably involves the accumulated imbalance between metabolic and environmental heat gain and decreasing or impaired heat loss.[18,19] The numerous contributing factors include: progressive volume depletion, alterations in cardiac output and skin blood flow, and decreasing or impaired sweat secretion or evaporation. Exertional heatstroke may occur in the presence of active sweating.[18,20,21] Recent reports of clinical heatstroke in runners have emphasized the finding of profuse sweating.[1,22,23] Anhidrosis *after* the onset of heatstroke may be a secondary response to severe central nervous system dysfunction.

Heatstroke in runners is usually preceded by significant disturbances in mental status ranging from disorientation and bizarre behavior to rapid loss of consciousness.[20,22] Any runner who exhibits a disturbance in thought or behavior or loses consciousness during a road race must be suspected of having significant hyperthermia or clinical heatstroke. It is of paramount importance to obtain vital signs and rectal temperature to differentiate heatstroke from other possible causes of mental aberration or unconsciousness, such as hypoglycemia, cardiovascular failure, or arrhythmia. If rectal temperature exceeds 41°C, immediate thermal resuscitation should be started.

Hemodynamic status is characterized by tachycardia (heart rate 120-140 beats per minutes) and normal or reduced systolic pressure (140-100 mm Hg) and low or absent diastolic pressure. These findings are consistent with a high-cardiac-

Table 8.1
Heat Injury Management in Runners or Athletes

	Hyperthermia-Heatstroke	Hypovolemia-Heat Exhaustion	Other "Exertional Syncope"
Clinical Findings	—Initial temp > 41°C (rectal) (May fall during transport) —Impaired consciousness—variable (Initial unconsciousness or severe disorientation) —Active sweating (may be found initially) —Cutaneous vasodilation (unless shock) —C-V: HR 120-160 BP wide pulse pressure 140-120/0 (shock may ensue)	—Initial temp 39-40° C (or less) —Mild disorientation —Active sweating —Cutaneous vasoconstriction, piloerection C-V: HR 120-140 BP 100-80/60-40 supine *Orthostatic ↓ prominent*	—Brief syncope or collapse associated with prolonged or intense exercise. May occur in cool weather (Usually "under-conditioned" person) —Temp < 39°C —C-V: HR < 120 *BP normal with mild orthostatic drop*
Initial Management	—TREAT AS TRAUMA CASE —Establish IV line —Use ECG monitor, Foley Cath —Do lab studies—STAT	—Establish IV line —Do lab studies—STAT Lytes, Glucose, U/A (expect ↑ WBC, RBC in runners)	—Determine volume status (Orthostatis Δ's) —Check Glucose, Lytes, U/A ECG

Peter G. Hanson, M.D.

CBC, Lytes, LFTS, PT, PTT Glucose, ABG, U/A BUN/Cr.
—Initiate cooling with ice on wet towels
—Continue active cooling to 39°C (rectal)
—Give IV: ½ NS/D5W to replete ECF vol. *Do Not Overload*
—Give mannitol 12.5 GM IV
—Maintain urine output and C-V status. Use Swan-Gantz to direct fluid therapy if shock develops
—Avoid vasopressors

—Cool if temp = 40°C
—Give IV: 1/2 NS D5W Give 1 liter 30 min.
—Continue volume repletion based on urine output and V.S.
—Add K^+ if depleted

—Treat as heat exhaustion

Complications
—HOSPITALIZE FOR 48-72 HRS
—Watch urine (hematuria, myoglobinuria) (Except WBC, RBC in runners)
—Expect hepatocellular damage Max 48-72 hrs.
—Expect PT, PTT and platelets Max 48-72 hrs.
—DIC—may develop
—Watch for occult sepsis

—Discharge if condition is uncomplicated. Warn patient to watch for urine changes in subsequent 48 hrs.

Watch for other causes of syncope in exercise:
—Hypertrophic cardiomyopathy
—Mitral valve prolapse
—Dysrhythmia
—Myocarditis—myocardial infarction
—Drug abuse

output, low-peripheral-resistance state.[23] Relative bradycardia and preservation of blood pressure may be seen in highly conditioned distance runners in spite of considerable hyperthermia.

The skin is usually vasodilated and warm. As previously described, active sweating is usually found on initial examination.

Rectal temperature in heat stroke may range from 40 to 43°C; however, the temperature may be influenced by the transport time from field to hospital. An average initial temperature of 41.5°C was found in several recent reports of heat stroke in runners.[3,20,22]

Effective treatment of heat stroke includes immediate cooling, appropriate rehydration, and treatment of circulatory status. Complications and mortality in heatstroke are directly related to the delay in achieving body temperatures below 40°C. Most authorities recommend rapid cooling to 38.5-39°C, followed by closely monitored passive cooling.[3,20,21,24] Thermal resuscitation, by means of wet ice towels applied to the neck, axilla, abdomen, and groin, may be started in the field and continued during transport to hospital.

Richards and colleagues pointed out that spot cooling of these regions maximizes cooling to superficial great vessels, while minimizing cutaneous vasoconstriction that tends to reduce heat loss.[3] Immersion therapy is effective, but cardiac monitoring may be difficult and resuscitation effects delayed or hazardous in the case of cardiac arrest or dysrhythmia.

For initial fluid therapy, a glucose-electrolyte solution such as half-normal saline with 5% dextrose should be used. Hypoglycemia is a common finding in hyperthermic runners, and may be quickly corrected with glucose-containing solutions.[4,22]

Extracellular volume depletion should be corrected so that urinary output is maintained. Mannitol (12.5 IV) may be administered intravenously as a prophylactic measure. Excessive administration of fluids, however, should be avoided to prevent circulatory overload and possible cerebral edema.[21,24] If severe hypotension is present, pulmonary artery wedge pressure monitoring may be required to evaluate ventricular function and guide fluid therapy.

Basic laboratory work must include electrolytes, hepatic and muscle enzymes, uric acid, BUN and creatinine, urinalysis, coagulation studies, and CBC with platelet count. A 12-lead electrocardio-

Peter G. Hanson, M.D.

gram, and cardiovascular monitoring are advisable during the initial period of treatment.

Hematologic and biochemical alterations and exertional heat stroke are complex, and reflect combined factors of tissue damage, dehydration, and disturbances of acid-base and renal function. Heatstroke victims should always be hospitalized and observed for 24 to 48 hours so that potential major complications may be identified and treated.

The time course and magnitude of serum enzyme concentration increase may be of prognostic value and should be closely monitored for evidence of continued hepatic or muscle damage.[6,211] Transient decreases in calcium and phosphate levels are apparently due to intracellular shifts of these ions secondary to cellular damage. Hypernatremia and hypokalemia may be found initially, probably secondary to volume depletion, although increased potassium levels may be related to muscle injury. Delayed coagulation times and thrombocytopenia are probably explained by a transient decrease in liver hepatic synthesis of clotting factors combined with increased peripheral platelet consumption due to tissue injury. The presence of fragmented red cells and decreased platelet and fibrinogen levels is suggestive of disseminated intravascular coagulation, which is a known complication of heatstroke. Shibolet and colleagues emphasized that the apparent coagulopathic changes may be transient and do not require heparin therapy unless changes in laboratory values indicate continued deterioration.[4]

Acute renal failure is also a frequent complication of heatstroke. Rhabdomyolysis with myoglobinuria and hyperuricemia are probably contributing factors to renal tubular damage.[25] This complication may be avoided by early rehydration and osmotic diuresis. The management of these complex problems in heatstroke has been detailed in several recent reviews.[3,14,20-24] Heatstroke victims should be evaluated for chronic heat intolerance after recovery. Recent reports suggest some persons remain susceptible to recurrent heat injury with exercise.[26]

Heat Exhaustion

Heat exhaustion is characterized by moderate-to-severe volume depletion, with water losses usually exceeding electrolyte losses during prolonged exercise. Characteristic symptoms of fatigue, nausea, and headache are often severe enough to limit further participation in a road race. Significant hypovolemia may be tolerated while running, but may be followed by acute hypotension while walking or standing. Heat-exhaustion victims are usually confused and irritable but maintain consciousness while supine.

Rectal temperatures are elevated (39-40°C), but should be below 41°C. Circulatory status is characterized by rapid heart rate (100-140 beats per minute), and prominent orthostatic hypotension. The skin is cool with marked vasoconstriction and pallor. Active sweating should be present.

Treatment of heat exhaustion also requires fluid therapy and moderate cooling. Normal or half-normal saline with 5% dextrose may be used for initial fluid replacement. Subsequent fluid therapy may be guided by levels of serum electrolyte and glucose levels, which should be obtained on all runners who are treated in an emergency department. Adequate clinical response should be evaluated by progressive improvement of orthostatic blood pressure and urinary output.

Routine laboratory studies are consistent with acute hyperosmotic volume depletion. Hematocrit, serum sodium, creatine, and BUN levels are increased. Urine is scant and highly concentrated with positive protein, granular casts, RBC, and WBC. Serum enzymes from muscle sources (LDH, SGOT, CPK) are moderately elevated, but such elevation may be due to exercise alone.

Most patients with heat exhaustion may be released after adequate fluid replacement. Patients should be warned to watch for unusual symptoms, especially alterations of urine appearance and output. Delayed rhabdomyolysis with myoglobinuria and acute renal failure is a potential complication.

Prevention of Heat Injury
Organization

The potential for heat injury may be greatly reduced by proper planning of the date, time, and route of a road race. Climatic data for the anticipated date of road race should be carefully screened for temperature and heat-stress index. The most commonly used heat index is the "Wet Bulb-Globe Temperature" (WBGT). This index was developed for use in military training camps by measuring wet bulb temperature (WB), dry

Peter G. Hanson, M.D.

bulb temperature (DB), and metal globe temperature (GT). The WBGT index is calculated as follows:

$$WBGT°C = 0.7\ WB + 0.3\ GT + 0.1\ DB$$

Using this index, the American College of Sports Medicine[27] established guidelines for conducting road races in warm weather conditions (Table 8.2). A maximum limit of 28°C WBGT (82°F) is recommended for races in excess of 16 km (10 mi). Despite close adherence to these guidelines, however, significant heat injuries have been

Table 8.2
The American College of Sports Medicine
Position Statement on
Prevention of Heat Injuries During Distance Running

Based on research findings and current rules governing distance running competition, it is the position of the American College of Sports Medicine that:

1. Distance races (16 km or 10 miles) should *not* be conducted when the wet bulb temperature—globe temperature* exceeds 28°C (82.4°F).
2. During periods of the year when the daylight dry bulb temperature often exceeds 27°C (80°F), distance races should be conducted before 9:00 A.M. or after 4:00 P.M.
3. It is the responsibility of the race sponsors to provide fluids that contain small amounts of sugar (less than 2.5 g glucose per 100 ml of water) and electrolytes (less than 10 mEq sodium and 5 mEq potassium per liter of solution).
4. Runners should be encouraged to frequently ingest fluids during competition and to consume 400-500 ml (13-17 oz.) of fluid 10-15 minutes before competition.
5. Rules prohibiting the administration of fluids during the first 10 kilometers (6.2 miles) of a marathon race should be amended to permit fluid ingestion at frequent intervals along the race course. In light of the high sweat rates and body temperatures during distance running in the heat, race sponsors should provide "water stations" at 3-4 kilometer (2-2.5 mile) intervals for all races of 16 kilometers (10 miles) or more.
6. Runners should be instructed in how to recognize the early warning symptoms that precede heat injury. Recognition of symptoms, cessation of running, and proper treatment can prevent heat injury. Early warning symptoms include the following: piloerection on chest and upper arms chilling, throbbing pressure in the head, unsteadiness, nausea, and dry skin.
7. Race sponsors should make prior arrangements with medical personnel for the care of cases of heat injury. Responsible and informed personnel should supervise each "feeding station." Organizational personnel should reserve the right to stop runners who exhibit clear signs of heat stroke or heat exhaustion.

It is the position of the American College of Sports Medicine that policies established by local, national, and international sponsors of distance running events should adhere to these guidelines. Failure to adhere to these guidelines may jeopardize the health of competitors through heat injury.

reported over a wide range of distances (10 km-42 km) and ambient temperatures (20° - 28°C).

Another important factor in planning a road race is the route. In many instances the route is established by tradition or logistic constraints. A properly planned closed loop may be easier to monitor, and will provide a central aid station at the beginning and end of the race.

Aid stations should be positioned at 4 to 5 km (2.5 to 3 mi) intervals for all races greater than 10 km (6.2 mi). Field aid stations should provide fluids (water and hypotonic electrolyte solutions) and minor first aid (bandages, towels, and ice). Personnel assigned to field aid stations should be well versed in spotting potential heat victims.

An emergency communication system is vital for large road races. Such communication should provide contact between race officials and medical personnel at the finish, mobile emergency units in the field, and local hospital emergency rooms or fire rescue units.

Medical Coverage

Medical personnel should include physicians, nurses with intensive-care experience, and emergency medical technicians. Skilled professional personnel are best utilized in a major aid station located at the race finish. Paramedical and other knowledgeable persons may act as spotters at field aid stations.[28,29]

The major aid station at the finish should be equipped with cots, blankets, water, ice, intravenous fluids, and general medical equipment necessary for triage and initial treatment of heat injuries or other anticipated medical problems. Details of the organization and equipment needs for a road race aid stations have been published.[28]

Local hospitals and emergency departments should be notified well in advance of the road race dates, so that personnel and supplies may be increased during the period of the race. Communication with medical staff in these hospitals is important for maintaining a consistent plan for management of persons with heat injury.

Advice to Runners

Printed pre-race instructions to runners should contain a section on medical self-care. Information should include recommendations for training and conditioning, pre-race
and conditioning, pre-race nutrition, and fluid intake; advice on clothing and footwear; guide-

Peter G. Hanson, M.D.

lines for consumption of fluids; and recognition of heat symptoms during the race (Table 8.3). Runners should also be advised not to participate during or immediately after a febrile illness. Medications that may influence thermal regulation should also be mentioned.

Immediately before the race, runners should be apprised of current ambient temperature and humidity conditions, and reminded of the symptoms of heat injury. This preparation is especially important whenever the temperature exceeds 21°C WBGT (70°F). They should be strongly encouraged to drink adequate volumes of fluid (200-300 ml) at each aid station. Alcoholic drinks should be discouraged. Finally, runners should be

Table 8.3
Warm-Weather Medical Self-Care
for Beginning Runners

Training and Preparation. You should be able to run ____* miles at 9-11 minutes per mile pace to finish this race comfortably. Try to train ____** miles per week for at least 4 weeks before this race. Drink about 8 ounces of fluid 1 hour before the race and up to twice that amount 10-15 minutes before race time. Start warming up—stretching and jogging—about 30 minutes before race.

Race of 6 to 9 miles:	12-22 miles	26 miles
*run 3/** train 18	run 6/tr. 25	run 12/tr. 37

Temperature is a critical factor. Significant heat injury may occur at all temperatures from 65-80°F. Above 80°F, novice runners should *reduce running pace by about 1 minute per mile.* Wear only light athletic clothing (shorts, T shirt, tank top, or topless). Body temperature will normally rise to 102-103°F during race due to exercise heat production. Further increases nay occur due to radiant sun exposure, dehydration, and decreased sweat rate.

Fluid Replacement is essential to restore sweat losses. The average-size man (140-160 pounds) may lose 1.5-2.0 quarts of sweat per hour. Drink 6-8 ounces fluid at *each* aid station. Stop to drink. Even then, you may replace only 50% of sweat loss.

Problems During Run may include muscle cramps, joint pains, blisters, fatigue. Heat symptoms are most dangerous—headache, dizziness, disorientation, nausea, decrease in sweat rate, pale, cold skin. Don't try to run through these symptoms. Stop, walk or rest, ask for help.

After Running. At finish, you may become dizzy or faint on coming to a stop due to a fall in blood pressure. To prevent this, *keep moving.* But, if symptoms develop, lie down, raise legs, call for help.

Chronic Medical Problems. If you have medical problems such as asthma, diabetes, hypertension or other cardiovascular problems, check with your physician before entering a race. Wear a 'medic alert' tag and I.D.

Remember, running is fun but it can be stressful. Listen to your body. Walk when you are tired. There is always another race.

Heat Injury in Running

warned not to attempt a substantial increase in pace to catch up or finish a race when symptoms of heat stress are present. Novice runners should be advised to voluntarily decrease their planned running pace by 1 mile/min if the ambient temperature exceeds 24°C WBGT (75°F).

Summary

Heat injury is a threat to all distance runners, regardless of experience. Sustained high metabolic rate and unavoidable dehydration are constant stresses to adequate temperature regulation. The best defense against heat injury is prevention. Heat casualities are inevitable, however, in large warm-weather races, and preparation should be adequate to handle these problems. Medical personnel who provide coverage for organized road races should familiarize themselves with the clinical syndromes of heat injury, and develop a well-coordinated plan for identification and immediate management of heat casualties.

References

1. Runners' World Update: Peachtree sued. Runners World I, 1979.
2. England AC, Varsha, RA, et al: Epidemiology of severe heat injury occurring among participants of the 1979 Peachtree Road Race. Med Sci Sports (Abst) Spring, 1980.
3. Richards D, Richards R, Schofield PJ, et al: Management of heat exhaustion in Sydney's Sun City-to-Surf fun runners. Med J Aust 2:457, 1979.
4. Sutton JB, Coleman MJ, Millar AP, et al: The medical problems of mass participation in athletic competition: the Sun City-to-Surf race. Med J Aust 2:127, 1972.
5. Nicholson MR, Somerville KW: Heatstroke in a run for fun. Br Med J 1:525, 1978.
6. Bynum GD, Pandolf KB, Schuette WH, et al: Induced hyperthermia in sedated humans and the concept of critical thermal maximum. Am J Physiol 235:F227, 1978.
7. Maron MB, Horvath SW: The marathon—A review. Med Sci Sports 10:135, 1978.
8. Rowell LB: Human cardiovascular adjustments to exercise and thermal stress. Physiol Review 54:75-159, 1974.
9. Greenleaf JE: Hyperthermia and exercise. Ann Rev Physiol (Environ Physiol III) 20:157, 1979.
10. Adams WC, Fox RR, Fry AJ, et al: Thermoregulation during marthon running in cool, moderate, and hot environments. J Appl Physiol 38:1030, 1975.
11. Mitchell JW: Energy exchanges during exercise. In Nadel E (ed): Problems with Temperature Regulation during Exercise. New York, Academic Press, 1977, pp 11-26.
12. Costill DE: Sweating, its composition and effects on body fluids. Ann NY Acad Sci 301:160, 1977.
13. Pugh LGC, Corbett JL, Johnson RH: Rectal temperatures, weight losses and sweat rates in marathon running.

Peter G. Hanson, M.D.

J Appl Physiol 23:345, 1967.

14. Syndham CH: Heatstroke and hyperthermia in marathon runners. Ann NY Acad Sci 301:128, 1977.

15. Nadel E: Control of sweating rate while exercising in the heat. Med Sci Sports, 11:31, 1979.

16. Gisolfi CV, Wilson NC, Claxton B: Work-heat tolerance of distance runners. Ann NY Acad Sci 301:139, 1977.

17. Hanson PG: Heat injury in runners. Phys Sports Med 1:91, 1979.

18. Gilat T, Shibolet S, Sohar E: The mechanism of heatstroke. J Trop Med 66:204-212, 1967

19. Hubbard RW: Effects of exercise in the heat on predisposition to heatstroke. Med Sci Sports 11:66, 1979.

20. Costrini AM, Pitt HA, Gustafson AB, et al: Cardiovascular and metabolic manifestations of heatstroke and severe heat exhaustion. Am J Med 66:296, 1979.

21. Shibolet W, Lancaster MC, Danon Y: Heatstroke, a review. Aviat Space Environ Med 47:280, 1976.

22. Hanson PG, Zimmerman SW: Exertional heatstroke in novice runners. JAMA 242:154, 1979.

23. O'Donnell, TF, Jr: The hemodynamic and metabolic alternations associated with acute heat stress injury in marathon runners. Ann NY Acad Sci 301:262, 1977.

25. Knochel JP: Environmental heat illness: an eclectic review. Arch Int Med 133:841, 1974.

26. Shapiro Y, Magazanik A, Udassin R, et al: Heat intolerance in former heatstroke patients. Ann Int Med 90:913, 1979.

27. American College of Sports Medicine position statement on prevention of heat injuries during distance running. Med Sci Sports 7:VII-IX, 1975.

28. Noble HB, Bachman D: Medical aspects of distance race planning. Phys Sports Med 1:78, 1979.

29. Richards R, Richards D, Schofield PJ, et al: Reducing the hazards in Sydney's the Sun City-to-Surf run, 1971 to 1979, Med J Aust 2:353, 1979.

9

Female Runners

Lyle Micheli, M.D.

The growing interest of women in sports competition of all kinds has attained its most dramatic expression in running and running competitions. The first Bonnie Bell Marathon championship for women only was held in Boston in 1977, with 1,329 entrants. In 1978, 4,524 women began the 10 km course, and entries were accepted until the day before the race. The 1979 Bonnie Bell championship had 5,045 entrants, and registration was closed six weeks before the race.

There are many reasons for this explosion of female runners. Women, like men, are interested in fitness as a means of improving health and preventing disease. Most current weight-reduction programs stress regular exercise in addition to caloric reduction, and even the cosmetic and beauty firms, as evidenced by the many sponsored women's races, are emphasizing the healthy and athletic look.

Whatever the reasons, more women of all ages and levels of athletic experience are taking to running, and physicians dealing with runners and running injuries are noting a dramatic increase in both the number and the variety of injuries sustained by women.[1]

Although there has been much interest in women's participation in sports in the past, two types of sports competition for women were interdicted until recently: contact sports and endurance sports, including distance running, biking, and swimming. Contact sports for women were prohibited for fear of impact injuries, and endurance sports were eliminated for fear that women, having "weaker hearts," could not sustain prolonged endurance stress.

In 1967, Kathy Switzer, the first official female

entrant in the Boston Marathon, ran only after successfully evading marathon officials who attempted to physically restrain her from starting the race (which she completed). Even today, in Olympic competition, this distance bias persists. Although men compete over distances from 100 meters to the marathon distance of 43.2 kilometers, the greatest distance permitted for female competition is 3,000 meters.

One of the historic bases for this concern dates to the 1928 Olympics in Paris. Up to that time, most female competitive running was over 300 meters. For some reason, with just three-weeks' notice, an additional competition of 800 meters was added to the Olympic slate. The entrants from the various competing nations had no opportunity to train over this distance, and the results were disastrous. Only nine women completed the race, from a field of 14. People were outraged that "fair maidens" were submitted to such stress. Alarmed Olympic officials responded by permanently barring further long-distance competition for women. This interdiction has persisted even to our own times.

Female Physiology versus Distance Running

The notion that women cannot safely sustain the cardiovascular and thermal stresses of long-distance running has been most recently addressed by a position statement of the American College of Sports Medicine (1979). In reviewing current studies of endurance training for women, it was concluded that women respond in much the same manner as men to systematic exercise training, including endurance training. Cardiorespiratory function is improved, as reflected by increased maximal oxygen uptake (VO_2 max), lowered blood pressure and pulse, and lowered percentage of body fat.[2]

In fact, Wilmore and Brown[3] studied 11 world-class female runners in 1974 and found a mean body fat of 15.2% of total body weight, which was about half that expected. In addition, the maximal oxygen uptake of this group measured 59.1 milliliters per kilogram per minute, which was much higher than that of nonrunning women, although still 16% lower than the maximal oxygen uptake of male runners of similar caliber. This difference, however, was reduced to 7.8% when expressed relative to lean body weight.

Another concern often expressed has been

Lyle Micheli, M.D.

related to the ability of women to sustain the thermal stress of long-distance running. For many years women were thought to have less tolerance to environmental heat stress than men. That observation appeared to be particularly true when studied in association with prolonged exercise. Long-distance running carries with it the potential for significant thermal stress, even in the most favorable climatic conditions of ambient temperature and humidity. The associated water loss and hypovolemia of distance running appears to increase the susceptibility of both heat and cold injury in runners.[4]

More recent studies on thermal regulation in women have been reassuring. The observed differences in thermal stress response between men and women appear more quantitative than qualitative. Although women, on the average, require a higher skin temperature before onset of sweating, thermal equilibrium maintenance in the physically fit woman is little affected. Recent studies showed that cardiovascular fitness is an important factor in the body's ability to respond to thermal stress.[5] This relationship provides a plausible explanation for the observed differences between men and women in some of these earlier studies: in many of the studies, physically active male subjects were compared with sedentary female subjects.[6] Ironically, in one study that compared physically fit female subjects, the tested women appeared to have better heat tolerance than the control male population.[7]

When women who are trained for long-distance running are compared with matched nonathletic women, the trained women show a significantly enhanced ability to handle heat stress.[5] Thus, the properly conditioned woman apparently has an adequate ability to handle the thermal stress of long-distance running. Of course, even well-conditioned female as well as male runners must be wary of lack of heat acclimatization in distance running. An unusually warm and humid April Boston Marathon in 1976 took a terrible toll on northern runners who were cardiovascularly and musculoskeletally fit, but not heat acclimatized; their counterparts from warmer climates were little affected.

In summary, then, recent studies have shown that the physiologic response of highly trained women to endurance stress is similar to that of their male counterparts and far exceeds that of the

Fig. 9.1: Shin splints in a young female runner who began rapid hill training over a three-week period.

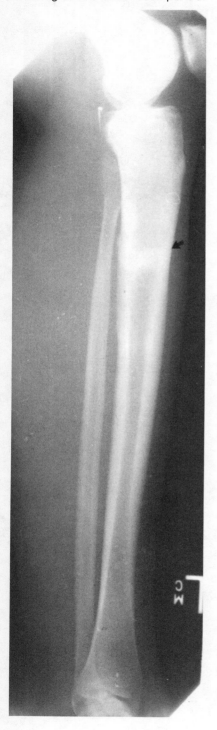

a.

Table 9.1
Women's Marathon Record Times (1967-1978)[16]

Year	Winning Time	Name of Winner (Country)
1967	3:15:22	Maureen Wilton (Canada)
1967	3:07:26	Anni Pede-Erdkamp (W Ger)
1970	3:02:53	Caroline Walker (US)
1971	3:01:42	Beth Bonner (US)
1971	3:00:35	Sara Berman (US)
1971	2:55:22	Beth Bonner (US)
1971	2:49:40	Cheryl Bridges (US)
1973	2:46:36	Miki Gorman (US)
1974	2:46:24	Chantal Langlace (Fr)
1974	2:43:54	Jacqueline Hansen (US)
1975	2:42:24	Liane Winters (W Ger)
1975	2:40:15	Christa Vahlensieck (W Ger)
1975	2:38:19	Jacqueline Hansen (US)
1977	2:37:57	Kim Merritt (US)
1977	2:35:15	Chantel Langlace (Fr)
1978	2:34:48	Christa Vahlensieck (W Ger)

untrained and physically unfit man in our society. In a further assault on historic views of male superiority and endurance fitness, Dr. Ernest Von Acken, a German physiologist, suggested that women, in addition to having a higher average percentage of fat in their body weight than do men, may have an enhanced ability to metabolize this body fat.[8] Thus, after two and a half to three hours of endurance stress, when the body supply of both muscle and liver glycogen have been depleted and lipids must be metabolized directly, the female may have a physiologic edge over the male. The main proponent of this view in our country, Dr. Joan Ullyot, herself a world-class marathoner, cites the dramatic performances of women in the ultra-marathon 50-mile competition in recent years.[8] Although this theory has yet to be proved, and although recent studies suggest that the highly trained male and female athlete are similar in their ability to metabolize lipids, such studies serve to further suggest that sex, per se, has little to do with a person's capability for high-level endurance stress. The dramatic and progressive decrease in the women's marathon record over a ten-year period reflects the untapped resources—both athletic and physiologic—in the female running population (Table 9.1).

Menstrual Problems

Studies of menstrual cycles in competitive female athletes suggested that a higher incidence of menstrual irregularity is found in these athletes than in the general population.[9] Amenorrhea and oligomenorrhea have occurred in a variety of situations characterized by loss of body weight and psychological stress.[10] Menstrual abnormalities have been recorded in ballet dancers and female athletes of all types, but endurance sports appear to have a particularly high incidence of these problems. This association may be partially explained by findings from studies being done at Harvard's Laboratory of Reproductive Science. Their studies show that lipid metabolism, and in particular, total percentage of body weight as fat, may be directly related to controlling the menstural cycle.[10] High-endurance athletes, including women, sustain the greatest decrease in total body fat, and this factor alone may explain observations that about one third of competitive female distance runners between age 15 and 45 experience amenorrhea or oligomenorrhea during training.[3] An additional factor may be that running long distances can result in decreased serum levels of pituitary gonadotropins in some women and may directly or indirectly contribute to menstrual irregularity.[11]

Although the long-term effects of these menstrual irregularities in young female athletes is unknown at this time, some reassurance is offered by Eriksson and his colleagues,[12] who did a recent follow-up study of competitive female swimmers in Scandinavia. These athletes were first tested in 1961 after being involved in competitive swimming for an average of 2.5 years. At follow-up, ten years later, all had discontinued high-level training and were indistinguishable physiologically from their less-athletic counterparts. Nine of the 12 had had children.

This type of information is reassuring, but we still cannot be certain that prolonged periods of endurance training accompanied by menstrual irregularities may not adversely affect subsequent gynecologic function. For the present, the safer approach would be to attempt to design training regimens and nutritional programs that avoid this development in the highly competitive female athlete.

Running Injuries

As women have become more active participants in running, some observers claim that they have a higher incidence of injuries from running than do

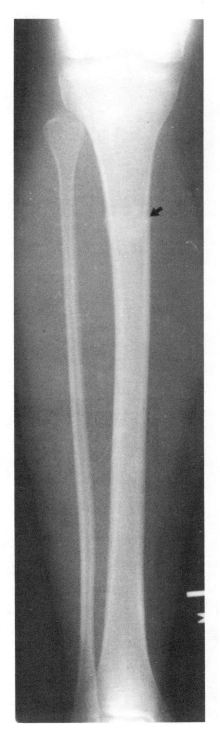

b.

men. Although this clinical observation has often been made by physicians caring for runners, clear support for this claim, based on sound epidemiologic information, is not available.[1,13]

Our own experience with sports injuries in women suggests that, although the rate of injury in certain women's sports programs, including running, may be relatively higher than that of similar men's programs at the initiation of such programs, this phenomenon is more likely due to undertraining and inappropriate training of a relatively greater number of under-conditioned and novice female athletes, than due to any real sexual difference in risk of injury from running.

Two examples that support this view come to mind. Four years ago, when women first began to play rugby football in the Boston area, the rate of overuse injuries from running training of these new ruggers was surprisingly high, and was actually greater than that of impact injuries sustained in this vigorous contact sports. This year, overuse injuries in these athletes are now at a minimum, reflecting, we believe, progressive improvement in the fitness level of the players as well as a more appropriate matching of training rate and intensity.[1]

Our second example comes from the previously cited Bonnie Bell championship races held in Boston since 1977. In 1978, when we had the opportunity to provide the medical supervision for this race, seven stress fractures directly attributable to this competition were identified after the race. Last year, with more entrants, we identified only one stress fracture resulting from the race.

Running, in particular, carries with it the potential for overuse injuries from the repetitive impact between foot and ground. The female runners appeared to be sustaining more than their share of these "microtrauma" injuries—including stress fractures, chondromalacia patella, multiple tendinitides, bursitis about the hip and knee, plantar fasciitis, and the ubiquitous shin splints (Fig. 9.1).

The occurrence of a given overuse injury in a given athlete at a specific time is usually the result of the interaction of several factors: an error in training, such as too much too fast; anatomic malalignment of the bones or joints, including the result of previous injury; imbalance of the muscle-tendon units of the extremity, either in flexibility or strength; improper equipment, such as poorly

Lyle Micheli, M.D.

Table 9.2

Risk Factors in Lower Extremity Overuse Injuries in Runners[17]

1. Training errors, including abrupt changes in intensity, duration, or frequency of training.

2. Musculotendinous imbalance—of strength, flexibility or bulk.

3. Anatomical malalignment of the lower extremities, including differences in leg lengths, abnormalities of rotation of the hips, position of the kneecap, and bow legs, knock knees, or flat feet.

4. Improper footwear: improper fit, inadequate impact absorbing material, excessive stiffness of the sole, and/or insufficient support of hindfoot.

5. Changes in running surface: concrete pavement versus asphalt, versus running track, versus dirt or grass.

6. Associated disease state of the lower extremity, including arthritis, poor circulation, old fracture, or other injury.

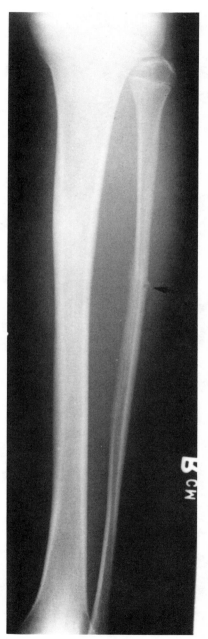

Fig. 9.2 Proximal fibula stress fracture in a young female "speed" runner. Note adjacent tibial sclerosis, the probable site of a prior tibial stress fracture.

constructed running shoes; or change in running surface, such as from dirt or grass to concrete. For the past two and a half years, we have used a simple checklist incorporating six possible causative factors in assessing each overuse injury seen in our own Sports Medicine Clinic, and have attempted to determine which risk factors were primary or secondary in the occurrence of a given injury (Table 9.2).

Female runners, particularly the newer ones, appear to be sustaining these injuries in high numbers. In the past, the relatively low level of athletic training and physical activity of women in our society rendered them significantly less fit. Cardiovascular fitness can be reached in a matter of months when a person is engaged in a fitness program. On the other hand, the musculoskeletal system and, in particular, the bones of the extremeities take much longer to remodel and strengthen themselves in response to increased physical demands.[14] Two of these overuse syndromes, in particular, are presently occurring with greater frequency in our female athletes. Although the explanation, at least in part, may be related to differences in athletic preparation and training, other factors may be working.

We did a prospective causative assessment of 53 stress fractures diagnosed in our Sports Medicine Clinic over a seven-month period (Fig. 9.2). Of these fractures, 18 occurred in men and 29 in women, whereas during the same period, only 40% of our clinic population was female. We cannot know, of course, the relative population at risk during the same period; ie, the numbers of men and women of similar age participating in running in the Boston area, but these data suggested that women were sustaining a higher rate of stress fractures than men in association with running.[15]

The other condition that is seen with a higher frequency than expected in young women athletes and runners is chondromalacia patella, or extensor mechanism stress syndrome. Once again, our ongoing prospective studies on the causative factors working in this condition often include an error in training or an associated direct blow to the extensor mechanism that initiates these symptoms. In addition, many of these athletes will have one or more of the anatomic malalignments of the lower extremity, including femoral anteversion, patella alta, genu valgum with tibia vara, or pes planus. Also associated with this condition in these women is imbalance of the muscle tendon units, especially relatively tight heelcords, perhaps reflecting the greater use by women of higher heeled shoes.

The high occurrence of chondromalacia patella in women has been suggested to be related to the greater width of the female pelvis compared with that of the male.[13] We have been unable to substantiate this finding. A comparison of the distance between the femoral head and the valgus angle at the knees taken from orthoroentgenogram studies of 25 men and 25 women from the Growth Study Clinic of our own hospital failed to show a significant difference between male and female, particularly when further compared by body weight.

We believe that the relatively higher incidence of this compaint in the female running population is related primarily to training error and lack of long-term running conditioning. We have also been impressed with the high incidence of musculoskeletal imbalances, such as relative weakness of the quadriceps muscle, and tightness of the hamstrings and gastroc-soleus muscles in these athletes.

We have used a combined therapeutic approach in this population to manage patello-femoral stress syndromes in association with running. A specific strengthening and stretching program to compensate for musculotendinous imbalance is instituted. The program consists of static straight-leg-raising exercises done in a progressive resistive fashion with the patient in a semi-Fowler's

Lyle Micheli, M.D.

position, supine and resting on the elbows. The exercise is done with the knee in full extension, with slow elevation of the extended leg to 45°. With this exercise, most of these patients will experience a significant decrease in pain and other complaints related to the extensor mechanism when they are able to lift 10 to 12 pounds in three sets of 10 repetitions. We maintain this program of progressive resistive exercises until the range of 18 to 25 pounds is reached, depending on the size and age of the patient. This level of resistance is then maintained for a minimum of six months. Dynamic resistive exercise to either quadriceps or hamstrings are not begun until the static straight-leg-raising program can be done without pain and without quadriceps lag in the range of 15 to 18 pounds.

In those patients with significant anatomic malalignment, we have also used orthotic devices combining forefoot and hindfoot posting to alter the ground-foot impact. We are uncertain as yet whether these orthotic devices serve primarily to compensate for anatomic malalignment, to provide additional heel cushioning, or to alter the time course of impact absorption by the lower extremity. We use only flexible orthotics for any condition in the female distance runner. Using this combined approach of exercises with or without orthotic devices, we have been able to successfully manage more than 90% of our young women patients with patello-femoral stress syndromes.[15]

Our own clinical experience with women's running injuries suggests that careful attention to slow and progressive training, in addition to instruction in running technique, is of prime importance in preventing these injuries. Next in importance is increasing the muscular strength and endurance of the back and lower extremities by means of resistive weight training and progressively intensified running training. As important, despite the somewhat increased general flexibility of women as compared with that of men, is attention to improving the flexibility of the lower extremities in these female runners through systematic stretching exercises. Although the overall flexibility of women may in general be greater than that of men, the gastroc-soleus mechanism in particular appears to be tighter in the woman than the man, and requires special attention in the female runner.

References

1. Micheli LJ: Injuries to female athletes. Surgical Rounds 44-55, May, 1979.
2. American College of Sports Medicine: Opinion Statement; The participation of the female athlete in long-distance running. Med Sci Sports 11:NO 4 (Winter, 1979) suppl ix-xi.
3. Wilmore JH, Brown HC: Physiological profiles of women distance runners. Med Sci Sports 6:178-81, 1974.
4. Gilofolvi CV, et al: Work-heat tolerance of distance runners. Ann NY Acad Sci 301:139-50, 1977.
5. Drinkwater BL: Physiological responses of women to exercise. Exercise Sports Sci Rev 1:125-153, 1973.
6. Wells CL: Sexual differences in heat stress response—do they exist? Phys Sports Med 5:78-90, 1977.
7. Weinman KP, Slabochova EM, Bernauer T, et al: Reactions of men and women to repeated exposure to humid heat. J Appl Physiol 22:533-538, 1967.
8. Ullyot J: Woman's secret weapon: fat. Runners World 22-23, 1974.
9. Erdelyi GJ: Effects of exercise on the menstrual cycle. Phys Sports Med 4:79-81, 1976.
10. Frisch RE, McArthur JW: Menstrual cycles: fatness as a determinant of minimum weight for height necessary for their maintenance or onset. Science 185:949-951, 1974.
11. Dale E, Gerloch DH, Martin DE, et al.: Physical fitness profiles and reproductive physiology of the female distance runner. Phys Sports Med 83-95, 1979.
12. Eriksson BO, Engstrom I, Karlberg P, et al: Long-term effect of previous swim training in girls. A 10-year follow-up of the "Girl Swimmers." Acta Paediatr Scand 67:285-292, 1978.
13. Haycock CE, Gillette JV: Susceptibility of women athletes to injury. Myths vs. Reality. JAMA 236:163-165, 1976.
14. Carter D, Spengler DM: Mechanical properties and composition of cortical bone. Clin Orth Rel Res 135:192-217, 1978.
15. Micheli LJ, Stanitski CL: Lateral retinacular release for parapatellar knee pain. Am J Sports Med (in press, 1981).
16. Kuscsik N: The history of women's participation in the marathon. Ann NY Acad Sci 301:862-876, 1977.
17. Micheli LJ, Santopietro FJ, Gerbino, PG et al: Etiologic assessment of overuse stress fractures in athletes. Nova Scotia Med Bulletin, April/June 1980, pp. 43-47.

Lyle Micheli, M.D.

10

Neurophysiology of Stretching

William D. Stanish, MD., F.R.C.S.(C), F.A.C.S.

Introduction

Historically, dancers and athletes have used techniques of stretching to enhance flexibility. These elite performers were intuitively aware that inadequate precompetition warm-up, including stretching, would impair body movement. Also, they perceived, albeit unscientifically, that improper stretching of soft tissues could lead to early fatigue, muscle soreness, and frequently, injury. The pre-performance ritual of muscle stretching for the ballerina has persisted to this day and clearly remains of unquestioned value.

The scientific arena of sports medicine, however, has approached stretching for flexibility differently (Fig. 10.1).

In the past, high school, collegiate, and professional athletic teams customarily spent relatively brief periods for pregame warm-up. Furthermore, most athletes were sometimes totally idle during specific games or practices but were expected to be totally prepared from a muscle-tendon standpoint when summoned for action. Indeed, performances were hampered and injuries were frequent when these essentially unprepared athletes were sent into competition. Epidemiologically, soft-tissue strains, or pulls, are still the most common injuries seen by sports medicine physicians.

The increasing prominence of sports medicine and sports science in the past 15 years has generated an attempt to provide a more scientific understanding of athletic performance and injury prevention. Fundamental to this renewed, and sometimes political, quest for enhancing athletic output has been research into the area of muscle and tendon mechanics. These moving units were,

Fig. 10.1: Stretching athlete

and still are, studied under varying static and dynamic circumstances so that we may understand more fully the traditionally appreciated value of warm-up and flexibility training. Of course, as with most research of this type, a proverbial Pandora's box has been opened. As more answers were sought regarding scientific stretching, more questions arose. Even now, only the surface is scratched in our attempt to add a scientific basis for stretching to enhance flexibility. Contemporary research in sports science has defined and elucidated satisfactorily how best to build strength and power. Comparable definitions, however, do not exist for stretching. The collective reviews of Wiechec and Krusen[1] and Holland[2] were valuable in pointing out the discrepancies in the research, but certain consistencies did exist. For instance, enhanced flexibility was found to be sport-specific, amplifying the fact that some athletes could be extremely flexible though the shoulders but very tight in the hip flexors and ankle regions. These excellent reviews also dispelled the concept that weight lifters became muscle-bound and sacrificed flexibility. Indeed, weight lifters and wrestlers have been reported to be remarkably flexible.[3]

In this chapter, I will discuss the practical techniques of stretching for flexibility and also present the current knowledge on the basic physiology of muscle and tendon under stress. Many points are theoretical; however, the ingredients of this chapter are the summations of research to date on the subject of flexibility, augmented with personal clinical experience.

Muscle-Tendon Unit
At Rest

The classical macrostructure of muscle has been more than adequately described in textbooks and manuscripts. Little material, however, is available on those structural elements within muscle that are responsible for its elastic properties. In 1938, A.V. Hill[4] suggested by theory that muscle possessed two components responsible for its elastic recoil characteristics: an actively contracting component and a passive elastic element located in series.

Further research demonstrated that the components of elasticity, acting in parallel with the contracting machinery, were present in the sarcolemma and fascia. D.K. Hill[5] in 1968, and Huxley and Simmons[6] showed that this characteristic of

William D. Stanish, M.D.

elasticity of muscle is a function of the cross-bridges between actin and myosin (Fig.10.2).

The muscle at rest can be clinically appreciated as a soft tissue with a constant desire to shorten. Athletic activities producing muscle hypertrophy will predictably produce transient, and sometimes permanent, muscle contracture, coupled with the subjective feeling of tightness. It has been our experience that if contraction is allowed to persist, the contracted soft tissue muscle, and tendon will be susceptible to injury when flexibility is demanded in the athletic challenge. Muscle and tendon are less likely to break down if their inherent characteristics of elasticity are consistently trained through stretching exercises.

Tendons have been singularly neglected in much of the clinical and research material related to flexibility training. Tendon injuries, however, are far more frequent than intrinsic muscle injuries with athletes. Since the work of Hill[7,8] in 1950, researchers have generally agreed that the elastic elements of the tendon component of the muscle-tendon unit exist intrinsically within the tendon and act in series with the contracting component of the functioning muscle-tendon complex.

It is beyond the scope of this chapter to discuss in depth the complex structure and mechanical properties of tendon. The interested reader is referred to the works of Harkness[9] and Viidik.[10,11]

Cross-sectioning of the tendon reveals progressively smaller subunits decreasing in diameter from the tendon bundle to the fibril, microfibril, and the smallest subunit, trophocollagen. The tendon fascicle is composed of many fibers, and in the unstretched condition it has a pleated, wavy appearance that disappears when the fascicle is stretched. This wavy configuration is due to the elastin content of the tendon, present either at the fiber level, or in the endotenon, which surrounds the fascicle. (Fig. 10.3)

Experimentally, when a tendon is stretched the resultant stess (ie, the load over a cross-sectional area) is not a simple linear function of the strain (ie, the increase in length over the original length x 100) applied. Stress of up to 1.5% results in little rise in strain within the tendon. The elongation is due to stretching of the elastin fibers, resulting in straightening of the wavy construction, possibly absorbing potentially damaging shock loads within musculature and skeleton. Within this elastic zone, tension is also related to the rate of strain. If the tendon is stretched rapidly, higher

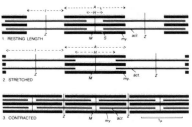

Fig. 10.2: The organization of striated muscle in longitudinal section under electron microscopy, showing the changes during stretch and contraction. 1) Elements at resting length in the body; 2) after passive stretch; and 3) after isotonic contraction to 40% of maximum. During passive stretch the actin filaments are partly withdrawn from the A band. In contraction the actin filaments are drawn into the A band. **Abbreviations:** A, anisotrophic (dark) band; act, actin filament; H, H zone; I,isotrophic (light) band; M, M line; my, myosin filament; Z, Z line. (Modified from Young JZ: The Life of Mammals and Clinical Physiology, Campbell EJM, Dickinson CJ, and Slater JDH (eds).)

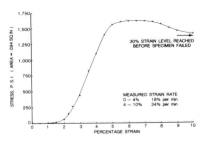

Fig. 10.3: Stress-strain curve for Achille's tendon from a 54 year old woman. Specimen was tested in Ringer's solution at 37° C, 24 hours postmortem.

strains will be induced than those induced during a slow stretch.

The quality of the elastic compliance of a muscle-tendon unit is proportional to the ratio of muscle to tendon in the contractural unit. For example, experiments with dogs have demonstrated the higher level of elasticity in the sartorius, which is muscle along its entire length with very little tendon, in contrast with the gastrocnemius, which has a long tendinous component.

Clinically, as previously stated, we have noted greater numbers of tendon injuries than intrinsic muscle breakdowns, suggesting that muscle, with its superior inherent compliance, is less likely than tendon to be disrupted under comparable stress.

In Action

The literature abounds with reviews of the mechanics of concentric, isometric, and eccentric modes of exercise. Nevertheless, only a few scientists have attempted to elucidate the behavior of the elastic components of the muscle-tendon unit under varying conditions. The mechanisms and techniques of improving muscle-tendon compliance are examined here under the assumption that the neurochemical status of the contractural unit is normal. The specifics of muscle contraction will be discussed later in this chapter.

When muscle shortens during concentric movement, in most instances positive work and heat are the predictable byproducts. During that type of muscle shortening, the elastic components (set in parallel and vital to muscle compliance) shorten simultaneously. On the other hand, when the muscle-tendon unit undergoes isometric or eccentric contraction, the elastic components of the muscle and tendon become strained like a spring and are said to be performing negative work. This negative work theory has experimentally and practically been exploited to enhance efficiency of the functioning muscle-tendon unit. Athletes who throw, jumpers, and even weight-lifters have improved their performances by maximizing the characteristics of elastic recoil that exist in muscle and tendon. Training these components with stretching techniques to enhance flexibility allows greater deformity (strain) of the muscle and tendon just before the abrupt shortening fundamental to throwing or jumping. The dividends from this stretched-shortened (abrupt) technique includes superior force, power, and performance.

William D. Stanish, M.D.

Also, in my experience, enhanced flexibility achieved through stretching allows the muscle-tendon unit greater properties of compliance. For a given load, this greater compliance allows the muscle to deform and recoil, achieving the ideals of improved work without structural breakdown (Fig. 10.4).

The tendon under stress behaves in a particularly interesting fashion. As previously stated, stresses of 1.5% cause a minimal rise in strain within the tendon. Stresses of 2.0 to 3.0% exceed the tendon elastic limit, resulting in permanent elongation and loss of the wavy pleating, causing irreversible structural damage. This structural damage is directly related to the elastic fibers, which have a lower tensile strength than collagen.

As the tendon is further stretched, stresses of 3.5 to 5.0% result in a linear rise in strain. The amount of elongation is determined by the behavior of the collagen alone under tension. Stresses greater than 5% rupture the collagen fibers, whereas complete tendon rupture does not occur until 10 to 30% stress exists.

The collagen fibers are not uniform in diameter or in tensile strength throughout the tendon. Consequently, some weaker fibers will rupture at tensions less than the reported maximum strength of the whole tendon ($5\text{-}10 \text{ kg/mm}^2$). Maximum values reflect the strength of the strongest fibers only. The tensile strength at the interfaces between the tendon body and the bone or muscle are reported to be less than the isolated tendon body preparation. Obviously, therefore, lesions to tendon-collagen ultrastructure may occur with tensions less than the reported maximal tensile values.

Tension produced during a concentric muscle contraction is transmitted via the tendon to the limb of its insertion. The tension produced is inversely related to the velocity of shortening, with maximum tension being produced during isometric contraction when the velocity of shortening is zero. The resting elastic component of the tendon is capable of absorbing any sudden jerking of the limb and the maximum tension is monitered by the golgi tendon apparatus. This golgi tendon apparatus reflexly inhibits agonist muscle groups if the tension is excessive. The maximum isometric tension is well below the tensile strength of tendon. Kamen reported values for eccentric tension production of 6-11% greater than for maximum isometric contraction.[12] Harkness pro-

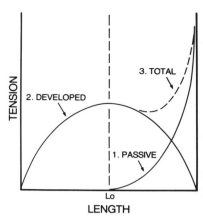

Fig. 10.4: Relationship between the length of a muscle fiber in tension. Curve 1 shows the result of applying passive stretch to a resting muscle until a peak tension develops; curve 2 shows the tension that is produced by contraction of a muscle after it has been stretched; and curve 3 is the summation of these two curves. (Modified after Duthie RB, and Ferguson AB: Orthopedic Surgery, seventh edition.)

posed that eccentric loads may be as much as twice maximum isometric values if applied rapidly.[9] Therefore, neither concentric nor isometric contractions appear to be likely causes of tendon breakdown.

Similarly, passive stretch of a tendon while the muscle is relaxed within physiological limits cannot be considered damaging to the tendon because the resultant strain is accommodated by the rather remarkable extensibility of relaxed muscle.

The Practical Value of Enhanced Flexibility Through Stretch

Clearly, enhanced flexibility has allowed athletes to achieve superior levels of athletic performance. Theoretically, according to the available literature, these improved performances have been accomplished partially as a consequence of training techniques to maximize the elastic recoil properties of muscle-tendon units.

Simultaneous with the concern for enhancing athletic performances, concern is growing over the upsurge of injuries secondary to recreational and sport challenges. The sport medicine literature is replete with reports of epidemiological injury profiles of various sports. Common to all these statistical analyses is the fact that soft-tissue injuries are most frequently encountered by sport physicians and thus, are a major concern. Compounding the issue is the undeniable fact of body physiology that "form follows function" and that complete rest for an injured athlete often leads to devastating atrophy. Also, surgeons are recognizing the limitations of surgical intervention in the management of soft-tissue injuries that are commonly microscopic.

Soft-tissue injuries to the muscle-tendon effector unit can frequently be prevented with structured flexibility conditioning programs. Various types of stretching programs have been devised and will be described later; however, the common denominator of them all is enhancing flexibility.

Once a muscle or tendon has been injured the pathophysiology of soft-tissue repair is always the same, with collagen being the final byproduct. For a high-level athlete that circumstance is fundamentally less than ideal because of the lack of inherent elasticity within the proliferating fibrous wad or scar. Thus, our practice has been to use graduated stretching techniques during the post-

William D. Stanish, M.D.

injury rehabilitating program for muscle and tendon trauma (Fig. 10.5).

Flexibility training is certainly not the panacea in the prevention or treatment of muscle and tendon injuries. Nevertheless, coupled with astute progressive strength retraining and muscle rebalancing, we can avoid many of these common soft-tissue injuries.

Physiology of Stretching

A clear scientific explanation of the physiology of stretching continues to elude contemporary research. Many creditable laboratories have worked tediously to elucidate the pathomechanics of stretching in an attempt to offer practical advice and explanations regarding the most effective techniques of enhancing flexibility. Their findings somewhat clarify the physiology of stretching for flexibility. Histologically, the muscle includes the extrafusal component that can be large or relatively small, depending on the task of that particular muscle. Simplistically, muscles are essentially divided into two fiber types, which from a laboratory standpoint, are differentiated by histochemical means. From a clinical standpoint, those muscle fibers that are slow-twitch in nature, are extremely high in aerobic potential, and carry the appropriate aerobic enzymatic package. The second fiber type, which stains according to its enzymes, is identified as being critical to aerobic function and is fast twitch in nature. Indeed, antigravity muscles, which are slow-moving, are traditionally slow-twitch in nature and have great endurance capacity. We know that these two fiber types are genetically determined and training is of little value in altering proportional fiber types.

These muscles are fired and controlled by rather complex neural influences. They work in parallel with the intrafusal muscle spindle that controls muscle tone. This unit sets the muscle in readiness for work. The intrafusal system conducts information to the central nervous system through the afferent unit. This unit is extremely responsive to passive stretch. As a passive stretch of the extrafusal muscle system occurs, the intrafusal system is triggered and the afferent unit stimulates an alpha efferent to facilitate contraction of the extrafusal system with a complementary inhibition to the antagonist muscle. The intrafusal system is complemented by a type 2 afferent that paradoxically conducts at a slower or weaker rate

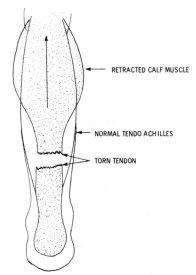

Fig. 10.5: Ruptured Achilles tendon

RETRACTED CALF MUSCLE

NORMAL TENDO ACHILLES

TORN TENDON

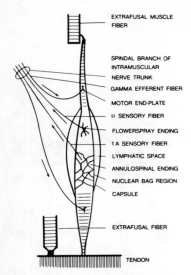

EXTRAFUSAL MUSCLE FIBER

SPINDAL BRANCH OF INTRAMUSCULAR NERVE TRUNK

GAMMA EFFERENT FIBER

MOTOR END-PLATE

II SENSORY FIBER

FLOWERSPRAY ENDING

1 A SENSORY FIBER

LYMPHATIC SPACE

ANNULOSPINAL ENDING

NUCLEAR BAG REGION

CAPSULE

EXTRAFUSAL FIBER

TENDON

Fig. 10.6: Intrafusal muscle system (Modified after Ganong: Review of Medical Physiology, third edition, Lange, 1967, and Chusid JG and McDonald JJ: Correlative Neuroanatomy and Functional Neurology, Lange, 1967.)

and coaxes the antagonist to fire, thus inhibiting the extrafusal agonist system. The intrafusal system, having been stretched, is encouraged back into readiness by the gamma efferent system. If for any reason the gamma system is obliterated, then muscle tone is rapidly reduced and no reflex (primary monosynaptic) can occur (Fig. 10.6).

Other structures within muscle units that are responsible for muscle tone are the golgi tendon organs (GTO). The GTO exist in series and require a major effort or contraction (usually voluntary) to be stimulated. They have an extremely high threashold, and respond most effectively with a human voluntary contraction of significant magnitude. As the extrafusal system contracts, the GTO fire and relax the extrafusal complex and simultaneously fire the antagonist system. If the stretch is too great, then the GTO fire simultaneously to the agonist and the antagonist muscle groups, yielding dual inhibition to both these units. The entire muscle complex will reduce their electromyographic activity. The GTO exist primarily in the slow-twitch units as well as in ligaments. They respond readily to movement but quickly become inactive once a new position has been achieved.

With this material, the proposed neural physiological features of various stretching techniques should be easily understood. In 1976, Jacobs[13] reviewed the physiology of slow active stretching and emphasized the intrinsic merits of that technique in contrast to passive stretching. Theoretically, passive stretching operates on the premise that the tension increase in the muscle-tendon unit (ie, the athlete's extremity passively forced by another person or machine) activates the GTO, which inhibit the extrafusal fibers via the alpha impulses. An important point to remember is that the alpha motor neurons and the GTO lie in series. Jacobs[13] elaborated that passive stretching should be condemned because:

1. Passive stretching can be painful;
2. Very little flexibility is retained with this technique;
3. Extreme stretch could cause the GTO to fire— however, the GTO are most sensitive to an active contraction;
4. If the passive stretching is done too rapidly, the muscle spindle complex would be activated and would contract rather than relax the muscle to be stretched.

William D. Stanish, M.D.

Active stretching offers the benefits of being voluntary, thus decreasing the likelihood of soft-tissue damage. De Vries reported that voluntary static stretching effectively reduced muscle spasm and soreness and enhanced flexibility.[14]

Many authors suggest that fundamental to this technique of stretching is the fact that movement encourages reciprocal inhibition and relaxation in the antagonist. Holt[15] and Jacobs[13] advocated and used variations of this neurophysiological principle, simultaneously improving muscle strength.

As the extrafusal muscle mass sits in readiness to do work, the intrafusal muscle spindle unit, lying in parallel, prepares itself also to moniter the behavior of the extrafusal muscles. For example, as the biceps contracts slowly, the intrafusal muscle spindle sends messages to the spinal cord primarily via the afferent unit. Eccles[16] emphasized that the afferent unit provoked a gamma efferent return to maintain intrafusal muscle integrity; simultaneously, however, the afferent unit provokes through disynaptic connections, inhibition of the antagonistic muscle—in this instance, the triceps. This process, through reciprocal inhibition, may, then, encourage stretching of the antagonist muscle, in this instance, the triceps. For these techniques of stretching to be useful, a slow movement is required (joint motion at 150° per second), rather than a more rapid movement. Fast movements of joints in the range of 270° precludes the reflex inhibition of the antagonist muscle mediated by the afferent unit. Indeed, with a rapid movement, the antagonist will respond with contraction rather than relaxation, thus aborting the effort to achieve stretch.

Holt and others[17] advocated a technique of stretching based on principles detailed by Kabat in 1952. Appreciating that Kabat's original work,[18] proprioceptive neuromuscular fascilitation (PNF), was designed for patients suffering from paralysis, these authors proposed that the same principles could be applied to athletes to enhance their flexibility. Holt advocated that through the 3-S system (scientific stretching for sport) the following factors would be improved (Fig. 10.7a and b).

1. Range of motion compared with results from other techniques;
2. Retention of flexibility;
3. Muscle strength.

Fig. 10.7: Stretching exercise a. A is standing on one foot, both hands on table, body straight, and the leg to be exercised straight and raised as high as possible. P is standing in front of A, holding the exercise leg with both hands, one above the ankle and the other on the foot. A attempts to push the exercise leg to the floor while keeping the knee straight. P resists. After a six-second isometric contraction, A lifts the leg toward the ceiling. P assists with light pressure. b. The procedure is repeated from the new lengthened position. (Taken from Holt L: Scientific Stretching for Sport.)

Neurophysiology of Stretching

The physiology of this type of stretching is described in a monograph by Holt.[15] He explains that with an isometric contraction of a previously passively stretched muscle, a firing of the GTO takes place within that stretched muscle, thus facilitating a relaxation within that group. If a particular muscle is to be stretched, then from a practical standpoint, it should be passively stretched to minimal discomfort and then exposed to an isometric contraction (which facilitates relaxation of the muscle); then further relaxation of the stretched muscle can be achieved if the agonist muscle contracts. This technique exploits the reciprocal innervation and contraction inhibition that was alluded to earlier in the text.

In review, if one stretches an antagonist muscle group and then encourages an isometric contraction within that prestretched muscle, relaxation will be induced within that same muscle and finally, as the agonist (ie, the non-stretched muscle) contracts, the antagonist will relax and stretch even further.

We have found the three-S technique superior in improving flexibility and range of motion. It is essential in using this technique that the athlete is well warmed up, that the movements are done slowly and deliberately and that the athlete's discomfort is closely monitered. The entire process must be totally pain-free.

References

1. Wiechec FJ, Krusen FH: A new method of joint measurement and a review of the literature. Am J Surg 43:659-668, 1939.
2. Holland GJ: The physiology of flexibility: A review of the literature. Kinesiology Review 1968, p 49.
3. Leighton L: A study of the effect of progressive weight training on flexibility. Physical Mental Rehab 28:101, 1964.
4. Hill AV: The heat shortening and the dynamic constance of muscle. Proc Royal Soc B 126:136-195, 1938.
5. Hill DK: Tension to interaction between the sliding filaments of resting striated muscle. The effect of stimulation. J Physiol London 199:367-684, 1968.
6. Huxley AF, Simmons RM: Mechanical properties of the cross-bridges of frog striated muscle. J Physiol London 218:59P-60P, 1971.
7. Hill AV: The series elastic component of muscle. Proc Royal Soc B 137:27-280, 1950.
8. Hill AV: The mechanics of active muscle. Proc Royal Soc B 141:104-117, 1953.
9. Harkness RD: Mechanical properties of collagenous

Special thanks to Howard Lamb Research Fellow, Nova Scotia Sports Medicine Clinic.

William D. Stanish, M.D.

tissues. In Gould BS (ed): Treatise on Collagen, Vol 2, pt A. Academic Press, 1968, pp 247-310.

10. Viidik A: On the correlation between structure and mechanical function of soft connective tissues. Verh Anat Ges 72:75-89, 1978.

11. Viidik A: The effect of training on the tensile strength of isolated rabbit tendons. Scand Plactic Reconstr Surg 1:141-147, 1967.

12. Kamen G: Serial isometric contraction under imposed myotatic stretch conditions in high strength and low strength men. European J Applied Physilogy 41:73-82, 1979.

13. Jacobs M: Neurophysiological implications of the slow act of stretching. Correlative Therapeutic J 30:151-154, 1976.

14. DeVries HA: Evaluation of static stretching procedures for improvement of flexibility. Res Quart 33:222-229, 1962.

15. Holt LE: Scientific Stretching for Sport. Sport Research Ltd, 1973.

16. Eccles JC: The Physiology of Synapsis. Berlin, Springer-Verlag, 1964.

17. Holt LE, Kaplin HM, Okita T, Hoshiko M: The influence of antagonistic contraction in hip position of the responses of agonistic muscle. Arch Physical Med Rehabil 50:279-283 passim, 1969.

18. Kabat H: Studies of neuromuscular dysfunction—The role of central facilitation in restoration of motor function in paralysis. Arch Phys Med 33:523, 1952.

11

Flexibility Conditioning for Running

Virginia B. Davis, L.P.T., M.A

Types of Stretching

Today, the sport of jogging seems to have captured the fancy of hundreds of thousands of individuals. Persons who were previously uninterested in physical activity or sport have taken to the city sidewalks, parks, and country backroads. Some of these enthusiasts were one-time high school or collegiate athletes, but the vast majority have never before participated in athletic endeavors to any great extent. They are encouraged in their sport by each other and by the proliferation of magazine "how-to" articles. Unfortunately, there seem to be as many different "how-tos" as there are authors, and the guidelines purported are often not founded on sound physiological principles.

It is no wonder then that our medical offices and physical therapy clinics are filled with seemingly healthy persons with a variety of orthopedic complaints. We find that many of their problems are related to inadequate preparation for the sport, including inadequate flexibility.

Traditionally, flexibility routines have centered around ballistic and static types of stretching.

Ballistic Stretching

This type of stretching is characterized by bouncing or quick, jerking movements in an attempt to produce maximum muscle lengthening. Physiologically, however this method has been demonstrated sometimes to do more to impede motion than to improve it. The muscle to be lengthened is quickly stretched, thus invoking a stretch reflex that then produces a recoil, or shortening reaction in the muscle, which actually reduces its overall length.

Static Stretching

This method of stretching emphasizes a gradual lengthening of a muscle group in an attempt to gain maximum length with as little accompanying muscle activity as possible, thus avoiding possible reflex stimulation of the involved muscle.

Neither of the above techniques use central mechanisms to achieve maximum muscle lengthening for improved flexibility. Types of stretch that are founded on neurophysiological principles are as follows:

3-S Stretching[1]

The muscles to be stretched are first contracted isometrically in a lengthened position, followed by concentric contraction of the opposite muscle group along with slight assistance from a partner. This method utilizes the reciprocal innervation and contraction inhibition described in detail by Holt in his monograph *Scientific Stretching for Sport*.[1] Stretching exercises as presented by Holt require the assistance of a partner.

Combo Stretching

This method combines the gradual lengthening of the muscle along with simultaneous isometric contraction of the opposing muscle group to produce relaxation in muscles being stretched, and further increase muscle length. This method utilizes the neurological principle of reciprocal innervation as described by Kabat[2] and further explained by Knott and Voss in their book *Proprioceptive Neuromuscular Facilitation*.[3] Assistance of a partner is not necessary with this method.

Holt's 3-S approach has been shown to be superior to both ballistic and static stretching methods. Athletes rapidly increased flexibility when exercises were carried out exactly as described by Holt, with participants working in pairs. Certainly some muscles cannot be adequately stretched without the assistance of a partner (hip flexors, low back extensors), but many runners or joggers prepare for their sport alone. The Combo stretching method has been developed out of the need for runners to be able to stretch independently while taking advantage of central mechanisms to achieve maximum flexibility. This method has been found to be superior to both ballistic and static stretching in producing increased flexibility.

Virginia B. Davis, L.P.T.

Techniques of Stretching

One does not prepare for running simply by running, just as a football player would not take to the field for a season opener without benefit of off-season training. A person who does not prepare for running by a program designed to promote muscle balance for strength and flexibility may be asking for a great many aches and pains due to musculoskeletal imbalance.

Central mechanisms play a paramount role in the fundamental aspects of exercise. Physical therapists have long used neurological treatment techniques in their practices, but only recently have these techniques been espoused for use in athletic conditioning.

The specific techniques of stretching to be illustrated in this text incorporate neurological principles to promote maximal muscle lengthening. Exercises have been designed specifically to meet the needs of runners. These exercises have been used in our physical therapy and running clinics in New Orleans as a part of our treatment regime, and also as a part of our program to prepare individuals for running by promoting the full range of motion necessary to prevent injury.

The limiting factor for flexibility is often the length of the muscles that are antagonistic to a specific movement. For example, if one first flexes his hip maximally with the knee fully extended and then flexes his knee, additional hip flexion may be appreciated. The initial hip-flexion limitation was due to the limited length of the hamstring muscles.

The converse is also true and may be appreciated by the runner who flexes his hip after toe-off with his knee simultaneously flexed. As the knee is extended towards heel strike, extension may be inhibited by the amount of hip flexion if limited hamstring flexibility exists. Inadequate hamstring flexibility in this instance may prove to be a mechanism for injury to the hamstring itself, the low back, the knee, the lower leg or the foot. This illustrates the importance of examining joint motions occurring simultaneously during running when evaluating flexibility.

We have found that many running problems center around the low back, hip flexors, adductors, hamstrings, and plantar flexors. The following exercises are presented as a means to promoting flexibility in those specific areas. The exercises do

Fig. 11.1

Fig. 11.1a

Fig. 11.2

Fig. 11.2a

Flexibility Conditioning in Running

149

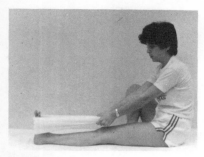

Fig. 11.3

Fig. 11.3a

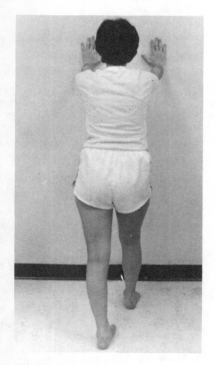

Fig. 11.4

not require special equipment and they may be done in most instances without the assistance of a partner.

Care should be taken that exercises are done as directed. Exercises may be used to gain flexibility as part of a conditioning program, a warm-up/cool-down routine, or a part of a rehabilitation program. In addition, exercises may be combined with other treatment modalities such as application of heat or cold. For example, ice massage or ice towels may be used just before, during, or after stretching.

The number of repetitions of each exercise may vary depending on the purposes of the program: ten repetitions may be adequate to maintain flexibility before and after running, whereas 70 repetitions twice a day of the hamstring stretch is advocated to produce flexibility where severe limitation exists.

Specific Stretching Exercises

Hamstring Stretch (Davis' Combo Stretch).
Sit with the leg to be stretched fully extended and the opposite leg flexed at the hip and knee (Fig. 11.1). 1) Tighten the quadriceps muscle (isometric contraction), 2) dorsiflex the foot maximally, and 3) then reach both hands toward the toes (Fig. 11.1a). Hold for six seconds. Relax. Repeat, each time trying to reach the hands farther towards and then *past* the toes. Do not hang on to the toes. It is extremely important to hold the isometric contraction of the quadriceps while maintaining maximum dorsiflexion throughout the six second stretch, thus allowing reciprocal relaxation of the hamstrings for maximal lengthening.

Hip Adductor and Internal Rotator Stretch (Davis' Combo Stretch).
Sit with the soles of the feet together. Let the knees fall apart as far as possible. Place the hands on the inside of the knees (Fig. 11.2). Attempt to move knees together while resisting movement with hands (isometric contraction). Hold this for six seconds, then let the hands move outward with the knees, assisting as the knees are actively moved farther apart for six seconds (Fig. 11.2a). Relax. Repeat, starting with knees in the new position farther apart and closer to the floor. As this exercise is repeated, the heels should be moved in closer to the body.

Virginia B. Davis, L.P.T.

Plantar Flexor Stretches (Davis' Combo Stretch).

1. Sit with legs extended. Place a towel, stirrup-like, around the ball of *one* foot (Fig. 11.3). Begin with the foot dorsiflexed to a comfortable position and the foot in a neutral position of inversion-eversion. Holding the ends of the towel securely, plantarflex the foot into the towel while not allowing the foot to move (isometric contraction). Hold for six seconds, then actively dorsiflex the foot slowly while assisting the motion with the towel for three seconds (Fig. 11.3a). Relax. Repeat, starting with the foot in increased dorsiflexion. Do not be tempted to do this exercise with both feet simultaneously because flexibility may differ between the right and left legs. Knees should be maintained in complete extension throughout the exercise to ensure maximal stretch of the gastrocnemius muscle.

2. Stand with one foot forward, hip and knee flexed. Hands should be placed against a wall. The toes of both feet should point *straight* forward (Fig. 11.4). Hold the back leg straight by tightening quadriceps muscle (isometric contraction) while lifting toes into maximal extension, thus forcing the heel to the floor while leaning the hips forward (Fig. 11.4a). Hold for six seconds. Relax, then repeat.
Note: Persons with pronated feet may need to "toe in" slightly to insure adequate stretch of the gastroc-soleus muscles.

Fig. 11.4a

Hip Flexors (Holt's 3-S)[1].
Lie prone with the leg to be exercised in a flexed knee position and thigh raised as high as possible. A partner, positioned behind, rests on one knee with the opposite foot on the floor, one hand under the subject's knee, and the other slightly above the buttock (Fig. 11.5). Attempt to pull the knee downward to the floor. The partner resists (isometric contraction). After a six-second isometric contraction, lift the bent leg higher with slight assistance of the partner (Fig. 11.5a). Repeat three more times, each time beginning the procedure from the new length-ened position.

Fig. 11.5

Fig. 11.5a

Low Back Extensors (Holt's 3-S)[1].
Sit with legs straight and trunk flexed comfortably forward as far as possible (Fig. 11.6). The partner kneels behind and slightly to the side and puts his hands on the subject's neck and central portion of the upper back. Attempt to

Flexibility Conditioning in Running

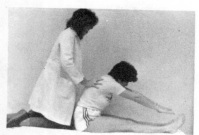

Fig. 11.6

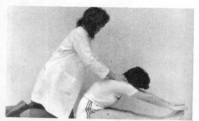

Fig. 11.6a

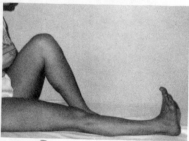

Fig. 11.7

Fig. 11.8

Fig. 11.8a

Fig. 11.9

straighten up (extend trunk).* The partner resists the movement (isometric contraction). After the six-second isometric contraction, pull the trunk down towards the legs with the slight assistance of the partner. (Fig. 11.6a). Repeat, starting from the new lengthened position.

Gross Assessment of Flexibility for Running

The discussion of flexibility and stretching exercises for runners would be incomplete without mention of the simple tests that may be used by the clinician or athlete to determine muscle tightness. Tightness noted on doing any of the tests will point out the necessity for stretching to improve flexibility. Hesitation in embarking on such a stretching program while running increased distances and/or faster times will almost certainly

1. *Plantar Flexors* (Gastrocnemius). Assume supine position. With the knee fully extended, maximally dorsiflex the foot in a neutral position of inversion/eversion. Measure dorsiflexion with long axes along the fifth metatarsal and the fibula. Active dorsiflexion should measure 10° (Fig. 11.7). If less than 10° of active dorsiflexion is present, gastrocnemius tightness exists. Test the opposite leg in the same manner.

2. *Hamstrings.* Assume supine position. Flex one leg to 90° at the hip with the knee flexed. Maintain 90° of hip flexion throughout the test by placing hands around thigh (Fig. 11.8). Extend the flexed knee as far as possible. Measure the angle at the knee to determine hamstring flexibility/tightness (Fig. 11.8a). The long axes are the fibula and the femur. This angle should be 0°. Thus, hamstring tightness is present if the angle is greater than 0°. Test the opposite leg in the same manner.

3. *Combined Hamstring—Plantar Flexor Assessment.* When doing the hamstrings test above, maximally dorsiflex the foot in the neutral position, then extend the knee with the hip held flexed to 90° (Fig. 11.9). Maximal dorsiflexion should be maintained throughout. Now measure the angle at the knee between the long axes of the fibula and femur as a measure of

This exercise should be done with less than maximum effort until the subject is well acquainted with the procedure and confident that no injury will result.

Virginia B. Davis, L.P.T.

combined hamstring-plantar flexor flexibility/ tightness. The angle should be 0° (Fig. 11.9a). If maximal dorsiflexion (as measured in #1) cannot be maintained with maximal knee extension (as measured in #2), combined tightness exists (Fig. 11.9b). Test the opposite leg in the same manner.

4. *Hip Adductors and Internal Rotators.* Sit with the soles of the feet together, heels about six to eight inches from the body, and let knees fall apart towards the floor. Knees should be three inches from the floor (Fig. 11.10). If knees are more than three inches from the floor, a lack of flexibility exists in the muscles being tested (Fig. 11.10a).

5. *Hip Flexors.* Assume supine position. Flex one leg maximally at the hip and knee by pulling the knee to the chest with hands. The opposite leg should remain relaxed, flat on the floor (Fig. 11.11). If the leg is raised from the floor with the action of the opposite, maximally flexed leg, then hip flexor tightness exists in the extended leg (Fig. 11.11a). Test the opposite leg in the same manner.

References

1. Holt LE. Scientific Stretching for Sport (3-S). Biomechanics Laboratory, Dalhousie University, Halifax, Nova Scotia.
2. Kabat H: Studies on neuromuscular dysfunction: XV. Arch Phys Med 33:521-533, 1952.
3. Knott M, Voss D: Proprioceptive Neuromuscular Facilitation. Harper and Row, New York, 1965.

Fig. 11.9a

Fig. 11.9b

Fig. 11.10

Fig. 11.10a

Fig. 11.11

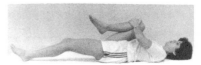

Fig. 11.11a

12

Orthotics

Robert D. D'Ambrosia, M.D.
Roy Douglas, C.P.

Introduction

An orthotic is used to bring the foot into proper alignment when it strikes the ground. The use of orthotics has become popular as a means of preventing and curing the stress-related injuries found in long-distance runners whose malalignment problems become manifested as injuries because of the high forces generated in running. Advocates of orthotics speculate that excessive foot pronation (Fig. 12.1) is the cause of most leg and foot problems among runners. They maintain that proper leg-foot alignment is critically important in running because the force on the foot is much greater in running than in walking; malalignment problems that may have been asymptomatic earlier are believed to be greatly magnified by the increased force. The use of orthotics is therefore espoused as a means of preventing excessive or abnormal pronation while preserving normal resupination.

To understand why some physicians use orthotics and why they are prescribed requires an understanding of the biomechanics of the subtalar joint, the joint the orthotic attempts to control. We shall briefly discuss biomechanics in this chapter, but the reader is referred to Chapter 1 and *The Joints of the Ankle*[1] for more detailed information on the subtalar joint.

Biomechanics of Orthotics

During running, the lower extremity joints not only go through flexion and extension, but also undergo considerable rotation.[1] Such rotation occurs at both the knee and the subtalar joint, not just at the hip (Fig. 12.2). The subtalar joint is an oblique hinge aligned 42° to the horizontal and deviating 16° medially to laterally.[2,3] Inward

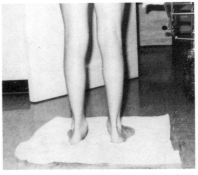

Fig. 12.1: Excessive foot pronation causing symptomatic plantar fasciitis.

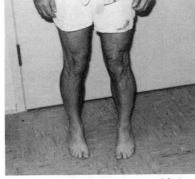

Fig. 12.2: Excessive femoral internal rotation (femoral anteversion) causing intoeing. Note the inward rotation of both patellae, implicating the femur as the cause of intoeing.

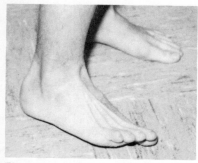

Fig. 12.3: a. Foot pronation. The heel (calcaneus) is everted (valgus). The arch is depressed.

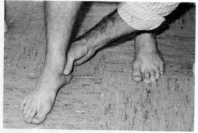

b. Foot supination. The calcaneus is inverted (varus). The arch is elevated.

Fig. 12.4: a. Excessive foot pronation from front.

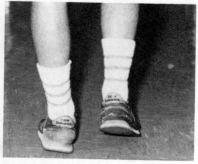

b. Excessive foot pronation from back.

rotatory motion at the subtalar joint is pronation (Fig. 12.3a) and outward rotation is supination (Fig. 12.3b).

Just before initial ground contact the talus is in slight outward rotation and the calcaneus is usually inverted with the foot in slight supination. On ground contact, internal rotation of the tibia occurs, and as the foot becomes loaded, the heel goes into eversion through an inward rotatory motion at the subtalar joint. The subtalar joint, acting as an oblique hinge, translates the internal rotation of the lower extremity into eversion of the calcaneus. As the calcaneus is everted at ground contact, the rest of the foot becomes pronated due to the inward rotatory motion occurring at the subtalar joint. This pronation of the foot unlocks the midtarsal joint, making the foot more flexible so that it can adapt to the underlying surface.

It is this pronation that an orthotic attempts to control. However, if the pronation is controlled completely, the foot becomes rigid and absorbs shock poorly. Therefore, an orthotic attempts to control only an excessive amount of pronation. Pronation is normal and an important factor in enabling the foot and body to absorb the force and shock of impact while running. Pronation results in a flexible transverse tarsal joint, allowing collapse of the longitudinal arch as the foot comes in contact with the ground. The normal factors limiting pronation are largely passive and controlled by supporting ligaments and bone contours in the joints. If pronation is excessive (Fig. 12.4a and b), characterized by a falling over on the medial side of the foot, then supporting ligaments and connective tissue may become strained as excessive stress is placed on them.

In the remaining part of the cycle, once the foot is firmly on the ground, another series of events occurs, beginning with external rotation of the lower extremity. As the tibia rotates externally, the talus at the subtalar joint rotates in the opposite direction so that inversion of the calcaneus occurs concomitantly with supination of the remainder of the foot. Supination stabilizes the transverse tarsal joint, helping to create a rigid longitudinal arch. This stabilization creates a more rigid lever for push-off. Several factors work to help this outward external rotation at the subtalar joint take place. The metarsal break, which has an oblique axis, causes calcaneus inversion and lower extremity external rotation. With toe dorsiflexion during

156

Robert D. D'Ambrosia, M.D., Roy Douglas, C.P.

the latter part of stance phase, the attachment of the plantar aponeurosis around the metatarsal heads elevates the longitudinal arch. Active firing of the intrinsic flexor musculature also helps stabilize the arch.

The mechanisms involved with supination are more active than the process of pronation. The resupination process, which begins in midstance and terminates with the foot acting as a rigid lever at toe-off, is also important in preventing overuse syndromes. If it does not occur normally, it places undo stress on the surrounding ligaments, capsule, and bone.

The advocates of orthotics theorize that overpronation or prolonged pronation greatly increases, both actively and passively, stresses to the supporting structures of the foot. Theoretically, abnormal rotation at the subtalar joint can cause injuries to the posterior tibial tendons, plantar fascia, tendoachilles, and iliotibial band, from stress translated to these structures. Thus by controlling and partially restricting the rotatory motion of the subtalar joint, orthotics can prevent undo stress to the active and passive supporting structures of the foot, ankle, and, indirectly, the knee.

If worn constantly, foot orthotics may cause the muscles and ligaments around the joints to weaken through disuse to the point that the orthotic device could become a detriment rather than an aid to better foot alignment. If worn temporarily, however, during periods of severe or repeated stress such as long-distance running, and if properly fitted, they can help prevent arch breakdown and excessive pronation.

Many contemporary foot orthotics for runners cannot hold the calcaneus in alignment to stabilize the subtalar joint adequately. Not until Henderson and Campbell's device, designed at the University of California Biomechanical Laboratory (UCBL), has there been an effective orthotic designed to control the subtalar joint.[4] An orthotic becomes effective when it creates an inner contour that is capable of giving the architecture of the foot maximum passive support. The orthosis must also be adequately stabilized in the shoe so that it cannot roll into varus or valgus. The UCBL design lends itself well to solving a wide range of malalignment and pressure distribution problems of the foot.[5,6]

Our orthotic design embodies the UCBL

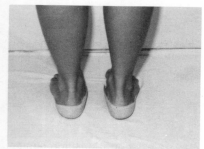

Fig. 12.5: Orthotic firmly gripping the heel of a runner with posterior tibial tendonitis secondary to excessive pronation.

Fig. 12.6: Neutral position standing.

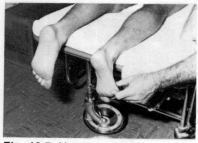

Fig. 12.7: Neutral position prone.

concept of firmly gripping the heel (Fig. 12.5) as the only effective way of controlling the subtalar joint.

Orthotic Casting Technique

To fabricate a proper orthotic, the physician/orthotist must know how to place the foot and subtalar joint in the "neutral position," the position in which the foot functions in its most efficient manner, thereby receiving the least amount of stress from the surrounding joints, ligaments, and tendons. The foot should be positioned so that, with weight bearing, the vertical axis of the heel is parallel to the longitudinal axis of the distal tibia and the plane of the metatarsal heads is perpendicular to the heel. To obtain the neutral position, from which the casting of the foot is made, the person taking the mold of the foot must accurately align the foreleg, heel, and heel-forefoot, which may be done by several techniques. This may be obtained with the patient standing, prone or supine (Fig. 12.6,7, and 8).

Neutral position with patient standing. With the patient standing and looking straight ahead, grasp the head of the talus between the thumb and index finger (Fig. 12.6). Instruct the patient to look behind him by rotating his pelvis as far as he can laterally while keeping his foot planted on the floor (Fig. 12.9). With the patient's upper torso rotated laterally and his feet and extremities straight ahead, his foot will supinate and the head of the talus will protrude laterally (Fig. 12.10). The patient is then told to look forward and to bring his upper torso back in level with his lower extremity. As he rotates his pelvis back over the fixed heel, the forefoot will pronate and the head of the talus will protrude medially. The point at which the foot seems to fall to one side or the other (Fig. 12.11) is the neutral position of the subtalar joint.

Neutral position with the patient prone. Have the patient lie prone on the examining table with his feet extending over the end. With index finger and thumb, grasp his foot at the fourth and fifth metarsal heads and gently dorsiflex it until some resistance is felt (Fig. 12.7). Then move the subtalar joint through an arc of pronation and supination; at one point during this rotatory arc, the foot will tend to fall more easily to one side or the other. The point where the talar head does not

Robert D. D'Ambrosia, M.D., Roy Douglas, C.P.

protrude medially or laterally is the neutral position.

Neutral position with the patient supine. With the patient supine, palpate the head of the talus with the index finger and thumb while pronating and supinating the foot back and forth through a rotatory arc (Fig. 12.8). With inversion of the calcaneus, the head of the talus will be felt as a bulge¬laterally (Fig. 12.12). With eversion of the calcaneus, the bulge will be medial (Fig. 12.13). The neutral position is that point at which the foot is positioned so that the talar head does not bulge either medially or laterally (Fig. 12.8). At that point the talus is anatomically aligned with the navicular and does not protrude in any direction.

Neutral Position Cast

The neutral position cast is best obtained with the patient lying supine, as described above. The patient is instructed to relax completely and to refrain from actively dorsiflexing his foot during the procedure. The neutral position cast is obtained by making a plaster mold of the patient's foot while exerting passive dorsiflexion force on the lateral column of the foot (basically the fourth and fifth metatarsals). This produces a locking position of bone against bone and the foot in its best functional position. If dealing with a patient who has a severely pronated flatfoot, the head of the talus will protrude markedly on the medial side and will not be palpable laterally. On the other hand, if dealing with a cavus or a highly arched foot, the head of the talus will protrude prominently on the lateral side and will not be easily palpable on the medial aspect.

To make the mold, have the patient lie supine on the casting table. A towel or pillow under the hip corresponding to the affected foot helps bring the foot up to a vertical position (Fig. 12.14a), and is the best position for obtaining a neutral cast. The mold is made with two 4 x 20 inch plaster-of-paris splints (Fig. 12.14b). If a 4 by 30 inch splint is wrapped around the foot it can be cut to the exact size needed. The splints are emersed in tepid water and placed on the foot so that they extend from the fifth metatarsal head around the heel (Fig. 12.14c) and up the medial aspect of the first metatarsal head (Fig. 12.14d). Next, one side of the plaster is folded over the sole of the foot (Fig. 14e) and the opposite side is folded over it as well

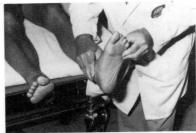

Fig. 12.8: Neutral position supine.

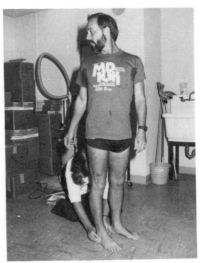

Fig. 12.9: Patient looks backward causing supination, higher arch, and heel varus.

Fig. 12.10: Looking backward causes foot supination and head of talus protrudes laterally.

Orthotics

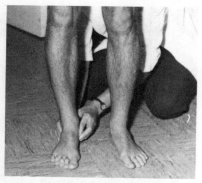

Fig. 12.11: Neutral position of subtalar joint. The talus is neither medial nor lateral.

Fig. 12.12: The talar head bulges laterally with heel inversion and forefoot supination.

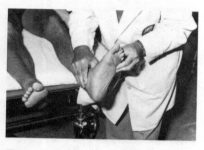

Fig. 12.13: The talar head bulges medially with heel eversion and forefoot pronation.

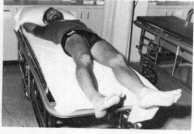

Fig. 12.14: a. Folded towel under hip brings the foot to a more vertical position.

(Fig. 12.14f). Then, with a gloved hand, smooth the plaster over the contours of the foot until the plaster is free of irregularities (Fig. 12.14g). Then, grip the fourth and fifth metatarsal heads with the thumb on the plantar surface and the index finger on the dorsal surface of the metatarsals (Fig. 12.14h), and with the opposite thumb and index finger feel for the head of the talus. With the head of the talus in the neutral position, pressure is maintained on the fourth and fifth metatarsal heads. The foot must not slip out of the neutral position while the cast is setting. The position of the cast must be maintained until the drying plaster is no longer pliable.

To remove the cast, pull it away from the dorsal aspect of the foot (Fig. 12.14i). Then grasp the cast on the medial and lateral sides of the heel and pull straight down; the cast will separate from the heel. As soon as the cast is off the heel, pull it forward, and it will slide off the plantar surface of the foot (Fig. 12.14j). The completed plaster molds of the foot are shown in Fig. 12.14k.

Orthotic Fabrication

A positive model is then made from the plaster mold of the foot. The modeling plaster is poured in and allowed to dry, and the plaster bandages are removed (Fig. 12.15). The positive model is then smoothed, and the plantar surface at, and just proximal to, the metatarsal heads and at the heel, is flattened precisely perpindicular to the vertical. If the deformity is especially severe, it is advisable to flatten the heel at a slight angle of 5-10,° depending on the amount of correction needed, by removing more plaster from the medial or lateral side to correct for supination or pronation, respectively. The forefoot is left alone.

Perhaps the most important phase in modification of the positive model is the exaggeration of the posterior aspect of the longitudinal arch and its blending with the medial support area above the calcaneal tuberosity. Locating the navicular and the calcaneal tuberosity are important because as much plaster as necessary must be removed from between these two positions to create the pressure needed for direct support of the calcaneus in the area of the sustentaculum tali.

The effectiveness of a good supporting inner contour of an orthosis should never be compromised by inadequate trimming of the model. Trim lines should be left as high as comfort will allow.

Robert D. D'Ambrosia, M.D., Roy Douglas, C.P.

This rule is important in order to obtain effective support around the subtalar joint.[6]

The mold is now ready for orthotic construction. Selection of material depends on the prescription (Fig. 12.16a). For correction of supination, pronation, pes cavus, heel spurs, or any deformity that needs solid support, a polyethylene material called vitrathene is used. This material is nontoxic, highly compressible, and easily reshaped with the use of a heat gun. After a blank is cut, it is then placed in an oven on a piece of aluminum coated with a parting agent, at 177° C, for 10 to 15 minutes to achieve optimal working temperature (Fig. 12.16b). The vitrathene is then removed from the oven, draped over the mold, and then placed in a vacuum-forming machine (Fig. 12.16c). Pressure of 25 lbs. per square inch is applied, and the material is then left to cool for ten minutes under that pressure (Fig. 12.16d). Finally, the form is released from the mold, (Fig. 16e), trimmed (Fig. 12.16f), and the surfaces sanded (Fig. 12.16g). The orthotic is now ready for fitting to the patient's foot (Fig. 12.16h).

If more cushioning is needed than is provided by a running shoe, Plastizote #2 or #3, depending on the density preferred, can be used (Fig. 12.16a). Plastizote is a lightweight, thermoplastic material consisting of a closed-cell-formed polyethylene sheet, cross-linked by irradiation. It is oven-heated for molding to 140° C. It is nontoxic, inert, and resistant to strong acids, alkalis, and solvents.

Patient Results

During the three years the Louisiana State University Medical Center Runner's Clinic has been in existence, more than 500 runners with stress-related injuries have been examined and treated in a team approach that includes an orthopedist, a physical therapist, and an orthotist. Ten percent of these runners received orthotics for stress syndromes that we were unable to relieve through modification of training techniques. Before an orthotic was prescribed, we first altered training techniques to avoid sudden increases in mileage and to see whether a more cushioned surface or shoe could be fitted to alter the stress pattern. Training techniques were modified to discourage rapid changes in mileage, avoid hill-running and hard-surface running, practice proper stretching techniques, and to encourage shoe modifications. The most common problem in

b. Materials necessary to obtain a neutral cast of the foot.

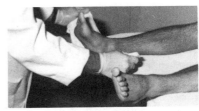

c. Beginning application of plaster splint.

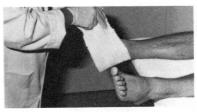

d. Plaster splint applied around foot.

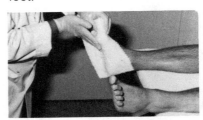

e. Plaster splint folded on medial side.

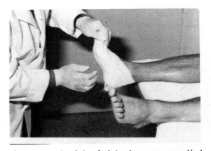

f. Lateral side folded over medial side.

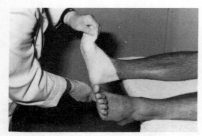

g. Plaster is smoothed of irregularities.

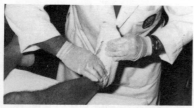

h. Grip the fourth and fifth metatarsal heads with thumbs on plantar surface and index and long fingers on the dorsal surfaces of the metatarsal. With the opposite thumb and index finger, feel for the head of talus.

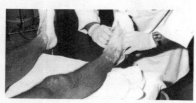

i. Cast pulled away from dorsal aspect of foot.

j. Plaster cast pulled from the foot of the patient.

k. Completed plaster molds of both feet.

Table 12.1
Type of Arch Related to Improvement

	Total	Improved	Unimproved
Flat arch	22	18	4
Normal arch	12	8	4
High arch	16	10	6
Total patients	50	36	14

runners is, of course, inadequate stretching, which is dealt with in Chapters 10 and 11. Only after we had carefully evaluated the patient's running techniques and could find no other means of help would we resort to an orthotic to help the runner with his stress problem.

We recently evaluated 50 runners who had been given orthotics over the past three years to determine whether their pain and discomfort from stress syndromes had improved. In this group of patients, 22 (44%) had flat arches, 16 (32%) had high arches (cavus), and 12 (24%) had normal arches (Table 12.1).

No specific diagnosis was associated with a particular type of arch. Diagnoses varied, depending on which part of the body was acting as the shock absorber when the foot struck the ground. It was usually in the tendons, fascia, and, less frequently, the bone. The diagnoses included iliotibial band tendonitis, posterior tibial tendonitis, tendoachilles tendonitis, plantar fasciitis, tarsal tunnel syndrome, metatarsalgia, heel spur, and chondromalacia patellae.

Thirty-six patients (72%) reported improvement after the use of the orthotic. Improvement was defined as a decrease or elimination of the pain associated with running. Fourteen patients (28%) reported no improvement, a worsening of symptoms, or the development of additional problems.

The flat or pronated foot was more apt to be helped by an orthotic than the high arch or cavus foot. The cavus foot, which is by far the most difficult problem to manage with an orthotic, is usually intractable, rigid, and poorly adapted to absorb the accumulated forces generated on impact with distance running. Since 42% of our patients with cavus feet were unimproved with the use of an orthotic, we recommend caution in prescribing an orthotic for this condition. The best results for cavus feet were obtained with the more cushioned orthotic materials, which, unfor-

Robert D. D'Ambrosia, M.D., Roy Douglas, C.P.

tunately, hold their contour poorly.

We evaluated the improved versus the unimproved groups in relation to several factors: age, sex, distance run, duration of participation in the sport, and type of running surface. The average age of both the improved and unimproved groups was 33.7 years (range: 14-52 years and 24-45 years, respectively). Twenty-eight (78%) of our improved group were men and eight (22%) were women. The unimproved group had 12 men (86%) and two women (14%). Overall, 80% of the women and 70% of the men showed improvement. The improved group of runners ran slightly less than did the unimproved runners. The 36 runners in the improved group ran an average of 23.6 miles per week; 32 (89%) ran less than 40 miles per week. The unimproved runners ran an average of 30 miles per week; half of these runners ran less than 20 miles per week (Fig. 12.17).

Most of the runners in both groups had been running for one to five years. Only four patients (11%) in the improved group and three patients (21%) in the unimproved group had been participating in the sport for more than five years.

The running surfaces used by the two groups differed considerably. Twenty-six of the improved patients (72%) ran on paved surfaces only part of the time or not at all. Ten patients (71%) of the unimproved group ran on *paved surfaces only*. Thirteen (36%) of the runners who showed improvement also decreased their speed and/or distance run. One runner changed completely from a paved to a clay surface. Five (36%) of the 14 patients who showed no improvement had extreme difficulty adjusting to the orthotic. This difficulty probably led to decreased usage of the orthotic device.

From our experience with prescribing orthotics for runners, we cautiously state that orthotics are a legitimate part of the runner's treatment program. Although we found no significant differences in many of the factors examined, the overall improvement rate was 72%, which probably justifies the use of orthotics. In analyzing our runners with orthotics, however, we could not find a precise means of determining which patients would benefit; we were able to make one generality, however: runners with flat feet and excessive pronation did much better than patients with rigid cavus feet. Almost half of our unimproved runners had cavus feet. In view of the 72% improvement rate, prescribing an orthotic for a

Fig. 12.15: Positive models made from the plaster molds of both feet.

Fig. 12.16:a. Three materials most commonly used for orthotic fabrication. Vitrathene, Plastozote #2, and Plastozote #3.

b. Blank cut of Vitrathene placed in oven on aluminum slab coated with a parting agent.

c. Vitrathene removed from oven and placed over the mold.

d. Vitrathene mold left in the vacuum-forming machine for ten minutes until cool.

e. Completed mold after release from the vacuum-forming machine.

f. Trimming of the orthotic.

g. Sanding of the orthotic.

h. Orthotic ready for patient fitting.

runner who has a stress syndrome secondary to a malalignment problem would seem appropriate. Its use is certainly more appropriate in the flat-footed or normal-arched runner than the runner with cavus feet.

The physician seeing running problems should be aware that orthotics are just one factor in the treatment of stress syndromes. Most stress syndromes are related to training errors and are improved with rest, reduced mileage, and a change to a more cushioned surface, or to a modified or more cushioned shoe. The next most useful therapy is instituting proper stretching techniques both in prophylaxis and in the treatment of specific injuries. It is only after the above treatments fail that an orthotic should be used to correct malalignment problems. Although the science of orthotics is inexact, when it is correlated with the biomechanics of the lower extremity, orthotics may be effective in treating recalcitrant problems that have not been helped by improved techniques, stretching, surface changes, or shoe modifications.

References

1. Inman VT: The Joints of the Ankle. Baltimore, Williams and Wilkins, 1976.
2. Manter JT: Movements of the subtalar and transverse tarsal joints. Anatomical Record 80:397-410, 1941.
3. Hicks JH: The mechanics of the foot. I. The joints. J Anat 87:345-357, 1953.
4. Henderson WH, Campbell JW: UC-BL shoe insert: Casting and fabrication. Biomechanics Laboratory, University of California, San Francisco, Laboratory, 1967. Reprinted in Bull Pres Thet Res 10-11:215, 1969.
5. Campbell JW, Inman VT: Treatment of Plantar Fasciitis and Calcaneal Spurs with the UC-BL shoe insert. Clin Orthop 103:57-67, 1974.
6. Colson JW, Berglund G: An effective orthotic design for controlling the unstable subtalar joint. Orthotics and Prosthetics 33:39-49, 1979.

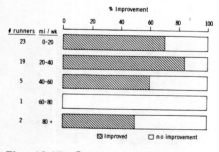

Fig. 12.17: Graph showing relationship of miles run with improvement or lack of improvement.

Robert D. D'Ambrosia, M.D., Roy Douglas, C.P.

13

Nutritional Needs of the Runner

Diane M. Huse, R.D., M.S.

Interest in the relationship between the athlete's diet and his performance is probably older than organized sports. Many of the dietary superstitions of primitive tribes are based on the idea that certain foods—in particular the meat of certain animals—endowed the consumer with the qualities of strength, endurance, and courage with which his prey was identified.[1] Perusal of the daily press leads one to believe that some special nutritional factors are responsible for the preparation and success of members of professional or Olympic teams. Proper nutrition all too often loses out to food fads, quackery, and superstition among athletes. Special properties are ascribed to specific foods and food supplements that have little scientific merit. Evaluating the effect of a single food on performance is extremely difficult because of the interference of such variables as motivation, differences in experimental conditions, types of work performed, and the wide range of individual response. The practices being followed may have potentially harmful effects (eg, megavitamin treatment) or may reinforce eating habits or attitudes about food that may be detrimental in later life (eg, inappropriate high calorie intake leading to obesity). The implications of dietary practices for future health should be carefully considered, especially when dealing with the young athlete whose growth and development must be protected.

The athlete's nutritional needs are similar to those of the nonathlete; he requires calories, proteins, fats, water, vitamins, and minerals in quantities determined by his age, body size, and activity level. These requirements can be met by a basic, well-balanced diet.

Calorie Needs

The calorie or energy requirement of a person is determined by his basal energy expenditure and the energy expended in physical activity. Basal energy expenditure is relatively constant and includes energy required for maintenance of muscle tone, body temperature, circulation, respiration, and other glandular and cellular activities, including those related to growth. The primary determinants of basal metabolic energy requirement are body size, age, and sex. With these determinants, basal energy requirement can be determined from a nomogram,[2] or can be estimated from the formula: basal needs equals one kilocalorie per kilogram of body weight per hour.[3] In general, the basal energy requirement increases as body size or surface area increases, is higher in young people than in older persons, and is higher in males than in females.

Physical activity is the major determinant of variation in energy expenditure among individuals. Whenever muscular work is done, energy is used, and the amount required is proportional to the work done. Estimates of energy needs are: for extremely light or sedentary activity, such as writing at a desk or standing in one place, add 30% of the basal metabolic energy needs: for light activity, such as filing or other office work, 50%; for moderate activity, such as that allowing for little sitting, 75%; and for strenuous activity, such as construction work or athletics, 100% or more.[4]

The nonathlete can, therefore, estimate his daily energy requirement by determining his basal energy requirement using 24 kilocalories per kilogram of body weight and adding to that the appropriate percent of the basal calorie needs for the level of activity selected by the person as most typical of his daily routine. The athlete also uses this method of determining calorie needs but must determine the additional calories required for his athletic activity by considering the frequency and duration of his participation in the activity. That amount can be approximated by knowing the caloric cost per minute of the activity. The athlete's daily energy requirement will change depending on whether the day is the day of competition, a training day, or a day during off-season. The duration of activity will differ in each of these situations. For the runner, the approximate calorie cost of cross-country running is 10.6 kilocalories per minute;[1] of long distance running

Diane M. Huse, R.D.

15.0 kilocalories per minute;[5] and, of marathon running, 20.7 kilocalories per minute.[6]

Estimates of energy expenditure in running are made more difficult by variations in terrain and air resistance. Various investigators have shown that the total energy expenditure in running on a level surface is constant and independent of velocity for a given person; pace has little effect on the caloric cost of running. Running up a hill with an incline of 6% requires 35% more energy than running on level ground. Running down a similar grade reduces the effort by only 24%. Studies of running in still air and against the wind suggest that in distance running about 5 to 8% of the energy spent is needed to overcome air resistance.[6] Of more importance, perhaps, is the energy cost based on the weight of the runner.

Because the work of exercise, as measured by oxygen consumption, increases as body weight increases, it is easy to understand the advantage attributed the runner who has small bones and minimal body fat. The less nonpropulsive weight or fat, the greater the efficiency of movement. Anatomically, marathoners are usually small and thin. The average height and weight of all the Boston Marathon Champions from 1897 to 1965 was 170 cm (range 155-188 cm) and 61 kg (48.8-78.2 kg).[6] An estimate of excess weight can be made by comparing the athlete's weight to a standard weight chart for height and age. A weight chart may give a false impression of overweight for the muscular athlete, because muscle tissue is heavier than fat tissue. A more accurate method to assess an athlete's excess weight is to measure the percent of body fat by use of calipers designed to measure the thickness of a fold of skin. Buskirk[7] advocated measuring the skin over the triceps muscle and advised that a skinfold less than eight millimeters thickness indicates a "lean" body build, eight to fifteen millimeters is "acceptable," and greater than fifteen millimeters (about one-half inch) is "over-fat." These measurements apply to highly trained athletes in top condition whose ideal fat content is 5 to 8%—the figures must not be broadly applied. When skinfold estimates of body fat were made on 114 competitors at the 1968 U.S. Olympic Marathon Trial, they showed that the marathon runners had about 7.5% fat or about 9% less than normally active men of comparable age.[8] Several of the top finishes were found to have less than 5% body fat.[6]

Cureton and co-workers investigated the effect of experimental alterations in excess weight on aerobic capacity and distance running performance.[9] Additional weight was found to decrease significantly maximal oxygen uptake (expressed relative to total weight carried), maximal treadmill run time, and 12-minute run distance. An increase of 5% additional weight was found, on the average, to decrease maximal oxygen uptake by 2.4 ml, the treadmill run time by 35 seconds, and the 12-minute run distance by 89 meters. These decreases were direct consequences of the increased energy cost of running at submaximal speeds.

The determination of and adherence to a daily caloric intake appropriate for body size and activity needs are, therefore, of great importance because if the runner's caloric intake exceeds his needs, his total body fat will increase. The increase in body fat resulting from caloric intake exceeding caloric needs will not only decrease the runner's performance by increasing the work of his exercise but will likely also create eating habits and attitudes about food that may contribute to the development of obesity in later life.

Caloric balance is especially important for athletes during the off-season and in the post-competitive years. Many athletes develop weight problems at these times because they fail to realize that when competition and training stops, habitually high calorie intakes must be lowered for adaptation to decreased energy demands.

Protein

Proteins are more complex molecules than either fats or carbohydrates. The molecules are similar in that they all contain oxygen, hydrogen, and carbon, but proteins (unlike fats or carbohydrates) also contain nitrogen; many contain sulfur, phosphorus, iron, and other minerals, as well. Proteins are made up of great numbers of relatively simple units, the nitrogen-containing compounds called amino acids.

The major roles of proteins in the body are for building new tissues in growing children, in athletic training, and after injury; for maintaining tissues already built and replacement of regular losses; as regulatory substances for internal water and acid-base balance; as a precursor for enzymes, antibodies, and some hormones; and as energy. If more protein is eaten than is needed for essential functions, the extra protein is oxidized to supply energy or is converted to body fat if the total energy

Diane M. Huse, R.D.

intake is excessive. If the energy control of the diet is inadequate (ie, if sufficient carbohydrates and fats are not supplied to meet the energy needs of the body), proteins are burned for energy because energy needs have a higher priority than does maintenance of some of the tissue proteins. In this event, building or repair processes will suffer. Nitrogen, which is indispensable as long as protein is used for tissue building, becomes a liabilty when protein must be used for energy. The nitrogen-containing substances (primarily urea) that result from amino acid oxidation must be excreted by the kidneys. Because energy is more economically supplied by carbohydrates and fats, the consumption of protein greatly in excess of body needs is usually disadvantageous.

The requirement for protein in the diet has been set at 0.8 grams per kilogram body weight per day for adults. Because of the additional need for protein for growth in children, the requirement decreases gradually from 2.0 grams per kilogram at ages 0.5 to 1 year to 0.8 gram per kilogram at age 18 years.

Increases in lean body mass, enzymatic proteins, and hemoglobin, all typical effects of training, may temporarily require greater than normal intakes of protein. Athletes who develop protein-uria, hemoglobinuria, or myoglobinuria as a result of high-intensity exercise may also require greater than normal levels of protein until these conditions subside. One recommendation has been that during training and competition the mature athlete needs 1 gram protein per kilogram body weight per day and the growing athlete may require up to 1.5 grams protein per kilogram per day to meet his greater demand for amino acid retention and protein synthesis.[10] The recommendations for increased protein intake during athletic training vary, however. Consolazio and Johnson believe than an increased dietary protein above normal intake for men in athletic training is not necessary.[11]

Although early workers thought that protein was the primary source of muscular energy, the work of Voit and Pettenkofer, as Mayer and Bullen[1] pointed out, refuted this theory, and this refutation has been well confirmed. Nitrogen excretion has been shown repeatedly not to increase during muscular work. As Consolazio and co-workers[5] mentioned, Atwater showed that nitrogen excretion was not above that in the resting conditions even when the metabolic rate was nearly doubled by physical work. Astrand cited data showing the combustion of protein was not higher during heavy exercise than during rest, even after glycogen depots have been depleted.[12] Pitts, Consolazio, and Johnson[13] examined the effect of variation in the level of dietary protein on the physical fitness (ie, treadmill runs of various speeds and grades followed by pulse counts) of three subjects studied under both temperate and tropical conditions while reclining, standing, and marching. There was no change in performance attributable to dietary protein level under any of these environmental conditions, although improvements due to training and acclimatization were observed.

Excess protein intake increases water requirements of the body because additional fluid is required to eliminate nitrogen by-products in the urine. Not only is excess protein unnecessary, it can be harmful, particularly when ingested during times of intense athletic competition when it can compromise body hydration.

Vitamins

Vitamins are organic compounds that occur in small concentrations in foods; they are necessary in small amounts in the diet for normal growth, maintenance, and reproduction. Their absence in the diet or improper absorption results in specific deficiency diseases. They differ from each other in physiologic function, in chemical structure, and in distribution in food. The vitamins are classified into two groups based on their solubility. The solubility characteristic is important in determining whether the body can store the vitamin or whether the supply must be replenished daily. Solubility also has implications for the vitamin's toxic potential when taken in excess of body needs. The four vitamins A, D, E, and K are soluble in fat and fat solvents and are therefore known as the fat-soluble vitamins. They can be stored in the body to some extent, mostly in the liver, and as a result, manifestations of deficiencies are likely to be slow. The water-soluble vitamins include vitamin C and the B complex vitamins. The body has limited ability to store water-soluble vitamins, except water-soluble vitamin B_{12}, which is stored extensively in the liver. Tissues are depleted of their normal content of these vitamins in a relatively short period if the diet is deficient, so supplies are needed regularly to maintain tissues levels. The tissues take up only as much as is needed, and

Diane M. Huse, R.D.

because water-soluble vitamins are freely soluble in water, most of the intake of these vitamins not required for day-to-day use is excreted in the urine.

Most B complex vitamins act as an organic catalyst or as a part of a catalyst. A catalyst is a substance that speeds up a chemical reaction without itself taking part in it. The special types of organic catalysts that promote these reactions in living tissues are known as enzymes and coenzymes, which aid enzymes in their tasks. Many of the vitamins occur in the body as coenzymes responsible for promoting some essential chemical reaction. For example, the cell gets much of the energy it requires through oxidation of the carbohydrate, glucose. This oxidation takes place in many intermediate steps, so that energy is gradually set free. Several of the B complex vitamins are coenzymes that catalyze specific steps in the oxidation of carbohydrates. The absence of any of these enzymes means a failure of some link in the chain of tissue oxidations. Therefore, the lack of a vitamin that is an essential part of such an enzyme can inhibit oxidative processes in cells.

As in the case of caloric undernutrition, the impairment of the ability to perform work efficiently in cases of frank vitamin deficiency is well known. No conclusive evidence, however, supports the theory that once vitamin requirements are met, supplementation will enhance athletic performance. Greater attention should be directed to the possible detrimental effects of their indiscriminate use.

Easy fatiguability, loss of appetite, irritability, and apathy are signs of vitamin B complex deficiency; the ability to perform work efficiently is impaired in this state. Review of the studies done on work efficiency of persons receiving diets adequate in B complex vitamin versus B complex vitamin supplemented indicate that supplementation does not enhance performance. In normal young men, in experiments lasting 10 to 12 weeks, intakes of thiamine at four different levels, from 0.23 mg per 1,000 kcal daily up to 0.63 mg per 1,000 kcal, exerted no beneficial effect on diets otherwise considered adequate. Muscular, neuromuscular, cardiovascular, psychomotor, and metabolic functions tested were in no way limited. Clinical signs, subjective sensations, and state of mind and behavior were likewise unaffected.[14]

Nicotinic acid, or niacin, is another of the B complex vitamins. It has been shown, in exercising men, to decrease mobilization of fatty acids

Nutritional Needs

from adipose tissue, resulting in increased utilization of muscle glycogen stores for energy.[15] The effects of large doses of niacin on myocardial metabolism in men, either at rest or during exercise, have been documented as undesirable on the metabolism of heart muscle.[16] Because fatty acids are important fuels for the heart, excessive consumption of niacin is contraindicated before endurance events.

Vitamin C supplementation is especially popular among athletes because of its known role in collagen synthesis and the poor quality of tissue repair associated with vitamin C defiency. The reasoning is that the athlete has perhaps a greater need for collagen synthesis and tissue repair, and thus athletic performance would benefit from supplementation. It has been found that vitamin C supplementation has a negligible effect on endurance performance and rate, or on severity or duration of athletic injury.[17]

Excessive vitamin C supplementation increases vitamin C destruction in the body. Scurvy has been noted in persons who have had a history of taking excessive amounts of vitamin C and who returned to a diet containing normal amounts.[18] Seventeen subjects consuming 1 to 3 grams of vitamin C per day over a period of three to 36 months were studied to determine the serum ascorbic acid levels. The subjects' intake was first standardized to 2 grams vitamin C supplement per day for ten days. The serum ascorbic acid level was found to be 1.45 mg per 100 ml. The serum ascorbic acid level of 16 normal controls not receiving supplemental vitamin C was 1.20 per 100 ml, and increased to 2.75 mg per 100 ml after the administration of 2 grams vitamin C supplement daily for eight days. Therefore, the serum ascorbic acid levels initially increase, reaching a maximum value after about eight days of supplementation. The continued use of supplemental vitamin C leads to a gradual decline of the serum levels that cannot be compensated by increasing the dosage.[18]

Because adequate saturation levels of ascorbic acid may be maintained on recommended dietary sources of vitamin C, the habitual intake of larger amounts is not advantageous, while posing the risks of causing an ascorbic acid deficiency on termination of the regimen.

On the basis of these data, one can no longer presume that excessive intake of a water-soluble vitamin will simply result in excess quantities

172

Diane M. Huse, R.D.

being excreted in the urine with no possibility for toxic effects.

Vitamin E is a fat-soluble vitamin. There is no evidence that the healthy human is susceptible to vitamin E deficiency; supplementation has, likewise, not proved to be advantageous. Vitamin E toxicity in humans has not been confirmed. An oxidation product of vitamin E has been thought to be an inhibitor of vitamin K and, therefore, responsible for a prolongation in blood clotting time. Large doses of vitamin E potentiate the affect of warfarin. A study conducted by the National Institute of Health on persons who had been ingesting up to 800 IU of vitamin E for more than 3 years did not find evidence of toxicity.[19] Although some athletes have taken vitamin E in hopes of improving athletic performance, vitamin E taken at a level of 900 IU daily for six months did not improve athletic performance in well-trained swimmers.[20]

Minerals

Sodium, potassium, and iron are the minerals most often affected by heavy exercise. Because sodium and potassium are intimately related to the athlete's state of hydration, these minerals will be part of the discussion of water requirement.

Iron is distributed through the body as a component of essential metabolic enzymes in every cell. About 65 to 70% of the iron in the body is present in the blood as hemoglobin in the red blood cells. Hemoglobin is essential for oxygen transport in the blood. The remainder of the iron stored in the body is found in combination with protein in the liver, bone, and bone marrow or found in other tissues such as myoglobin in muscles. In all sites, the iron-containing compounds are involved in the vital processes of cells and tissues. The body guards its iron stores carefully and reuses any iron that is broken down in the body over and over again. Only small amounts of iron lost in the urine, sweat, hair, sloughed-off skin, and nails and by menstruation need to be replaced—normally only about 1 or 1.5 mg a day. About one-tenth of the iron in the diet is absorbed, which means that about 10 times the amount of iron must be eaten than the 1 or 1.5 mg a day that the body actually uses in its tissues. The 1979 National Research Council's recommended dietary allowances are 18 mg of iron per day for women and 10 mg per day for men.

Iron needs are greater during periods of growth, including pregnancy, lactation, and infancy through adolescence. Iron deficiency is the most common nutritional deficiency in the United States.[21]

Bunch states that the low or low-normal hemoglobin or hematocrit values commonly found in runners or other endurance-trained persons seldom reflect true anemia and do not indicate a need for folate or vitamin B_{12}.[22] To advise oral iron therapy for women runners would seem reasonable because of menstrual loss.

In the past decade, interest has increased among athletes in the use of iron to improve performance. Low serum iron values and subnormal hemoglobin values have been demonstrated among athletes who are involved in intense physical activity. That finding has been looked on as a possible factor responsible for suboptimal oxygen transport and hence lower capacity for physical performance. A plausible explanation for these suboptimal values might be a slightly increased destruction of the red blood cells during heavy training.

The iron status and the possible effect of training on iron metabolism of a group of extremely hard-training long-distance runners has been reported from Sweden. A depressed absorption combined with an increased elimination were thought to explain these runners' suboptimal iron state.[23] Iron loss via sweat is usually considered to be negligible in humans. Vellar showed, however, that in cases of extreme sweating as much as 40 μg of iron per 100 ml sweat might be lost.[24] Runners have been shown to lose between 1 and 3 liters of fluid a day as sweat, resulting in, perhaps, an extra iron loss of 0.4-1.0 mg per day. The increased elimination rate of iron found in the runner could be explained by the profuse sweating that occurs.

From the practical standpoint, the runner should be advised to include adequate quantitites of iron in his diet. As recommended for individuals in the general population, greater attention to good sources of iron in the diet seems reasonable. The best dietary sources of iron are meat, especially organ meats, fish, poultry, and eggs. Green leafy vegetables, potatoes, dried fruits, and enriched bread and cereal products are the best plant sources.

Diane M. Huse, R.D.

Water

Humans can live for about 30 days without food, but will die in 5 to 6 days if deprived of water. Water is lost from the body constantly from the skin, as perspiration; from the lungs, as water vapor in expired air; from the kidneys as urine; and from the intestines in feces. A minimum of 800 ml of water is lost daily through the skin and lungs and this amount may increase in hot, dry environments. The kidneys eliminate about 1,000 to 1,500 ml of water in urine; fecal losses approximate 200 ml daily.

Fluids are replaced by the ingestion of liquids and foods containing water. To ensure sufficient water, adults should drink 2,000 to 2,500 ml of water or other liquids daily.

Body water serves many functions. Nutrients, hormones, waste products, and antibodies are all transported in the water of the blood plasma. All of the body's chemical reactions are carried out in water and are significantly less efficient when an adequate amount of body water is not available.

The role of water in regulating body temperature is of particular importance to the athlete. The excessive heat generated by exercise must be dissipated and the most effective way is through evaporation of sweat. This mechanism fails to function effectively, however, if the water supply is inadequate to meet the needs of the sweat glands.

When fluid losses exceed supply, dehydration follows. Dehydration is characterized by loss of appetite and limited capacity for work. Physiological changes that impair performance are detectable with losses no greater than 3% of body weight. When losses are 5%, evidence of heat exhaustion becomes apparent and at 7% hallucinations occur. Losses totaling 10% are hazardous and lead to heat stroke, a sudden collapse, and loss of consciousness. Persons in excellent physical condition can perform adequately until body water equal to 4 or 5% of body weight is lost.[25] Generally, with the loss of water amounting to 4 to 5% of body weight, the capacity for hard muscular work declines by 20 to 30%.[26]

During exercise and muscular work, changes take place in the distribution of body water. When exercise begins, water is immediately transferred from the extracellular fluid space to the intracellular space within cells. This transfer facilitates the utilization of energy. The extracellular fluid that moves into the muscle cells is rapidly replaced by water from blood plasma, thereby reducing the volume of circulating blood. The amount of blood plasma that is available to flow to the kidneys is thus reduced and urine production is decreased.

Once exercise begins and water is lost through sweating and increased breathing, this reduced excretion of urinary water provides a control mechanism that helps to conserve body water. Mechanisms for increased water intake are not nearly as effective. After a period of exercise and resulting dehydration, the average thirst response will not in itself call for complete replacement of body water for a considerable time, often up to several days. The need for a prescribed schedule for water intake to maintain hydration is important for the athlete.

The athlete who is well conditioned will voluntarily drink more often than one who is not well trained. The acclimatized athlete will also sweat more profusely and will thus more effectively dissipate his body heat. Even the well-condtioned athlete, who drinks more, and more nearly compensates for his water losses, may spontaneously replace only one-half to one-third of his sweat losses within 24 hours of a vigorous workout or competition.

Distance runners may lose 8 to 13 pounds of water during a marathon run. That loss causes dehydration of 13 to 21% of plasma water and 11% of muscle water.[27] All athletes should weigh in before and after each event or practice. The difference in weights before and after the event or competition represents water loss, and the proper amount of water replacement required can be determined.[25] Weight loss may be a guide to water replacement. The athlete should take 2 to 3 cups of water or liquid supplement for each pound of weight loss.

In addition to their role in maintaining acid-base balance, sodium and potassium exert a primary influence on the distribution of body water. Sodium is concentrated primarily in the extracellular fluid, whereas potassium is concentrated in the intracellular fluid. Any salt ingested in excess of salt losses will cause a trapping of water between cells and deplete the intracellular supply. When water is in short supply in the body, the most critical need is to maintain the metabolically active water within cells.

Sweat is hypotonic compared with the body fluid so that relatively more fluid than salts, such

176

Diane M. Huse, R.D.

as sodium and potassium, is lost from the body during sweating. Athletes in training do not require electrolyte supplements to replace perspiration losses because healthy kidneys automatically compensate by conserving sodium and potassium. Clearly, the body has highly effective mechanisms for regulating its supply of sodium and potassium.

Specific salt replacement is rarely needed during athletic activity, even if excessive sweat loss occurs. About 20 to 30 milliequivalents of sodium are lost per 1,000 ml of perspiration. Excessive sweating can lead to sodium losses of 350 milliequivalents (8 grams) per day in the acclimated person.[28] The usual dietary sodium intake of the adult is 100 to 300 milliequivalents (2 to 7 grams) per day.[28] Americans eating a varied diet generally get more than enough sodium in their daily foods to meet even the extraordinary needs of vigorous athletic activity. As a general guideline, however, Smith[25] recommends that, if water loss exceeds 5 to 10 pounds in a given workout, some consideration may be given to specific salt replacement. This replacement can be made by liberally salting a normal diet or it can be provided by a highly dilute salt-containing fluid, whose concentration should not exceed 1.5 grams of salt per liter of water (or 1/3 of a teaspoon per quart). Smith states that the use of salt tablets is inappropriate because they provide a high concentration of salt and may complicate the state of dehydration.

Williams believes that salt tablets may not be necessary to restore lost electrolytes if the weight loss is less than 6 pounds per day.[27] The person who is not acclimatized to heat will lose about 4 to 5 grams sodium with a 6 pound loss; the acclimatized person will lose only about 3 grams. Because the average meal contains as much as 3 grams of sodium, normal food intake should suffice. Williams recommends that one salt tablet should be taken per pound of weight loss over 6 pounds and that a pint of water be taken with each 7 gram tablet (200 mg sodium). This dosage is consistent with the Food and Nutrition Board of the National Research Council recommendation of a 2-gram salt (800 mg sodium) replacement per liter of extra water lost in sweating.[28]

Potassium losses in sweat are negligible, under any but the most extreme conditions, and potassium deletion is not a primary concern. The need for potassium has been suggested because of the low serum levels found in some athletes after exercise. Now, however, it is thought to be due to hemodilution rather than actual depletion of body potassium. Muscle weakness could result from excessive potassium losses. If additional needs do exist because of exercise losses, potassium may be increased in the normal diet by the inclusion of foods high in potassium, such as oranges, grapefruit, pineapples, apricots, bananas, and dried fruit.

Basic Diet

Optimal nutrition is one of the basic conditions necessary to maintain top performance for the athlete and nonathlete alike. As the previous review indicates, the athlete, aside from possible increases in caloric intake, necessitated by increased energy expenditure, and in water intake, to ensure adequate hydration, does not need additional nutrients beyond those found in a balanced diet.

The diet recommended for the athlete, and for the population in general, is one in which about 15% of calories are derived from protein, 30 to 35% from fat, and 50 to 55% from carbohydrate. This distribution of nutrients will allow for a moderate intake of protein, which easily meets requirements during training and is reasonable in terms of the athlete's appetite for meat. It provides a fat intake that is less than that currently consumed in this country but meets the recommendations of the American Heart Association.

No single food or category of foods contains all of the nutrients in amounts sufficient to maintain life. The key to balancing the diet is combining different foods so that nutrient deficiencies in some foods are made up for by nutrient surpluses in others. Each nutrient performs specific functions in the body and each needs to be present for the body to be in peak condition. Eating a proper variety of foods at each meal is the secret.

An adequate guide on which an athlete should base his food selection is the use of food groups. These food groups include milk and milk products; meat and meat substitutes; fruit and vegetables; and cereals and grains—the Basic Four Food Groups as established by the United States Department of Agriculture in 1956. For a diet selected to meet high evergy needs, such as the athlete's diet, additional groups such as fat, desserts, and sugars and sweets are also appropriate. Foods included in each of these groups, the major nutrients supplied in each group, and the

178

Diane M. Huse, R.D.

quantity of each food constituting a serving size are illustrated in Table 13.1.

Foods are classified into groups on the basis of similarities in nutrient composition; foods in a group are comparable in calories, protein, minerals, and vitamins and can be interchanged if taken in the suggested serving sizes. There is a vast leeway in the choice of the foods within each of the groups. The diet is flexible enough to adapt to an almost unlimited range of conditions and circumstances.

A reference runner, male, 29 years old, 170 cm in height and 61 kg in weight, would require about 1,500 kcal for daily basal needs (24 kcal/kg). Calorie needs on a day when he is engaged in light activity would be met by the addition of 50% of basal needs or about 2,200 calories. A sample menu illustrating this calorie level with a nutrient distribution of 15% of calories as protein, 35% as fat, and 50% as carbohydrate is shown in required by the athlete if he ran 60 minutes at a colorie cost of 15 calories per minute, increasing his calories needs to 3,100 on that day.

As the calorie level of the diet is adjusted depending on the daily calorie demands for activity, the distribution of protein, fat, and carbohydrate should remain relatively constant so that the diet remains well balanced nutritionally. That is, the intake of calories should not be increased by merely adding more meat or decreased by eliminating bread or potatoes (Tables 13.3 and 13.4).

Optimum body weight is important for the runner. If the reference runner weighed 70 kg and wished to reduce to 61 kg at a comfortable rate of about 1 kg per week, he must reduce his daily calorie intake by 1,000. Because 0.5 kg body fat equals 3,500 calories, a deficit of 7,000 calories a week would result in 1 kg of body fat. To maintain this rate of weight loss, on light activity days, the reference runner's calorie intake should be about 1,200 and 2,100 on days when he runs about 60 minutes. In the weight-reduction diet plan, less emphasis is placed on foods from the desserts and sugars and sweets food groups because they tend to be higher in calories and lower in essential nutrients than are appropriate at low calorie intakes. The percent of calories derived from protein is likely to be greater to meet the person's protein requirement of 0.8 gram per kilogram body weight (Tables 13.3 and 13.4).

Weight reduction efforts by means of starvation

Nutritional Needs

Table 13.1
Food Guide

Food Group	Foods Included	Major Nutrients Supplied	Serving Size
Milk Group	Milk (skim, buttermilk, 2%,* whole*), yogurt	Calcium, protein, riboflavin, vitamin A and D (all milk should be fortified with vitamins A and D)	1 serving is 1 cup (8 ounces)
Meat Group	Beef, pork, lamb, veal, organ meats,* poultry, fish, shellfish, egg,* cheese,* cottage cheese. As alternates—dry peas, dry beans, lentils, peanuts,* peanut butter*	Protein, thiamin, riboflavin, niacin and iron	1 serving is —1 ounce lean cooked meat, fish, poultry —1 egg —½ cup cooked dry peas, beans or lentils —2 tablespoons peanut butter (25 peanuts) —1 ounce cheese or ¼ cup cottage cheese
Bread-Cereal Group	All whole grain or enriched breads and cereals, macaroni, grits, spaghetti, crakers, noodles and rice	Food energy (kilocalories), protein, B complex vitamins	1 serving is —1 slice bread —½ cup cooked cereal, rice,

Diane M. Huse, R.D.

Group	Food	Description	Serving
		macaroni, grits, noodles, spaghetti	—1 ounce ready-to-eat cereal —4-6 crackers
Vegetable Group	Vegetables, cooked or raw	Vitamins A and C primarily as well as other vitamins and minerals Good sources of vitamin C are broccoli, brussels sprouts, green peppers	1 serving is —½ cup cooked —1 cup raw
		Good sources of vitamin D are deep yellow or dark green vegetables such as carrots, pumpkin, spinach, sweet potato, winter squash, broccoli, beets, collards, turnip and mustard greens, kale	Each day have one serving high in vitamin C; at least every other day have 1 serving high in vitamin A
Fruit Group	Fruits Fresh or cooked Fruit juice	Vitamins A and C primarily as well as other vitamin and minerals	1 serving is —½ cup juice —1 medium piece fruit —½ cup cooked
		Good sources of vitamin C are cantaloupe, strawberries, grapefruit, lemon, oranges	
		Good sources of vitamin A are cantaloupe and apricots	

(Table Continued)

Fat Group	Butter,* margarine, cooking fats* and oils, salad dressing, mayonnaise, sour cream,* gravy,* cream sauce,* cream*	Food energy (kilocalories) Carries of fat-soluble vitamins A, D, E	1 serving size is —1 teaspoon butter, margarine, oil, mayonnaise —2 tablespoons gravy, cream, sour cream, cream sauce —2 teaspoons salad dressing
Desserts	Ice cream,* frosted cake,* cookies,* pie,* sweet roll,* chocolate*	Food energy (kilocalories)	1 serving is —1/12 of 9-inch fruit pie —¾ cup ice cream —2" x 3" x 2" piece frosted cake —1½ ounces chocolate —2 - 2" cookies
Sugars and Sweets	Sugar, jelly, syrup, honey, hard candy, carbonated beverage	Food energy (kilocalories)	1 serving is —1 tablespoon sugar, jelly, syrup, honey —3 pieces hard candy —4 ounces carbonated beverage

*Omit to reduce cholesterol and/or saturated fat content of diet.

Diane M. Huse, R.D.

Table 13.2
Sample Menu
2200 Calories

Breakfast

Orange Juice	1 cup
Ready-to-Eat Cereal	2 ounces (about 1½ cups)
Milk	1 cup
Sugar	1 teaspoon
Ham	1 ounce
Toast	2 slices
Margarine or Butter	2 teaspoons
Jelly	2 teaspoons

Lunch

Roast Beef Sandwiches	2
Bread	4 slices
Roast Beef	4 ounces
Mayonnaise	2 teaspoons
Lettuce	
Celery and Carrot Sticks	
Fresh Pear	

Dinner

Baked Chicken	3 ounces
Rice	½ cup
Dinner Roll	1
Margarine or Butter	1 teaspoon
Broccoli	
Green Salad	
Salad Dressing	4 teaspoons
Ice Cream	3/4 cup

Evening Snack

Peanut Butter	2 tablespoons
Toast	2 slices
Margarine or Butter	2 teaspoons
Apple	1

or fad diets that emphasize the omission or encourage the increased use of a particular group of foods are never appropriate. Fad diets are usually nutritionally inadequate and will compromise not only athletic performance but general health. Weight loss from starvation involves loss of protein, glycogen, potassium, sodium, phosphorus, sulfur, enzymes, and other important cell constituents. Fifty percent or more of weight loss induced by total starvation involves fat-free protoplasm. The result of these responses is diminished body reserves for athletic demands. Weight reduction effort should include increased physical activity and a calorie-controlled, nutritionally well-balanced diet.

If the athlete eats a varied diet that meets but does not exceed his calorie, protein, vitamin, and mineral requirements, he need not take protein, vitamin, or mineral supplements; his nutrient requirements will be met by food. A dietitian

Nutritional Needs

Table 13.3
Nutrient Content of Meal Plans at
Sample Calorie Levels

	Protein		Fat		Carbohydrate	
Calories	grams	% of kcal	grams	% of kcal	grams	% of kcal
1200	60	20	40	30	150	50
2200	80	15	85	35	275	50
3100	115	15	120	35	390	50

should be consulted if there are questions about the formulation of the diet.

Carbohydrate Loading

The key role of carbohydrate in exercise performance has been emphasized for several decades. The main source of carbohydrate was thought to be local glycogen stores in muscle tissue, which was confirmed by Bergstrom and co-workers[29] by direct determinations of glycogen content in human muscle tissue during exercise. In 1967, Bergstrom and co-workers[29] and Hermansen, et al,[30] reported studies on young men on the effect of muscle glycogen levels on physical performance and endurance. The results indicated that performance time to exhaustion averaged 59, 126, and 189 minutes after three days on a high fat-high protein diet, a mixed diet, and a high carbohydrate diet, respectively. Muscle biopsy measurements indicated that the nutrient composition of the diet could affect the muscle glycogen stores. These stores were observed to be reduced during strenuous exercise, and when the muscle glycogen drops to a critical level, work usually stops or the physical activity rate is decreased. In this instance, an increased energy yield from free fatty acids results. These studies show that the working muscles have a requirement for carbohydrate as an energy source and that carbohydrate is obtained directly from the muscle stores of glycogen.

In the well-trained athlete, in brief high-intensity exercise (eg, tennis, sprinting), the size of the glycogen store is not a limiting factor, provided that it is not grossly subnormal at the beginning of the exercise. On the other hand, with high-intensity exercise of long duration, glycogen stores can be a limiting factor for the endurance capacity, especially considering that at the end of the competition a capacity to increase the performance (spurt) may be decisive for winning. Such

Diane M. Huse, R.D.

Table 13.4
Number of Servings of Food
at Sample Calorie Levels

Food Group	1200 Calorie	2200 Calorie	3100 Calorie
Milk	1	1	3
Meat	7	7	9
Bread-Cereal	4	12	12
Vegetable	2-3	2-3	2-3
Fruit	8	4	9
Fat	1	9	14
Dessert	0	1	1
Sugar-Sweet	0	1	4

long-duration, high-intensity exercise includes long-distance running, cross-country skiing and possibly some team sports such as soccer and ice hockey. The amount of glycogen stores must also be considered when athletes perform repeatedly during one day.

Bergstrom et al, observed that after the muscle glycogen stores had been depleted by previous exercise, a high-carbohydrate diet for one to three days greatly enhanced the synthesis of muscle glycogen.[29] They also showed that when carbohydrate was given without any previous exercise, muscle glycogen stores only moderately increased.

Slovic confirmed that carbohydrate loading does improve performance, with the improvement most pronounced in the final stages of the event.[31] The available information indicates that the glycogen content of the working muscle is one of the most important factors for prolonged exercise.

The carbohydrate loading technique[32] has been published in many forms but essentially consists of three phases: phase I, the depletion phase, consists of days 7 to 4 before the event; phase II, the glycogen synthesis phase, days 3 to 1 before the event; phase III, the day of the event.

In phase I, the specific muscles to be used must be exercised to exhaustion by the same type of activity as performed during the event to deplete them of their glycogen stores. Phase I is done about six to seven days before the day of the endurance event so that the muscles can be rested before the event. The diet during this phase is crucial. While depleting the muscles of glycogen, a high-fat, high-protein, low-carbohydrate diet is followed for three days. The glycogen content of the muscles is kept low during this time. One possible problem during phase I is a feeling of fatigue, irritability, nervousness, or nausea due to

Nutritional Needs

the low carbohydrate intake. During this phase, many athletes will refuse all forms of dietary carbohydrate and eat only protein and fat, resulting in ketosis. Intake of carbohydrate should be kept at about 100 grams per day.

After three days on the low-carbohydrate diet, the athlete begins the high-carbohydrate diet of phase II. This diet is adequate in protein and fat but the major source of calories is carbohydrate. A minimum of 250 to 525 grams of carbohydrate is needed each day in phase II. During this period, glycogen synthesis is enhanced and is localized to the muscles that were depleted during phase I. Exercise is not recommended at this time because it depletes the glycogen stores. Diets during phases I and II should be similar in caloric value and should be designed to meet the athlete's protein and energy needs.

Phase III is the day of the event. The athlete may eat anything he wishes. If an athlete thinks any one food will help his performance, he should eat it. The pre-event meal should be eaten three to four hours before the event so that the stomach is empty at the time of competition. Intake of food or fluid is necessary during an endurance event to maintain hydration and blood glucose.

A shorter method of carbohydrate loading would consist of the exhausting exercise on day 4 before the event, followed by three days of high-carbohydrate diet. Many misconceptions exist about diet for carbohydrate loading. Many equate carbohydrate with foods containing simple sugar such as candy, soft drinks, and honey, neglecting the complex carbohydrate sources such as vegetables, breads, and cereals.

Several investigators believe that the carbohydrate loading technique should be used with caution. In addition to glycogen, water is also deposited in muscle in amounts equal to about three times the amount of glcogen deposited. While this deposit of water may contribute to a sensation of muscular heaviness and stiffness, some believe that it partly compensates for the evaporative water losses experienced during the event. It does, however, result in increased body weight. For example, with glycogen storage of 700 grams, there is an increase in body water amounting to about 2 kilograms. In activities in which the body weight must be lifted, an excessive glycogen store should be avoided.

Athletes who are at risk for cardiovascular

Diane M. Huse, R.D.

disease should consult their physician before attempting endurance exercise or carbohydrate loading. There is little evidence of adverse effects of carbohydrate loading on the heart muscle except for one report[33] of a 40 year old marathon runner who suffered angina-like pain and electrocardiogram abnormalities presumably as result of glycogen and water deposition in the cardiac muscle. It has also been suggested that athletes using carbohydrate loading may be destroying muscle fibers due to the high glycogen stores or to the heavy exercise. Because no evidence supports this theory, no definitive statement can be made concerning possible muscular breakdown.

The purpose of carbohydrate loading is to supersaturate with glycogen the muscles to be used in competition. The competition should be longer than 30 to 60 minutes to fully utilize the glycogen stores. The complete technique of carbohydrate loading should be used only for endurance events and because of the demands on the muscles, it should be used sparingly, possibly two to three times a year. For shorter events, phase I can be omitted and phase II can be followed to fill but not supersaturate glycogen stores.

The effects of using the technique over a competitive lifetime are unknown. Adverse effects are suspected but full knowledge of possible dangers is lacking at this time because of the limited duration of use. If this dietary manipulation is practiced by many athletes to enhance their endurance and achieve better performance, the nutritional adequacy of the diet should be carefully considered.

Precompetition Meals

Unfounded beliefs have probably placed greater restrictions than necessary on food choices for the precompetition meal. The rigidity of some well-known recommendations is obviously extreme and limited in the light of what is known about food and its digestion. There is no reason that an athlete should not enjoy his pre-event meal and have the privilege of selecting the customary food he enjoys at other times during training. Probably more important than the foods consumed during this meal is the psychologic significance ascribed to foods or combinations of foods by the athlete.

The relative composition or size of the meal

preceding an event of short duration has little influence on improving performance. The main concern is that the meal be consumed at a reasonable time, usually three hours before the competitive event, which allows for digestion and absorption but is not long enough for feelings of hunger to develop.

In long-duration events,[34] the meal should also be consumed about three hours before the event. The fat content of the meal should be kept at a minimum, however, because fat in any form slows stomach-emptying time. Protein intake should also be limited because most protein sources contain fat. The athlete will want digestion in the stomach to be complete before the competitive event begins. Protein also yields the nitrogen by-products of digestion, which can only be eliminated by urinary excretion, therefore requiring fluid loss. The carbohydrate content of the meal should be higher than normal because it is easily digested and readily absorbed and will ensure adequate glycogen stores. The meal should exclude foods that are likely to cause flatulence and discomfort. To compensate for sweat losses, the athlete should drink 2 to 3 cups of water to insure adequate hydration. An additional cup of water should be taken 1½ hours before competition. Ingestion of bouillon, broth, or consomme' at least three hours before the event will ensure adequate salt intake. Because of its potientially detrimental effect on coordination and its dehydrating effect, alcohol should be avoided. Caffeine in coffee and tea should also be avoided because it has a diuretic effect causing a depletion in body water and because it is a central nervous system stimulant that may impair the athlete's awareness of fatigue.

Costill believes that an experienced runner will generally learn when and what to eat during precompetition.[35] For a race that begins at noon, the runner generally eats his major meal at about 6 o'clock the night before, followed in 4 hours by a snack. Breakfast should be taken about 4 hours before the race. All of these meals and snacks should be high carbohydrate, defined by Costill as being 60-70% of calories as carbohydrate.

To maintain energy and prevent dehydration in long-duration events, runners need to drink during competition. Excess amounts of glucose, dextrose pills, sugar cubes, honey, or hard candy should be avoided because they draw fluid into the intestinal tract and may add to the problem of

Diane M. Huse, R.D.

dehydration. A concentrated sugar solution may also cause distension of the stomach, cramps, nausea, and diarrhea.

The American College of Sports Medicine position statement on prevention of heat injuries in distance running suggests that fluids containing less than 2.5 grams glucose per 100 ml of water and less than 10 mEq sodium and 5 mEq potassium per liter of solution be used.[6] These proportions are recommended as sufficiently dilute to allow for rapid gastric emptying. Commerical solutions are generally more concentrated than the recommended solution. The role of the electrolytes, sodium, and potassium in the recommended fluid is primarily to improve absorption; these electrolytes do not appear to need to be replaced during exercise.

The addition of glucose increases the blood glucose level and thus increases the insulin level, which may increase the utilization of glucose. The ingestion of glucose may decrease the rate of of utilization of glycogen and thereby improve endurance. The position paper also states that runners should be encouraged to ingest fluids frequently during competition and to consume 400 to 500 ml of fluid 10 to 15 minutes before competition. In races of 16 km (10 mi) or more, fluid should be consumed every 3 to 4 km (2-2.5 mi).

References

1. Mayer J, Bullen B: Nutrition and athletic performance. Physiol Rev 40:369-397, 1960.
2. Committee on Dietetics of the Mayo Clinic: Mayo Clinic Diet Manual, Ed 4. Philadelphia, WB Saunders Co, 1971, p 160.
3. Mitchell HS, Rynbergen HJ, Anderson L, et al: Nutrition in Health and Disease. Philadelphia, JB Lippincott Company, 1976, p 121.
4. Bogert LJ, Briggs GM, Calloway DH: Nutrition and Physical Fitness. Philadelphia, WB Saunders Company, 1973, p 39.
5. Consolazio CF, Johnson RE, Pecora LJ: Physiological Measurements of Metabolic Functions in Man. New York, McGraw-Hill Book Company, 1963, p 505.
6. Costill DL: Physiology of marathon running. JAMA 221:1024-1029, 1972.
7. Buskirk ER: Diet and athletic performance. Postgrad Med 61:229-236, 1977.
8. Costill DL, Bowers R, Kammer WF: Skinfold estimates of body fat among marathon runners. Med Sci Sports 2:93-95, 1970.
9. Cureton KJ, Sparling PB, Evans BW, et al: Effect of experimental alterations in excess weight on aerobic capacity and distance running performance. Med Sci Sports 10:194-199, 1978.

10. Serfass RC: Nutrition for the athlete. Contemporary Nutrition 2:May, 1977.
11. Consolazio CF, Johnson HL: Dietary carbohydrate and work capacity. Am J Clin Nutr 25:85-90, 1972.
12. Astrand PO: Nutrition and physical performance. World Rev Nutr Diet 16:59-79, 1973.
13. Pitts GC, Consolazio CF, Johnson RE: Dietary protein and physical fitness in temperate and hot environments. J Nutr 27:497, 1944.
14. Keys A, Henschel AF, Mickelsen O, et al: The performance of normal men on controlled thiamine intake. J Nutr 26:399-415, 1943.
15. Bergstrom J, Hultman E, Jorfeldt L, et al: Effect of nicotinic acid on physical working capacity and on metabolism of muscle glycogen in man. J Appl Physiol 26:170-176, 1969.
16. Niacin and myocardial metabolism. Nutr Rev 31:80-81, 1973.
17. Gey GO, Cooper KH, Bottenberg RA: Effect of ascorbic acid on endurance performance and athletic injury. JAMA 211:105, 1970.
18. Rhead WJ, Schrauzer GN: Risks of long-term ascorbic acid overdosage (letter to the editor). Nutr Rev 29:262-263, 1971.
19. Farrell PM, Bieri JG: Megavitamin E supplementation in man. Am J Clin Nutr 28:1386, 1975.
20. Lawrence JD, Bower RC, Riehl WP, et al: Effects of α tococopherol acetate on the swimming endurance of trained swimmers. Am J Clin Nutri 28:205-208, 1975.
21. United States Department of Health, Education and Welfare: Ten-State Nutrition Survery in the United States. DHEW Publication No. HSM 73-8704 Washington, DC, Government Printing Office, 1972.
22. Bunch, TW: Blood test abnormalities in runners. Mayo Clin Proc 55:113-117, 1980.
23. Ehn L, Carlmark B, Hoglund S: Iron status in athletes involved in intense physical activity. Med Sci Spor Exer 12:61-64, 1980.
24. Vellar OD: Studies on sweat losses of nutrients. Iron content of whole body sweat and its association with other sweat consitutents, serum iron levels, hematological indices, body surface area, and sweat rate. Scand J Clin Invest 21:157-167, 1968.
25. Smith NJ: Food For Sport. Palo Alto, CA, Bull Publishing Company, 1976, p. 90-103.
26. Bergstrom J, Hultman E: Nutrition for maximal sports performance. JAMA 221:999-1006, 1972.
27. Williams MH: Nutritional faddism and athletics. Nutr and MD IV:1-2, 1977.
28. Food and Nutrition Board, Recommended Dietary Allowances, 1980, National Research Council-National Acadmey of Sciences, Washington, DC, 9th ed.
29. Bergstrom J, Hermansen L, Hultman E, et al: Diet, muscle glycogen and physical performance. Acta physiol scand 71:140-150, 1967.
30. Hermansen L, Hultman E, Saltin B: Muscle glycogen during prolonged severe exercise. Acta physiol scand 71:129-139, 1967.
31. Slovic P: What helps the long distance runner run? Nutr Today 10:18-21, 1975.
32. Forgac MT: Carbohydrate loading—a review. JADA 75:42-45, 1979.

Diane M. Huse, R.D.

33. Mirkin G: Carbohydrate loading: a dangerous practice (letter to the editor). JAMA 223:1511-1512, 1973.
34. Nutrition for Athletes: A Handbook for Coaches. Washington, DC American Association for Health, Physical Education, and Recreation, 1971.
35. Costill DL: Get a load of this. The Runner, May 1980, p. 68.
36. American College of Sports Medicine: Prevention of heat injuries during distance running. Med Sci Sports 7:7-8, 1975.

Index